*Estates and Revolutions*

ESSAYS IN EARLY
MODERN EUROPEAN HISTORY


VOLUME XL

OF

STUDIES PRESENTED TO THE INTERNATIONAL COMMISSION
FOR THE HISTORY OF REPRESENTATIVE AND
PARLIAMENTARY INSTITUTIONS

# ESTATES AND REVOLUTIONS

*Essays in Early Modern European History*

BY H. G. KOENIGSBERGER

## CORNELL UNIVERSITY PRESS

ITHACA AND LONDON

*First published 1971*

THIS BOOK HAS BEEN PUBLISHED WITH THE AID OF A GRANT FROM THE HULL MEMORIAL PUBLICATION FUND OF CORNELL UNIVERSITY

International Standard Book Number 0-8014-0605-6
Library of Congress Catalog Card Number 71-13214

Printed in the United States of America by Vail-Ballou Press, Inc.

*To Renate and Otto*

# Acknowledgments

I WISH to thank the following for their kind permission to reprint material first published elsewhere: Editions Nauwelaerts, for Chapter 1, reprinted from *Studies Presented to the International Commission for the History of Representative and Parliamentary Institutions,* Vol. XI (Louvain, 1952), for Chapter 4, from Vol. XVIII (1958), for Chapter 7, from Vol. XXIV (1961), and for Chapter 6, from *Anciens Pays et Assemblées d'Etats,* Vol. XXII (Louvain, 1961); the Istituto di Storia Medievale of the University of Palermo, for Chapter 2, from *Studies Presented to the International Commission for the History of Representative and Parliamentary Institutions,* Vol. XXXIV (Palermo, 1967); the editors and Messrs. Longmans, publishers, for Chapter 3, from *The English Historical Review,* Vol. LXII (1947); for Chapter 5, the editors and publishers of *The Economic History Review,* Ser. 2, Vol. IX, No. 1 (1956); Edward Arnold (Publishers) Ltd., for Chapter 8, from *The Reformation Crisis,* ed. J. Hurstfield (London, 1965); for Chapter 9, the University of Chicago Press and the editors of *The Journal of Modern History,* Vol. XXVII, No. 4 (1955), copyright 1955 by the University of Chicago; the editor of *The Historical Journal,* for Chapter 10, from the *Cambridge Historical Journal,* Vol. VIII, No. 3 (1946); and the Council of The Royal Historical Society, for Chapter 11, from *Transactions of The Royal Historical Society,* Ser. 5, Vol. 10 (1960).
A number of minor changes have been made in the essays

and some bibliographical citations added. I have deleted some quotations in foreign languages in the footnotes and have translated all others. In Chapter 10, on the revolt of Palermo in 1647, I have incorporated new material, which I found in Simancas and Madrid after the publication of the essay in 1946. This material concerns mainly the reaction of the Spanish government in Madrid to the events in Sicily.

H. G. KOENIGSBERGER

*Ithaca, New York*
*November 1970*

# Contents

# Estates and Revolutions

## ESSAYS IN EARLY MODERN EUROPEAN HISTORY

# State and Society in Early Modern Europe (Fifteenth to Seventeenth Centuries)

AT THE END of the Middle Ages the structure of European society had become highly complex. There was a simple and fundamental division between the great mass of the population, living at little more than subsistence level, in their villages and small towns, and a small upper stratum of society who could afford the leisure for pursuits other than the work necessary to satisfy the most basic needs. The low level of technology, and the low economic productivity which was its consequence, allowed of no other basic division of society. It was therefore natural that the upper stratum of society should control its political organization, the state. But within this simple framework there existed an almost infinite gradation of wealth and social status, and a rich variety of social and political institutions.

Even the lives and activities of the great mass of the common people were enormously diverse, from plowman to fisherman, or from shepherd to laborer or craftsman; nor were these activities at all easily interchangeable. This was true even of similar professions in different parts of Europe. The English copyholder or tenant farmer, living under the common law, had little in common with the French *métayeur* or Italian *mezzadro*, sharecropping under the jurisdiction of his local seigneur and, despite personal and legal freedom, still owing feudal dues and services. None of these, in their turn, would live at all like the Polish or East German *lassit*, working on his lord's estate and rapidly being depressed into a new serfdom. A peasant might grow foodstuffs mainly for himself, and a craftsman work for his village customers; but he might equally produce grain or wine, wool or cloth, for an international market of which he had dimly heard but whose fateful fluctuations he could neither control nor understand.

The status and activities of the other strata of European society, and the political institutions under which they lived, were even more varied and complex. The Italian and German city-republics were radically different from the great monarchies of France, Spain, and England. These, in turn, differed from such unions as the socially and linguistically diverse but contiguous provinces which formed the House of Burgundy's *pays de pardeça,* i.e., the Low Countries, or from the disjointed personal empires of the kings of Aragon or the Habsburgs, or again from the vast aristocratic kingdoms of the Poles and Hungarians on the central European plains and forests, and the even vaster and more heterogeneous empires of the Muscovites and the Turks, farther east. The different political organizations of the European states were related to the economic structure of society in their respective regions. But these relationships were complex and subtle; they were often shaped by traditions that had arisen under quite different conditions and sometimes in different places; above all, these relationships were institutionalized. It is the nature of institutions, whether they take the form of social and political organizations, of customs and laws, or of intellectual, artistic, and religious traditions, that they tend to follow their own inherent laws, or at least their own inherent logic, of development. Such laws, or logic, cannot therefore be deduced from the purely economic relationships of society; but, no more than the institutions themselves do they function apart from the economic relationships.

It is the purpose of this book to show the nature of these interactions in western Europe, from the fifteenth century to the seventeenth. I have concentrated on two major fields: first, the relations of parliaments and assemblies of estates with their respective monarchies and, second, revolutions and revolutionary parties.

No aspect of the social, political, and intellectual structure and tradition of western Europe remained unchallenged between the fifteenth and the seventeenth centuries. Peasant revolts and urban rebellions abounded. Many, perhaps most, had purely local and temporary causes, such as famine, unemployment, or excessive taxation; and the aims of the rioters or rebels rarely went beyond remedies or vengeance for their immediate miseries. It was characteristic of such movements that they were often directed against the Jews—convenient scapegoats, or so it often seems to have appeared to the privileged and educated—whose perhaps regrettable destruction happily left the existing order of society untouched. But there were also popular movements whose aims were more far-reaching and which presented much more serious threats to the established order. Such were the German peasant revolts in the first third of the sixteenth century, culminating in the frighteningly communistic and polygamous "kingdom of God" of the Anabaptists in Münster (Chapter 8). Such also were the guild-organized popular dictatorships in Ghent and Bruges, in 1578 (Chapter 9), and the revolutionary regimes in Naples and Palermo, in 1647 (Chapter 10), and the *ormée* of Bordeaux, in 1652.

All these attempts to invert the fundamental power structure of European society failed, either at once or after a very short period of time. The ruling strata—monarchies, aristocracies, and urban patriciates—remained the ruling strata, although in the Netherlands, and for eleven years also in England, the old monarchy was abolished. By 1660, they were more firmly established than ever. Even those remnants of medieval democracy that had been institutionalized and achieved some degree of respectability had all but disappeared. The powers which the guilds had won in city councils in Italy, Germany, and the Netherlands during generations of bitter struggle in the fourteenth century, were lost to the alliance of princes and patricians in the fifteenth and sixteenth. In Dithmarschen the free peasant communities which had held out for centuries against their hostile neighbors were finally defeated by the king and nobility of Denmark and Holstein. In the Swiss cantons the patricians and large landowners had long since gained a decisive ascendancy over the peasant communities and confirmed their predominance in the last "peasant war," of 1652–1653. In England, the Leveller movement produced the most interesting democratic theories of the period but never got nearer to power than a series of debates in the army.

In this respect, and in this respect only, that is in its basic power structure, the society of early modern Europe was stable. It could not easily have been otherwise. Those with property and privilege had all the advantages: education and religious tradition, the habit of command and the expectation of being obeyed, the ability to organize, and the cash or credit to employ professional troops. In the defense of their privileged positions against any serious threat from below they would forget all their other quarrels and enmities. Catholic and Lutheran authorities anxiously assisted each other against Müntzer and John of Leiden. The Castilian grandees rallied to the defense of their detested new king, Charles of Burgundy, against the native *comunero* movement as soon as this latter began to show radical popular tendencies. William of Orange overthrew the popular Calvinist dictatorship of Ghent, even when it was still fighting the Spaniards; the duke of Mayenne acted similarly against the organization of the popular Holy League in Paris, and Cromwell and Ireton were in complete agreement with their royalist enemies when it came to the defense of property and political privilege for property owners against the Levellers and the Diggers. It seems unlikely that the members of the privileged orders of the thirteenth and fourteenth centuries had looked any more kindly on popular movements than their descendants of the sixteenth and seventeenth. Such popular successes as had been won in the earlier period—in Flemish and Rhenish cities, in Alpine valleys, or in the tidal marshes of Schleswig—were perhaps due to geographical isolation and the consequent inability of the ruling strata to cooperate as effectively as they were able to do two hundred years later.

In every other respect, the forces making for instability in early modern Europe were very strong. In the first place, the economy of Europe was highly dynamic. Population growth, newly mined silver from central Europe and America, and greatly increased velocity of circulation, all these together caused an unprecedented inflation throughout Europe, lasting from about 1500 to 1620. It disrupted traditional price and wage structures, bore hard on those with fixed rental or wage income, and provided golden opportunities for those who were clever or lucky enough to profit from the rapidly changing economic conditions. Not for centuries had European society been as fluid as it became in the sixteenth century. At all economic and social levels new men were rising: the small English copyholder whom rising wool prices could carry to the position of a substantial farmer, or the respectable Augsburg woolen merchant who became the millionaire banker of kings and emperors. All over Europe towns and cities were growing rapidly. No fewer than twelve rose to over 100,000 inhabitants, and neither the lamentations nor the decrees of conservative princes and statesmen could stop the migration to the cities; for to thousands upon thousands of young villagers the city meant opportunity for economic and social betterment, even if only relatively few managed to fulfill their hopes. But life in the cities was precarious. Producing commodities for a European or even transoceanic market, the cities were subject to the slumps and mass unemployment caused by famine and war, and they were especially vulnerable to the periodic epidemics and plagues which, during the period, could still decimate whole populations.

Thus the cities were, and were seen to be, growing centers of instability and potential unrest, doubly dangerous to the established order because subversive and revolutionary ideas could spread so much more easily and quickly among its rootless masses than among the more scattered and tradition-bound country population.

Second, tremendous social changes had been taking place since the central Middle Ages. Almost everywhere in western (but not in eastern) Europe serfdom and other forms of personal unfreedom were disappearing. Feudal relationships of military service, fealty, obligation, and loyalty, based on landholding, were dissolving into much more fluid relationships. Land still played an important part in these relationships, but they tended to depend more and more on market values of property and labor, and on a system of patronage and clientage between powerful men and their followers, and this was happening at almost every level of society. Traditions of personal loyalty, while still very strong, were visibly weakening, and, as contemporaries saw it, this weakening was affecting the stability of society (Chapter 6).

These social changes necessarily affected the internal political structure of the European states. The dissolution of the older, feudal relationships between liege lords and vassals, and the opportunities provided by an ever more sophisticated money and credit economy, opened for the monarchies the possibility of greatly increasing their power and authority over their subjects. The success which different monarchies achieved in this direction varied from country to country; but the methods they used to attain their ends were remarkably similar. Instead of standing at the apex of a feudal pyramid, kings now came to stand at the apex of a pyramid of a complex patronage system; or, to use a more appropriate metaphor, at the center of a nationwide network of patron-client relations. The greater a king's resources, the more easily he could bind his subjects to his service. It followed that a prince must strive to expand these resources, and this could be done most easily in three directions: by the extension of the competence of royal courts at the expense of municipal or seigneurial jurisdiction, by the extension of royal control over the church within the boundaries of the kingdom, and by the extension of the king's dominions, either through inheritance or through war.

To follow such policies systematically it was necessary to improve or replace the traditional organs of government by institutions that were both functionally more efficient and personally more dependent on the king than the traditional royal council of feudal magnates had been. It was also necessary to greatly expand the king's financial resources in order to pay for the expanding machinery of government in an age of rising prices and, even more important, to pay for the armies of professional mercenaries which had shown themselves vastly superior to the traditional feudal levies.

This pattern of royal policy, or at least considerable parts of it, can be observed in most states of Europe from the fifteenth century onwards and, sometimes, even earlier; nor is there, in this respect, a great deal of difference between Catholic and Protestant states after the Reformation. On this very general level of historical analysis there is some justification for the traditional term "the new monarchies." Undoubtedly, the later fifteenth and early sixteenth centuries saw a great increase in the power of many European monarchies. But it turned out to be an increase in political and military power, and not nearly so much an increase in administrative effectiveness and political and social stability. In spite of rapidly increasing numbers of royal officials, there was nothing like a modern bureaucracy in any European country. In France and Italy men bought offices for income and prestige, and they treated them as private property. In England the crown appointed the justices of the peace, the most important local officials, but paid them no salaries. In neither case was it at all easy for the central government to control and discipline individual officials, and it was virtually impossible to pursue effectively policies which ran counter to the interests of the royal officials as a group or to those of the social strata from which they were recruited. Thus the series of well-meaning English enclosure acts remained largely unenforced and unenforceable, just as did the equally well-meaning legislation of the Spanish crown for the protection of the American Indians. In France royal officials often simply acted as a local power group, maneuvering and struggling against other local power groups, without materially increasing royal authority in the provinces. The control of royal officials, indeed the protection of the king's subjects from their acts of tyranny, became one of the most characteristic preoccupations of the central governments of the period (Chapter 6).

If such preoccupations were characteristic, they were, however, rarely consistent. Just as frequently, the king's subjects felt that they had to look after their own protection. They did not willingly pay the constantly increasing taxes. They resented growing royal interference with their traditional rights and powers. Provinces and cities, corporations and magnates fought hard to preserve their former privileges and autonomy. Absolutism in the early modern period meant the attempt of the monarchies to make themselves supreme over all autonomous centers of power within the state. Inevitably, these centers resisted such attempts. To do so effectively, however, they had to match the increased political and military powers of the monarchies. This meant that resistance had to be organized on a basis geographically and socially much wider than had been necessary for a group of rebellious medieval barons. The form of such resistance could vary, from peaceful constitutional action in representative assemblies to open rebellions and civil wars. In these struggles the enmities and alliances of different power groups and social strata were not determined by some simple schema, such as the opposition between a "rising" bourgeoisie or gentry and a "reactionary" or "declining" nobility. The pattern of such struggles varied with time and place and has to be determined, in each case, by detailed historical analysis; for it depended on local tradition, immediate political and social problems, and, not least, on personalities (Chapter 9).

In Chapters 2 and 5, I have attempted to find some correlation between the economic fortunes of different social groups and, more especially, of the nobility of Piedmont and Hainault

with their political activities. In Piedmont an economic upswing for the nobility and the urban patriciate, during the last
quarter of the fifteenth century, coincided with an attempt by
these classes to use parliament in order to increase their political power as against the monarchy, the dukes of Savoy. But this
political movement lacked persistence and, it would seem, conviction. The dukes kept it within bounds without great difficulty. In Hainault a similar economic upswing for the nobility,
during the last quarter of the fifteenth century, coincided with
the nobility's active support for the regent, Maximilian of Austria, against a series of popular rebellions in Flanders—something which, in the absence of large cities, never occurred in
Piedmont. In the middle decades of the sixteenth century,
however, the Hainault country nobility were losing ground
as against those who owned medium-sized properties in land,
probably bourgeois from the towns. In these difficult economic
conditions (which, however, can hardly be characterized as an
economic crisis), many of the Hainault country nobility joined
the noblemen's protest movement, the Compromise. But their
number was distinctly smaller than that of some other provinces, notably Brabant, Holland, and Friesland,[1] and when the
image breaking started, in August, 1566, they rallied to the
support of the government almost to a man.

The evidence for the motivation of political action provided
by the statistical analysis of the economic fortunes of different
social groups therefore is suggestive but not conclusive. It is
not sufficient in itself to explain the causes and results of political actions and affiliations. But it does help to build up the
complex pattern of the social and political development of
early modern Europe, and it helps to demonstrate the powerful elements of instability within this society.

The social and political instability of the European states
was compounded by the fact that their very existence and identity was not at all firmly established. Nation-states, in the nine-

[1] Tentative and certainly incomplete figures are in F. Rachfahl, *Wilhelm von Oranien* (Halle, 1908), II, 567, n. 1.

teenth-century sense of an identity between a self-conscious nation or people and its independent political organization, simply did not exist. All the great states of Europe were multi-lingual and few included all those speaking the same language. Some, such as Spain, Poland, and the Ottoman Empire, were also multiracial and multireligious. None had obvious and un-contested frontiers, and there were few monarchies that did not have legal claims to lands outside their actual frontiers, and sometimes at great distances and beyond an intervening stretch of sea. Unions of crowns in the same ruling family could create wholly new political organizations which might then develop some form of national feeling, or at least a sense of belonging together, quite rapidly (as did the duchies and counties of the Netherlands), rather slowly (as did the kingdoms of Castile and Aragon), not very much (as did England and Ireland) or hardly at all (as in the case of Denmark and Sweden, and Sweden and Poland). Age-old peasant xenophobia mingled with a rather newer and sophisticated patriotism that grew with the spread of classical education, to form the beginnings of nationalism. But the objects and direction of such early forms of nationalism were often far from clear. They might be harnessed to the mili-tary proclivities of the European nobility who saw war and warfare as the ultimate justification of its existence; but they could also be diametrically opposed to the policies of central governments. Ferdinand and Isabella found the peculiar Span-ish mixture of national, religious, and racial pride among their subjects most useful in their wars against the Moors of Gra-nada; but when they carried their "crusade" to the shores of North Africa, the differences of interest of their Castilian and Aragonese subjects became immediately apparent, while their successor, Charles V, found it not at all easy to reconcile tra-ditional Spanish feelings and aspirations with his own supra-national policies in Christian Europe (Chapter 7). When he eventually did achieve such a reconciliation, Spanish patriotism was transformed into an aggressive and self-righteous imperial-ism which made the Spaniards feared and hated throughout western Europe, just as, later, the French and, later still, the Germans came to be feared and hated.

There were few years, from the fifteenth to the seventeenth century, when at least some of the states of Europe were not engaged in warfare. Every aspect of public life was affected by this fact (Chapter 3). It has often been argued that it was warfare, the needs of defense, and, especially, the establishment of standing armies which enabled princes to found absolutism in their countries. This could, indeed, happen. Emmanuel Philibert of Savoy, returning from exile to his country at the head of a professional army, gave a classic demonstration of how this could be done by double-crossing his ultraloyal parliament (Chapter 1). But such actions were rare. More often, warfare, and the enormous sums of money which it demanded, left princes and their governments vulnerable to counterattacks by the parliaments or forced them to sell or give away important prerogatives, such as rights of jurisdiction or the control over recruitment and organization of their armies. This could happen even in countries such as Castile where the crown had previously defeated the specific challenge of a representative assembly and reduced it to political impotence (Chapter 7). And where such assemblies had not yet been decisively defeated, even a standing army was not necessarily a guarantee of princely absolutism—as several German princes found out to their cost, as late as the seventeenth century.

The armies themselves were unreliable. Princes habitually overextended their resources by overrecruiting. Sooner or later, the unpaid armies would mutiny or refuse to fight or, worst of all, take matters into their own hands, as did Charles V's army which sacked Rome in 1527, and Philip II's army which sacked Antwerp, in 1576. In the following century, armies, and especially their commanding generals, began habitually to play independent politics, and in 1649 a regime set up by an army horrified respectable Europe by cutting off the head of the king of England.

External wars and their attendant hardships of high taxes,

interrupted trade, destruction of property, unemployment, and famine, together with the availablity of weapons presented fertile fields for anyone preaching subversion for whatever reason. But while members of the propertied and privileged strata of society viewed all popular movements with alarm and horror, many ambitious aristocrats were willing to play with fire and attempted to use popular discontent for their own purposes (Chapter 9).

A particularly vulnerable point for the monarchies of the period was the moment of succession. At the death of any prince the chances were no better than even that he would be succeeded by an unequivocally legitimate adult male heir.[2] When John Knox called for the "blast of the trumpet against the monstrous regiment of women" he simply voiced his and his contemporaries' characteristic antifeminism. But they knew what they were talking about. The succession of a woman or a child was an all too common experience. In a social setting whose ethos was essentially masculine and military such a succession was, with very few exceptions such as that of Elizabeth of England, an unmitigated disaster; for it led to bitter faction fights for the control of the central government, and often to civil war.

Such events were certainly not new in this period. England, France, Castile, Naples, Milan, and several of the German principalities all experienced them in the latter half of the fifteenth century. In 1560 England, Scotland, France, Portugal, and the Netherlands were again being ruled by women or boys. What was new at this date, however, was the injection of religious passions into traditional political quarrels. The results were a terrible aggravation of the crisis. Political and legal pretensions could now shelter behind the respectable and emotionally much more satisfying banner of the defense of the true religion. Personal loyalties, which had become conveniently flexible and negotiable in the postfeudal age, now either dissolved

2 H. G. Koenigsberger and George L. Mosse, *Europe in the Sixteenth Century* (London and New York, 1968), p. 249.

altogether or suddenly hardened into new, rigid, and unpredictable patterns, as Margaret of Parma and Catherine de Medici both found to their great dismay. Simple struggles for political power were transformed into wars *à outrance* in which one or the other side—and sometimes both of them—felt itself fighting for sheer survival. Such desperation drove the antagonists to seek allies abroad, and thus they involved their local civil wars with the international power politics of the great monarchies. This was the basic pattern of European political history during the hundred years between the Peace of Cateau-Cambrésis (1559) and the Peace of the Pyrenees (1659).

Parliaments represented, to a varying but always considerable degree, the more important privileged strata or orders of the different European countries. They existed in nearly all of these countries, except for the city states. Inevitably, the parliaments became involved in the social, political, and religious conflicts of the period. At some time, during the two hundred years from the middle of the fifteenth century to the middle of the seventeenth, nearly all the parliaments found themselves engaged in struggles for ultimate political power with their respective monarchies. In this book I present a case study of one parliament, that of Piedmont, which was deliberately killed by its prince (Chapter 1). Such a clear-cut and unequivocal result in the political competition between princes and parliaments was not common. More usually, the political victory of the monarchy left parliament intact as an institution but, to a greater or lesser extent, without effective power. Even under the house of Savoy the assemblies of the Val d'Aosta continued to function, mainly, it seems, because their authority was so localized that they could not possibly rival the duke's power for whom it was therefore simply not worthwhile to antagonize the inhabitants of this remote region. In composite monarchies, such as the Spanish, the struggle for ultimate political power was likely to occur only in the major dominions, such as Castile (Chapter 7). In the lesser dominions the king had the advantage of being able to call on outside resources, and the estates of these dominions could only effectively challenge the authority of the king if they were prepared to go to the length of deposing him and calling on the help of a major power.

This was, usually, clearly recognized at the time, and it accounts for the reasonably stable balance of power between the king and the estates of Catalonia, Naples, Sicily, and Sardinia. Since its ultimate authority was never in question, the monarchy found it wise to allow the estates the enjoyment of their local privileges and, especially in Sicily, the relatively innocuous game of forcing the recall of successive viceroys every three or six years (Chapter 2). Only when the financial strains of the Thirty Years' War forced the Spanish monarchy to put ever more intolerable burdens on its smaller dominions did the normal balance of power break down: in 1640 in Catalonia and in 1647 in Naples and Sicily (Chapter 10).

In this context the history of the estates of the Netherlands is particularly significant; for here the contemporaries misjudged the strength of the political forces involved. At first it seemed as if the situation of the Netherlands was similar to that of Catalonia or Sicily, i.e., that of an outlying dominion in which the power of the crown was sufficiently secure to allow the estates the luxury of overthrowing an unpopular minister, Cardinal Granvelle. But religious divisions made the opposing parties virtually irreconcilable, and the Netherlands were much too important for the king to allow his authority to be seriously challenged. Philip II sent the duke of Alva with his best army to the Netherlands, and the duke abolished the former balance between crown and estates in favor of the absolute supremacy of the crown. Or so he thought when he assured his much more sceptical master that the States-General of the Netherlands would cause him no more trouble than the long-since-tamed Cortes of Castile.[3] It was a natural enough

[3] Alva's view was so definite and so wrong that it is worth quoting his letter to Philip II (Brussels, Jan. 19, 1568): "Although Your Majesty has commanded me that, for dealing both with this and other matters, it is

assumption but it proved to be wrong. The estates were still very much alive, able effectively to block Alva's tax plans and, ultimately, to organize armed resistance against the king.

Some years later, the estates of the Union of Utrecht also misjudged the situation. Having deposed their legal sovereign, they tried for many years to acquire a new one in the person of a foreign prince. Only repeated disillusionment with their candidates finally convinced them that they had to fend for themselves; or rather, that they had to create their own, substitute monarchy; for this was what they did, by the special position which they accorded, first to William of Orange and then, successively, to his sons Maurice and William Henry. Much the same happened, later, to the only other parliament which decisively won its struggle with the monarchy and deposed its king, the parliament of England. For in England, as in the Netherlands, it was found necessary to set up a substitute monarchy, that of Lord Protector Cromwell. In both countries the estates or parliaments then found that they still had to engage in the old struggles with these substitute monarchs, just as if they had been legitimate princes.

This apparently paradoxical phenomenon suggests that there may have existed, during this period of European history, certain recurring functional patterns. Such patterns seem to have arisen, both from certain intellectual preconceptions and from the recurrence of certain practical problems in the running of any political organization. Thus, men accustomed to think of the state in terms of a "body politic" found it difficult to visualize such a body without a head. This was so even in the United Provinces of the Netherlands, where a quite specific theory of the sovereignty of the estates, without reference to any head, had been formulated (Chapter 7). To practical men

not expedient that the States-General should be summoned, yet when they should be assembled Your Majesty may rest assured that times have changed from what they were, and that the States-General can be assembled just as the procurators of the [Castilian] cities in Valladolid" (Duque de Alba, *Epistolario del III Duque de Alba* [Madrid, 1952], II, 11).

it was also only too apparent that a large parliament or assembly of estates did not function very efficiently as a government. When, moreover, such an assembly was fighting a civil or foreign war for its very existence, a unified direction of both civil government and army were clearly essential for survival. Both in the Netherlands and in England the new heads of state, the princes of Orange and Cromwell, started their careers as politicians and ended them by finding their principal support in their armies. The interests of the armies together with the leaders' own dynastic ambitions—ambitions which were taken completely for granted during this period and which were still prominent in Napoleon but which have disappeared from the careers of most twentieth-century dictators—were bound to lead the new rulers into opposition to the very assemblies that had raised them to power.

Parliamentary history seems to be particularly rich in such patterns (although other fields of history, such as economic history, international relations, and wars certainly provide further examples).[4] Very few comparative studies of such problems have as yet been made.[5] Chapter 7, on the powers of deputies in sixteenth-century assemblies, is an attempt to study one of them.

Much more than the history of parliaments, that of the revolutions of this period has been studied on a comparative basis. Nevertheless, a fully satisfactory typology of these revolutions has not yet been worked out by historians or sociologists.[6] Ex-

[4] I have discussed some of these in chapter 3 of *The Habsburgs and Europe, 1516–1660* (Ithaca, 1971).

[5] An important start has, however, been made by G. Griffiths, *Representative Government in Western Europe in the Sixteenth Century* (Oxford, 1968), which provides both comparative source material and comments. Cf. also E. Lousse, *La Société de l'Ancien Régime* (Bruges-Louvain-Paris, 1943); and A. Marongiu, *Il Parlamento in Italia* (Milan, 1962), trans. as *Medieval Parliaments* (London, 1968).

[6] Cf. J. H. Elliott, "Revolution and Continuity in Early Modern Europe," *Past and Present*, No. 42 (1969); and L. Stone, "Theories of Revo-

cept for the millennarians (Chapter 8), the leaders of political movements in this period rarely argued that they wanted to set up a new and better order of things. Rather, they usually claimed that they were returning to an old and better order which the existing powers had perverted. The distinction was real enough, and it was psychologically important because it was genuinely believed and because it lent an air of respect-ability to the most far-reaching demands. To the other side, however, to the established authorities and their supporters, the opposition's claim to be only restoring the good old order appeared as not very subtle hypocrisy; for, whether revolution-aries looked forward or backward, whether their ideal was a utopia of the future or a golden age of the past, they were only too plainly intent on changing the existing order of state and society. To Philip II it was quite immaterial whether his op-ponents in the Netherlands were conservatives, seeking to res-urrect the medieval autonomies of the provinces, or whether they were forward-looking champions of political liberty.[7] What mattered to him, and he said it time and again, was that they rebelled against his lawful authority. The state which they set up, a state without a legitimate monarchy, without an established church, and with no privileged place for the old nobility—this state was in effect something quite new, what-ever may have been the intentions of its founders. "It were full strange," Charles I said to his judges, "that they [the House of Commons] should pretend to make laws without King or Lord's House, to any that have heard speak of the laws of England."[8] It was an accurate characterization of revolution-ary action. From the king's point of view it did not matter at

---

lution," *World Politics,* vol. 18 (1966). Both authors give comprehensive bibliographies of this topic.

[7] Cf. the recent controversy between Pieter Geyl, L. J. Rogier, and H. A. Enno van Gelder in *Bijdragen voor de Geschiedenis der Neder-landen,* vols. 9, 10, and 11 (1955–1957).

[8] Quoted in S. R. Gardiner, *The Constitutional Documents of the Puritan Revolution,* 2d ed. (Oxford, 1962), p. 375.

all whether his opponents were trying to return to a mythical former stage of the English constitution or whether they were trying to set up a new regime of the elect, or even just of the elected representatives of the country. Without a legitimate monarchy, without an established church, and without a House of Lords, the England of the Commonwealth was indeed as different from a traditional state as were the United Provinces of the Netherlands. To contemporaries, these revolutions were certainly real enough, whatever word they used to describe them.

For the historian it therefore seems legitimate to characterize as revolutions all those movements which succeeded, at least for a period of time, in overthrowing the existing political authority and of significantly changing the structure of the state. Those movements which attempted but failed to do this may then be characterized as revolutionary movements. But before we can succeed in constructing a generally acceptable pattern for all revolutions and revolutionary movements, from the Hussites to the English civil war, or even only for the contemporaneous revolutions of the mid-seventeenth century, it may be useful to concentrate on partial and functional patterns as I have attempted to do in Chapter 9.

The last essay in the book is an attempt to correlate creative activities, especially in the arts and in music, with changes in the social and political structure of different countries, and with their artistic, religious, and philosophical traditions. This is a vast and highly complex subject, and the present chapter does not attempt to do more than outline the field of investigation, suggest certain methods of handling the historical problems involved, and put forward some first conclusions. Just as in the political and economic essays in this book, I have here tried to show the interaction between the autonomous laws or inherent logical developments of institutions and cultural traditions with the changing social and intellectual conditions of European society.

# CHAPTER 1

# The Parliament of Piedmont during the Renaissance, 1460–1560

"Hence, to continue my argument, is there a king or other lord who has power, outside his domain, to levy even a penny on his subjects without the grant and consent of those who have to pay it, unless it were by tyranny or violence?"
(Philippe de Commines, *Mémoires*, Bk. 5, chap. 19)

THE GREAT KINGDOMS of modern Europe have owed much to the Italian republics and city-states of the Renaissance: secular government and Roman law, capitalist finance and systematic diplomacy, modern democracy and modern despotism—all these have spread from Italy beyond the Alps. Only representative assemblies did not enter firmly into the Italian political tradition. Neither the democracy of Florence, nor the oligarchy of Venice had any need for parliaments; and the rulers of Naples and Milan, together with the host of smaller despots, were never willing to accept limitations of their personal powers. Machiavelli thought that the existence of a lazy and turbulent nobility, with its private castles and retainers, made genuine political life impossible in those states.[1] Parliaments,

---

[1] N. Machiavelli, *Tutte le Opere* . . . G. Mazzoni and M. Casella, eds. (Florence, 1929), *Discorsi*, I, 54, p. 127: "Gentlemen is the name given to those who live without working from the income of their properties. . . . These same are pernicious in every republic and in every province; but even more pernicious are those who, apart from having these fortunes, also command castles and have subjects who obey them. These two types of men abound in the kingdom of Naples, the Papal States, the Romagna, and Lombardy. This is the reason why in these provinces there has never appeared any republic nor any real political life. . . . Where the substance is so corrupt that laws do not suffice to restrain it, there it is necessary to order matters with greater force; this is the hand of a king and such absolute power as will restrain the excessive ambition and

and the vital role they were to play in modern history, arose out of feudal and transalpine institutions.

There were, indeed, representative assemblies in some of the Italian states in the later Middle Ages, just as there were in almost every other European country. Yet when, in the age of Lorenzo the Magnificent, the civilization of the Renaissance reached its most dazzling heights, and when the influence of Italian political institutions and practices began to make its greatest impact on the non-Italian world, only three Italian parliaments had survived.[2] As the transalpine monarchies followed the Italian states on the road to despotism, their representative assemblies were defeated and abolished; or they decayed, until they became mere ghosts of their former selves. The victory of the English parliament over the monarchy and the gradual evolution of parliamentary government represented transformations virtually unique in European history, parallelled, to some extent, only in the Netherlands and Sweden. These transformations were accomplished only where powerful social, political, and religious forces infused new life into the old feudal assemblies and where, moreover, a favorable geographical position conferred a certain degree of immunity from outside interference. This chapter attempts to show the reasons for the defeat of the most successful of the Italian parliaments.

Significantly, the three Italian parliaments had survived in the most feudal, the least "Italian," of the Italian states. The

---

corruption of the overmighty." Quoted also by F. Braudel, *La Méditerranée et le Monde méditerranéen á l'époque de Philippe II* (Paris, 1949), p. 628.

[2] The parliament of Friuli virtually received its deathblow when that province was incorporated in the Venetian Empire, in 1420. Cf. P. S. Leicht, "Parlamento Friulano," in *Atti delle Assemblee Costituzionali Italiane*, ser. I, sec. 6. The assemblies of the Papal States were never very important and had virtually died out, and the irregular meetings of nobles and representatives of cities in the kingdom of Naples never became a regular institution. Cf. A. Marongiu, *L'Istituto Parlamentare in Italia dalle Origini al 1500* (Rome, 1949), pp. 134, 203.

*stamento* of Sardinia was called into being by an act of grace of the crown of Aragon. It was a creature of royal policy, without roots in the independent rights of the Sardinians, and it could never seriously hope to influence or rival the Catalan and Spanish government of the island.[3] By 1460 only Piedmont and Sicily could still boast of powerful parliaments. The Sicilian parliament survived longer than any of the others, defending, not without success, the country's privileges against the encroachments of Castilian absolutism, and its people against the rapacity of the Spanish treasury. Yet the much-vaunted comparison of the assemblies of Palermo and Westminster in the seventeenth century as the only surviving effective parliaments was a Sicilian misconception. From the fifteenth century onwards, the Sicilian parliament remained nearly always on the defensive (much more so than the assembly of Piedmont), and it signally failed to initiate those constitutional changes which in England led to the transformation of a feudal into a constitutional monarchy.[4]

The assembly of the three estates of Piedmont was the only parliament functioning in an independent Italian state. While the Sicilian parliament could look for inspiration and precedent only to its own, somewhat mythical, past and to the rapidly declining cortes of Aragon and Catalonia,[5] the Piedmontese assembly was open to the influence of the political ideas of French and Swiss assemblies. It had, moreover, within the

[3] A. Marongiu, *I Parlamenti di Sardegna nella storia e nel diritto pubblico comparato,* Studi dell' Istituto di Diritto Pubblico e Legislazione Sociale della R. Università di Roma (Rome, 1932), p. 234 and *passim.*

[4] Marongiu, *L'Istituto,* p. 213, speaks of "the undoubted confusion of the constitutional powers of the state. In fact, it is possible to say that this latter rests on a diarchy of powers (king and parliament) in a state of equality or little less." I think this is much too optimistic a view of the powers of the Sicilian parliament. Cf. my *The Practice of Empire,* emended ed. of *The Government of Sicily under Philip II of Spain* (Ithaca, 1969), chap. 6, sect. 2, and pp. 7 f.

[5] The influence of the Aragonese cortes was of very doubtful value to the Sicilian parliament: it was, *inter alia,* probably responsible for the change in Sicily from a two- to a three-chamber system.

Savoyard monarchy, the example of the unusually strong representative institutions of the county of Bresse and the Pays de Vaud.[6] The assembly of the estates of Piedmont achieved its greatest power in the last hundred years of its career, before its death at the hands of Emmanuel Philibert in 1560. During the minorities and regencies of the last four decades of the fifteenth century it came to be regarded as the ultimate arbiter of the will of the country, consulted on important matters of state by the ruling house, and flattered by bribes to its members from the courts of Milan and France. Luigi Talliandi, one of the most experienced politicians of the time, told the Milanese ambassador "that although they [the Piedmontese] have a prince, nevertheless, in every important case, it is the three estates which deliberate, make decisions, and govern this country; and by himself the prince is incapable of pursuing a course of action, unless the three estates help him; and the three estates always deliberate and decide what the greatest men in the country have persuaded them to do for the peace and welfare of the country. . . ." [7]

Talliandi may have exaggerated the importance of the three estates. Later, in the sixteenth century, the assembly was no longer capable of increasing its political power; yet it held its

[6] A. Tallone, *Parlamento Sabaudo*, VIII, *Patria Oltramontana*, Vol. I; *Atti delle Assemblee* (Bologna, 1935), pp. ci ff. and cxlix ff.

[7] The Milanese ambassador, Bianco, to the duke of Milan, Sept. 21, 1476. Tallone, *Parlamento Sabaudo (Parl. Sab.)* V, *Patria Cismontana*, V, 180. Also quoted by M. C. Daviso, "Considerazioni intorno ai Tre Stati in Piemonte," *Bollettino storico-bibliografico subalpino* (1947), p. 23. This short article is, by far, the best that has been written on the parliament of Piedmont. Tallone's work is a monumental collection of documents in 13 volumes and in two parts: one, of documents referring to the assembly of the *patria Cismontana,* i.e., Piedmont; the other, of documents of the assemblies of the *patria Oltramontana,* i.e., Savoy, Nice, Bresse, and Pays de Vaud. This collection must remain the basis for all work on the parliaments of the states of the Savoy dynasty. Considering the vast number of documents, the number of mistakes in transcription and explanations is very small. Both parts of the collection are prefaced by lengthy historical introductions. But Tallone the historian was not the equal of Tallone the palaeographer and editor.

ground until the French invasion of 1536. And even when, for more than twenty years, the country was divided and occupied by foreign troops, meetings of the three estates continued to take place in both the French and the Spanish parts of Piedmont. Contemporaries expected that the restoration of Emmanuel Philibert to his dukedom, after the Treaty of Cateau-Cambrésis in 1559, would be followed by the restoration of the three estates to their traditional position. There were good precedents for such an expectation. At the end of the fourteenth century, for instance, Martin of Aragon had restored both monarchy and parliament in Sicily, after nearly a century of anarchy. But Emmanuel Philibert decided to put an end to the assemblies of the three estates after only one meeting, in 1560.

The hagiographers of the House of Savoy have hailed this move as the statesmanlike act on which the national greatness of Piedmont and Italy was founded, and they have represented the assembly of the sixteenth century as a decadent, factious, and unpatriotic body which had fallen far below the standards it had reached in its earlier career. Such views, however, are not supported by the evidence.

The civilization of the Renaissance was an essentially urban civilization. Its material basis was the trade and the manufacturing industries of the great cities of northern and central Italy. Piedmont, too, was a country of cities; yet its character had remained predominantly agricultural, and its social organization medieval and feudal. The master of the mint of Bourg-en-Bresse rejoiced that Savoy and Piedmont could more easily dispense with foreign merchants than a manufacturing country, such as Flanders, and moreover acquired large quantities of money from the export of foodstuffs. The chestnuts of Piedmont alone were worth more than 100,000 *écus*, he said.[8] Toward the end of the sixteenth century, Giovanni Botero

[8] "Discorso del Maestro della Zecca del Borgo in Bressa . . . ," c. 1530, Turin Archivio di Stato (from now to be quoted as A.S.T.), MS, Sec. Riun. A (III), Zecca e Monete, Mazzo 4A, No. 81.

claimed that "it was generally accepted that there was no part of Italy that was more pleasant [than Piedmont], more fertile in grain, wine, fruit, meat . . . and which, relative to its size and condition, provided its prince with a greater revenue." [9]

Other observers agreed with these views on the preponderance of agriculture in the principality; but they saw much more clearly the weakness of this one-sided economy. The author of a memorial addressed to Emmanuel Philibert in 1559 [10] stated that there were no mines in the country, nor gold and silver, neither were there industries which would help to earn money from elsewhere; everything needed for the clothing of men and women had to be imported at high prices, and in effect, he concluded, "all that is produced in this country goes to the greasing of the gullet." [11] The Venetian ambassadors, writing in the following thirty years, made similar observations.[12] The best parts of the plain and of the Alpine foothills were very fertile. In good years Piedmont had a large surplus of corn and meat for export to Milan, Genoa, and France, and even at that time the Piedmontese and Asti wines were famous.[13] But not all dis-

[9] G. Botero, *Relationi Universali, Relatione di Piamonte* (Venice, 1640), pp. 683 f.

[10] Printed in E. Ricotti, *Storia della Monarchia Piemontese* (Firenze, 1861), I, 291–340. For the disputed authorship of this document cf. F. Patetta, *Di Niccolò Balbo . . . e del "Memoriale" al Duca Emanuele Filiberto che gli è falsamente attribuito.* Studi pubblicati dalla R. Università di Torino nel IV Centenario della nascità di Emanuele Filiberto (Turin, 1928), pp. 426 ff.

[11] *Ibid.,* p. 304.

[12] Correr, *inter alia,* quotes the common saying about the character of the Piedmontese: "Piedmontese and Montferrese, Bread, wine, and tambourine." E. Albèri, *Relazioni degli Ambasciatori Veneti al Senato durante il secolo decimosesto* (Florence, 1858), ser. 2, V, 12.

[13] In 1560 Boldù estimated that a good harvest produced foodstuffs sufficient for three years. A. Boldù, "Relazione della Corte Savoia," in Albèri, *Relazioni,* ser. 2, I, 442 f. Writing in 1566, Correr put the surplus of an average year at about 150,000 sacks, or 230,000 Venetian *stara;* but he thought the country badly cultivated and at that time many parts were not cultivated at all. *Ibid.,* V, 10.

tricts were equally fertile. A report of 1615 described the country around Turin as so sterile and unfruitful that landowners were compelled to provide their *massari* (the peasants working on the métayage system) with all the capital needed for the working of the land, for the peasants would otherwise refuse to work the holdings, and there was a proverb that "he who passes the Dora [the river joining the Po at Turin] loses his cart and plow within a year." [14] In some densely populated Alpine valleys little could be grown but some barley, oats, and a few chestnuts; and whatever the master of the mint's opinion about the commercial value of chestnuts, they could feed the population of such valleys for barely two months in the year, so that the majority of the young people had to seek work or beg elsewhere for the remainder of the year.[15] Even the economy of the numerous towns of Piedmont differed little from that of the open country. Some, indeed, had old-established industries. Vercelli produced cloth and Pinerolo even boasted of a guild of wool merchants, the *arte del lanificio,* and held two annual fairs.[16] Perhaps the richest town was Chieri, once a leading member of the Lombard League. Before the French invasion, Chieri was said to have produced more than 100,000 pieces of fustian each year.[17] Her patrician families had made their fortune as cloth and silk merchants, importers of metal, and, above all, as moneychangers and bankers. Some of them

[14] Discourse of Paolo Contari to Carlo Emanuele I. Turin, Archivio Communale (Arch. Com.), MS, Category 46, No. 179. Conditions were certainly no better in the fifteenth and sixteenth centuries. I would like to thank the archivist, Cav. Gino Pastore, for drawing my attention to this interesting document.

[15] Appeal by the men of Val di Ponte for tax relief, c. 1560, and report of the ducal commissioner, Obertitus Marruchi, 1545. A.S.T., MS, Paesi, Provincia d'Ivrea, Mazzo 11, No. 8; Pont e Valle, No. 6. Marruchi described similar conditions for Castelnovo e Valle. *Ibid.,* Mazzo 5, Castelnovo e Valle, No. 1.

[16] A. Caffaro, "L'Arte del Lanificio in Pinerolo," *Miscellanea di Storia Italiana,* 30 (Turin, 1893), 493 ff.

[17] "Memoriale" to Emmanuel Philibert, Ricotti, *Storia,* I, 335.

were established in France and the Netherlands, as the Villa family who owned a banking business in Bruges and had financial dealings with the dukes of Burgundy. The chapels of the wealthy citizens of Chieri, decorated by Flemish masters, still bear testimony to Chieri's connection with transalpine Europe.[18] Yet Chieri remained a city built of brick, and the habitations of her patricians could not compare with the villas and *palazzi* of the merchant princes of Florence and Venice. In the capital, Turin, "few palaces were to be seen, and the houses were not very beautiful," even in the second half of the sixteenth century.[19]

Piedmontese merchants traveled to the Geneva and Lyons fairs and imported salt from Nice and Genoa,[20] and merchants and landowners in the border districts engaged in a lucrative smuggling trade in corn and livestock, varied with cattle raids into the Milanese.[21] But most of the country's export and import trade seems to have been carried on by foreigners. The duke imposed tolls on all goods which passed through his dominions and claimed that these *pedazzi* and *dazi* represented an insurance premium in return for which he guaranteed the safety of the merchants' persons and goods and promised to pay

[18] N. Gabrielli, "Opere di Maestri Fiamminghi a Chieri nel Quattrocento." *Boll. stor.-bibl. subalp.* (1936), pp. 427 ff.

[19] Relation of Cardinal Bonelli, 1571, quoted in M. Chiaudano, "Le condizioni economiche di Torino ai tempi di Emanuele Filiberto," *"Torino,"* 2 (1928), 467.

[20] E.g., the treaty of 1467–1468 between Genoa and the duke of Savoy calling off mutual reprisals on merchants and restoring the former freedom of trade between the two states. Genoa, Arch. di Stato, MS, Serie Segreto, Materie Politiche, Mazzo 13, N.G. 2732; and protests by Charles III to Genoa about the arrest of Piedmontese merchants, and the seizure of the goods of others by Genoese privateers. Probably April and Aug., 1515, respectively. *Ibid.*, Arch. Segr. 2791, Lettere Principi alla Repubblica di Genova, Mazzo 15, folder: Lettere di Carlo III . . . 1505 in 1539.

[21] Galeazzo Maria Sforza to his mother, Bianca Maria, Aug. to Oct., 1468, Milan, Arch. di Stato, MS, Box "Savoia, 483," folder for 1468; also Box "Novara, 1458–1461, No. 742," folder for 1461, Carteggio Interno, Novara.

an indemnity in case of loss.[22] Yet, communications were poor; most foreign merchants were engaged in transit trade only, which barely affected the Piedmontese economy; and the Genoese frequently complained of the difficulties put in their way.[23] The Milanese regarded their westerly neighbors as savages, as unreliable, and as "causing every day some new trouble to our merchants." [24]

The prosperity of the Piedmontese communes depended mostly on the land their citizens owned and on the sale of its produce. In Moncalieri, one of the relatively wealthier communes of the principality, industry and commerce were insignificant, and the inhabitants lived almost entirely by the cultivation, or from the rents, of their vineyards.[25] Turin, situated in poor agricultural land, was important mainly as a university town, the seat of an archbishop and of the Cismontane council (the highest legal and governmental authority in Piedmont) and, from the end of the fifteenth century, as the permanent residence of the dukes. Savigliano, on the other hand, owed its populousness and ease mainly to the fertile holdings of its citizens, and to its feudal lordship over a number of villages and smaller communes.[26]

In a country where most economic activity was centered on land, social position and political power were necessarily based on land as well. The duke himself derived most of his revenue from his domain lands and from feudal dues and services.[27]

[22] M. C. Daviso, *La Duchessa Iolanda* (Turin, 1935), p. 135.

[23] Genoa, Arch. di Stato, MS, Segr. 2707, Folio Istruzioni e Relazioni Politici, 1500–1558, Nos. 62, 78.

[24] Galeazzo Maria Sforza to E. di Iacopo, his ambassador in France, Jan. 14, 1469, Tallone, *Parl. Sab.*, IV, 300.

[25] Instructions to Moncalieri's delegates to the assembly of Oct., 1533, Tallone, *Parl. Sab.*, VII, 122 ff.

[26] Cf. the attempted *coup de main* by the citizen guard of Savigliano against Genoa, in 1490. F. Gabotto, *Lo Stato Sabaudo da Amedeo VIII ad Emmanuele Filiberto* (Turin, 1893), II, 463.

[27] Daviso, *La Duchessa*, pp. 133 ff.

He was, however, only one of many landowners, and hence his revenues and powers were severely limited. As elsewhere in Europe, government expenditure was increasing rapidly during the age of the Renaissance, and the ever more pressing calls on the ducal treasury could often be met only by the mortgage or sale of crown land. The long series of statutes against the alienation of ducal domain illuminates both this process and the insufficiency of legislative action to arrest it.[28] In the second half of the fifteenth century, the situation was further aggravated by the grant of great feudal appanages to the younger sons of duke Louis.[29] Bresse, the Pays de Vaud, the Genevese, and Chablais, were not, it is true, parts of Piedmont. Their alienation, however, meant that the duke's possessions outside Piedmont did not greatly strengthen his position in the principality.

Piedmontese trade was limited, and so too, therefore, was the possibility of exploiting it financially. There was no wealthy wool trade and no Company of the Staple to help a needy gov-

[28] A.S.T., MS, Segr. I, Materie Economiche: Demanio, Donativi, Sussidi. Mazzo without number, 1360–1799, "Ordini ducali per quali si prohibisce et si dichiaran vuotte l'alienationi de beni demaniali," 1590. There were edicts in 1445, 1470, 1490, 1496, and 1509 (probably not 1506 as stated on the folder). The preamble of the last edict stated that nobles, communes, and private persons had extended their jurisdiction over public waterways and mineral deposits, and had appropriated taxes on animals and foodstuffs.

In the Inventari di Paesi of the A.S.T. there are many documents of the grant or sale by the dukes of fiefs, or the jurisdiction over fiefs, to nobles and others.

[29] Jacques Lambert, "Régistres des choses faictes par . . . madam Yolant de France . . . ," in L. Menabréa, *Chroniques de Yolande de France . . . Documents Inédits* (Chambéry, 1895), p. 34: "One should realize . . . that the late duke Louis during his lifetime held not only the territories, lands, and lordships, which my lord duke Philibert now holds but also . . . all the territories, lands, and lordships which at present are held by my lords the counts of Geneva, Bresse, and Romont. And of these my lady [Yolanda] and my lord duke Philibert never have any revenue nor profit, even though they make up the greater part, indeed almost the whole, of the revenue of Savoy on this side of the mountains."

ernment as there was in England. Though the duke imposed taxes on the import and export of foodstuffs in certain frontier towns, such as the *dazio* of Susa,[30] he could never make control of the export trade in corn into a major source of revenue, as the viceroys of Sicily had done.[31] The length of the frontiers, the ease of smuggling, and the resistance of the communes rendered such a scheme impossible.

For communes and nobles relied on rights which were anterior to those of the crown. Their privileges were immemorial, whereas the claims of the House of Savoy to the whole state were comparatively recent.[32] Many towns had voluntarily submitted to Savoyard rule on the expressly stated condition that their local rights and administrative independence and all other privileges would be faithfully maintained.[33] As late as 1517, Vercelli and the smaller towns of the Vercellese protested against the government's proposal to raise 10,000 troops and reminded the duke that they had transferred their allegiance from Milan because they had been too heavily taxed and were promised better government by Savoy.[34]

The one important branch of trade which the dukes attempted to control and exploit financially was the import of salt. No other action by the government caused such constant friction with towns and nobles in the three estates. Successive assemblies petitioned, and almost always obtained, the promise of freedom to buy this vital mineral where they chose.[35] Yet

[30] A. Garino Canina, "La Finanza del Piemonte nella seconda metà del XVI secolo," *Miscellanea di Storia Italiana,* 52 (Turin, 1924), 547.

[31] Koenigsberger, *The Practice of Empire,* chap. 4, sec. 3, and chap. 5.

[32] G. Pérouse, *La Savoie d'autrefois: Etudes et tableaux* (Chambéry, 1933), p. 37.

[33] E.g., Savigliano in 1320, A.S.T., MS, Provincia di Fossano, Mazzo 4, No. 6. In this document there is the express reservation of the rights and jurisdiction of Savigliano over a large number of castles and villages. Turin, however, never possessed municipal independence.

[34] Vercelli council minutes, April 3, 1517, Tallone, *Parl. Sab.,* VI, 334.

[35] E.g., Assembly of Turin, Oct., 1481, *ibid.,* V, 287. Assembly of Vigone, Jan., 1522, *ibid.,* VI, 421 ff.

successive dukes tried as tenaciously to use this gabelle on salt for the establishment of a state monopoly. Neither side was wholly successful.

With the authority of the crown thus limited by the narrow basis of its resources, the residue of power within the state lay with the other landowners: the church, the nobles, and the communes. These were the classes represented in the assemblies of the three states. Since the average revenue of the dukes in the second half of the fifteenth century was little more than 50,000 florins, and since expenditure was nearly always higher,[36] the duke had to recur to his vassals for money grants. Since the duke ruled over nobles and communes who prided themselves on their voluntary allegiance to the House of Savoy, he had to recur to the assembly for advice and support in important matters of state.[37] This was the basis for Talliandi's description of Piedmontese politics.[38]

Nevertheless, Piedmont was not a parliamentary monarchy. The assembly of the three estates, though a recognized part of the constitution, was not a clearly defined body. There were meetings in which representatives of all three main orders of society took part.[39] But these were not the rule. In most assemblies the clergy does not appear to have taken part, or the intervention of the ecclesiastical members of the duke's council —nearly always several of the Piedmontese bishops—may have been deemed sufficient representation for the first estate.[40] This

[36] Daviso, *La Duchessa,* pp. 136 f. Toward the end of the century, the revenue was higher.

[37] Cf. a typical summons issued by the Cismontane council to Ivrea, for the assembly of Oct., 1468, Tallone, *Parl. Sab.,* IV, 270 f.

[38] Cf. *supra,* n. 7.

[39] E.g., the assembly of May 4–8, 1470, in which the Milanese alliance was discussed. Tallone, *Parl. Sab.,* IV, 351 ff.

[40] This is, indeed, an argument from the absence of evidence, and such an argument cannot be entirely conclusive. At least on one occasion the bishops claimed that decisions taken without the heads of the clergy were invalid (G. L. Bossi, Milanese ambassador, to Bona di Savoia, Sept. 8,

meant that the most powerful single group in the state, the owners of at least a third of all the land in Piedmont,[41] were not regularly represented in the assembly at all.

There was, indeed, no need for such representation. Ducal decrees exempted ecclesiastical land from liability to parliamentary taxation,[42] and prelates might well spare themselves the expense and trouble of attending the meetings of a body one of whose main functions was the granting of money. At the same time, the higher clergy maintained a much more direct control over the government of the country through membership of the duke's councils than they could have hoped to

1478, *ibid.*, V, 237 f.); yet, even there, one suspects resentment of a personal slight. But the complete absence of documents on ecclesiastical representation, in contrast to the mass of documents on the towns, seems most convincing. Moreover, in Beatrice of Portugal's detailed description of the differences between towns and nobles in the assembly of Oct., 1535, there is no mention of the attitude of the clergy which one would have expected if they had been present and had either supported or opposed the government (letters to Charles III; *ibid.*, VII, 153 ff.). Tallone comes to a similar conclusion, remarking that the name *"Tre Stati"* lost its numerical significance (*ibid.*, I, 106).

[41] There are no exact statistics for this estimate. But all contemporary sources agree that the clergy owned $\frac{1}{3}$ of all land or even more, e.g., the "Memoriale" for Philip Emmanuel, Ricotti, *Storia*, p. 293. The council of Turin declared in 1517 that "the greater part of the land of Turin is held by the church or others who are exempt (from taxation)" (Tallone, *Parl. Sab.*, VI, 336 ff.). and in Vercelli the church owned as much as $\frac{2}{3}$ of all property (memorandum for assembly of Jan., 1522, *ibid.*, pp. 415 ff.). In the A.S.T. there are a great number of inventories of the property of ecclesiastical estates (*Inventario delle Abbazie, Inventario della Citta e Provincia d'Asti*, etc.) which bear out these views. The bishop of Asti, for instance, was lord over 16 fiefs, and some abbacies owned a dozen or more villages and manors.

[42] Decree of Yolanda of 1475 and similar decrees in 1485, 1487, 1488, 1503, 1505, 1507, 1509, 1512 exempting the abbacy of S. Maria of Pinerolo from payment of parliamentary grants. Pamphlet printed in Turin in 1622, A.S.T., Abbazie, Pinerolo, Mazzo 1, No. 4, p. 14. From sixteenth-century complaints of communes it appears that such exemptions were very common, if not universal.

exert through the three estates. The duke, in his turn, could rely upon the steady support of the clergy against all possible rivals. There existed, therefore, a permanent alliance between the crown and a force whose material strength in the dukedom could be measured by an annual income estimated at 80,000 ducats, as against the government's 50,000.[43] This alliance was permanent, troubled only by personal jealousies and rivalries between Piedmontese and Savoyards.

In the sixteenth century, and especially just before and during the French invasion, there was a growing resentment against the exemption of ecclesiastical land from taxation. Turin and Vercelli refused to grant the government's demands unless the clergy contributed.[44] By 1542, mutual bitterness had reached such an alarming pitch that the commune and the cardinal of Ivrea called upon the Spanish commander in chief and the pope himself to support their rival stands. The struggle ended with a substantial victory for the commune, although the cardinal himself escaped taxation by the payment of a mere 100 scudi.[45] In the same year Moncalieri for the first time compiled a register of ecclesiastical property to serve as a basis of tax assessments.[46] But only the restored monarchy of Emmanuel Philibert was strong enough to modify its policy toward the clergy.

The clergy were thus only spasmodically represented in the assembly of the three estates and were never an effective parliamentary force. The power they wielded through their great wealth and by their hold over men's minds was either neutral in the constitutional struggle or at the service of the monarchy. The nobility, on the other hand, attended the assemblies more

[43] Report of the Venetian ambassador Bertuzi Valier, March 19, 1498, in M. Sanuto, *I Diarii*, F. Stefani, ed. (Venice, 1879), I, 908.

[44] Minutes of council of Turin, April 18, 1517, Tallone, *Parl. Sab.*, VI, 336 ff. Vercelli, memorandum for session of Jan. 22, 1522, *ibid.*, pp. 415 ff.

[45] Tallone, "Ivrea e il Piemonte al tempo della prima dominazione francese (1536–1559)," extr. of *Biblioteca della Società Storica Subalpina* (Pinerolo, 1900), VII, 95 f.

[46] Moncalieri, Arch. Com., MS, Ser. A, vol. 78.

regularly; yet they never formed a distinct upper house in the English sense, nor a closed estate like the *braccio militare* of the Sicilian parliament. No summonses to members of the nobility have survived,[47] and it seems doubtful whether any baron could claim a technical right to membership of the assembly, in contrast to his feudal right and duty of owing support and counsel to his liege lord. Of the thousands of Piedmontese nobles, lords of some 800 castles,[48] only a few of the greater barons seem to have been regular parliamentarians. While all baronial land was liable to its share of taxes imposed by the assembly,[49] the right to grant these taxes in the name of the whole estate was in practice concentrated in the hands of a comparatively small number of great baronial families. For, as elsewhere in Renaissance Italy, it was as families that the barons were to be reckoned with. On the basis of his private estates, no single vassal of the duke of Savoy could play in Piedmont the role of a duke of Bourbon in France. But the combined possessions of the Valperga, the Piosasco, the Romagnano, or the Seyssel made their power supreme in their own province and formidable in the principality. Single baronial estates were comparatively small and were generally split up into small holdings worked by peasants on the métayage (*mezzadria*) system.[50] Alternatively, the lords obliged their tenants

[47] Tallone, *Parl. Sab.*, 270 f., says that the letter of the lieutenant-general of Piedmont, asking Ivrea to send two representatives, was addressed to the signori di Montaldo (letter of Sept. 28, 1468). This seems to be the only such letter addressed to members of the nobility directly. But in the MS copy, in the A.S.T., Paesi, Provincia d'Ivrea, Mazzo 10, No. 13, the Montaldo are mentioned only on the modern folder and not at all in the document. It is conceivable, however, that they are mentioned in the copy of the letter in the Archivio Communale of Ivrea.

[48] G. Lippomano, *Discorso seu Relatione*, 1573, *Tesoro Politico*, Pt. 3 and 4 (Frankfort, 1612), p. 374.

[49] The lists of contributions to parliamentary grants by communes and baronial fiefs are published in Tallone, *Parl. Sab.*, passim.

[50] E.g., "Patto Colonico tra l'Arcivescovo di Torino e i Massari della Badia di Stura," (1519), printed in A. Caviglia, *Claudio di Seyssel* (1450–

to pay rents in money and kind, and almost universally they exacted feudal dues such as a third of the value on the sale of holdings, payments on the marriage of the tenants' daughters or sisters, tithes on the sale of grain and wine, as well as labor and carriage services on the demesne or the lord's castle. These rights were enforced by the lord's possession of local jurisdiction, often in both first and second instance.[51]

Such resources, together with the feudal service owed to the barons by their own noble vassals and retainers, enabled the Piedmontese magnates to take the field with considerable fighting forces, at least for short periods. Thus, in 1470 the Roero of Sommariva del Bosco disputed certain fiefs with duke Amadeus IX and resisted his officials by force of arms. Fifteen years later it needed a regular campaign to make Claudio di Racconigi give up the same town which he had acquired on a mortgage from the duchess Yolanda.[52] When, in 1535 the communes refused to grant money for the defense of the duchy, a number of barons (most of them, however, Savoyards) presented themselves to the duchess-regent with several thousand foot and horse.[53]

It was the representatives of the communes who constituted the most regular element of the assemblies of the three estates.

---

1520), *Miscellanea di Storia Italiana,* ser. 3. vol. 23 (54) (Turin, 1928), pp. 604 ff.

[51] E.g., Marruchi's report on the county of Valperga, 1545, A.S.T., MS, Paesi, Prov. d'Ivrea, Mazzo 13, No. 1, Valperga e Contado, No. 27. Marruchi's other reports reveal very similar conditions, although in some villages peasants were freer than in others.

[52] A. Leone, "La Famiglia di Roero," in "Sommariva del Bosco nei secoli XVI e XV," *Boll. stor.-bibl. subalp.,* 17 (1912), 347, 353 ff.

[53] Beatrice of Portugal-Savoy to Charles III, Oct. 25, 1525, Tallone, *Par. Sab.,* VII, 156 f.
The imposing force of over 3,300 cavalry which the adherents of Philip of Bresse brought into the field in 1463 were also all Savoyards. The Milanese ambassador, Z. Oldoini, to duke of Milan, Aug. 29, 1463. Milan, Arch. di Stato, MS, Savoia, Box 480, folder 1463, July–Dec.

It was the towns which were most immediately concerned with taxation; for, unlike the nobles, they could not shift to the shoulders of their vassals the burden of the taxes they granted. The towns, indeed, did not represent themselves only, but also their surrounding countryside. But, at least in the case of Vercelli, the representatives received their instructions not only from the city council, but sometimes also from a preliminary assembly of the representatives of the whole district.[54] When a number of small towns under the jurisdiction of Biella quarreled with that city about the distribution of taxes, the duke's lieutenant-governor held that, if they so wished, they might send one or more representatives to accompany the members for Biella to the assembly.[55] When a town had not taken part in an assembly, it might not recognize a parliamentary grant, as did Cuneo in 1506.[56] For important assemblies it was, therefore, more convenient for the duke to summon as many towns as possible, both independent and baronial. On the other hand, the burden of the salaries and expenses of members, sometimes attending several times a year, was often too much for small towns, so that they were only rarely directly represented.[57] There was little that small baronial towns could hope to achieve, when even the bigger cities had to instruct their mem-

[54] Minutes of council meetings of Vercelli, Aug. 28, 1517, March 9, 1518, July 7, 1536, etc. Tallone, *Parl. Sab.*, VI, 355, 372; VII, 164 and *passim*. This practice seems to have started only in the sixteenth century.

[55] Claudio di Seyssel to Biella, May 17, 1469. *Ibid.*, IV, 321.

[56] Council minutes, March, 27, 1506: "Item, because the principality of Piedmont is said to have granted our illustrious lord duke of Savoy a certain subsidy . . . as to this, it is lawful that this commune is not bound." But, to acknowledge the duke's authority, they sent two ambassadors to him with the offer of a grant. *Ibid.*, VI, 222.

[57] Since we have lists of membership for only a few assemblies and are otherwise dependent on the minutes of town councils, it is not possible to decide definitely whether our ignorance of the names of representatives on any particular occasion is due to the failure of the town in question to return members, or simply to lacunae in the documents.

bers at times to oppose grants, but vote for them with good grace if opposition proved fruitless.[58] In an age where influence and prestige counted for more than numbers of votes, fifteen or twenty of the bigger towns could represent the totality of the communes as effectively as a larger number so long as their interests were common.[59]

The representatives of the communes were elected in various ways by the town councils. In Chieri the council empowered the governor and the two principal executive officers, the rectors of the Society of the Blessed Giorgio, to make the appointments.[60] In Turin there was a similar delegation of the powers of appointment to the *clavarii,* the highest treasury officers,[61] although at times the council chose the members itself, and on at least one accasion one member thus elected was allowed to choose his companion.[62] Savigliano had its own complicated system of indirect election by which two electors were chosen in the council either by lot or by vote; these then had to elect the representatives.[63] In most other communes, and sometimes in Savigliano too, the whole council voted on the proposed members.

In practice, it mattered little what form the election took. The burden and dignity of membership was reserved, almost exclusively, to a small oligarchy of leading families. Between 1460 and 1471, and again between 1481 and 1490, Turin sent 27 members of 20 families to at least 49 sessions of the assembly

[58] E.g., Instructions of the members for Pinerolo, Feb. 18, 1475. *Ibid.,* IV, 37. Or the representative for Moncalieri who was instructed that "he should insist that the gift and subsidy which has been demanded should not be granted except in return for the petitions presented by the country; yet, nevertheless, if others of the country and the principality should accede, he should do what the others do and act as best he can" (June 13, 1461, *ibid.,* p. 111).

[59] In the sixteenth century, however, the interests of the larger and the smaller communes began to diverge.

[60] *Ibid.,* V, 53, also pp. 199 f., 333, etc.     [61] *Ibid.,* IV, 120 d.

[62] Thomas de Gorzano, Dec. 4, 1469. *Ibid.,* p. 340.

[63] *Ibid.,* VII, 82 f., 85, 89, etc.

of the three estates.[64] There were never fewer than two representatives at a time, sometimes more. Yet, of these 27, twelve were elected only once and another five only twice. In fact, ten persons coming from eight families virtually monopolized the representation of Turin. Thomas de Gorzano, "in whose virtue and prudence the whole council trusted," [65] represented his native city no fewer than 21 times before the end of 1471. Giorgio de Becuti and Vauterio de Ruori had ten sessions, Piero de Brossulo and Borbone de Strata had nine sessions each to their credit. The Gorzano, the Becuti, the Strata, the Scaravelli, the Ruori, the Ferreri and the San Giorgio were all noble families, owning property at least four to six times as large as the average of the citizens of Turin. Only Brossulo was a commoner, but he, too, was wealthy; and of those who were elected only once or twice, the majority were nobles, and nearly all appear in the *catasti,* or land registers, of Turin as owning very substantial estates.[66]

In other towns the situation was similar.[67] Luigi Talliandi represented Ivrea in over thirty sessions of the assembly from 1468 to 1512—a record of which a parliamentarian in any country might be proud. When he himself was not chosen or was abroad, another Talliandi nearly always took his place. In Moncalieri, the Degle, the Caburretto, the Marchoaudi, the Vagnoni, the Gramaya and the Duchis featured prominently both as members of the assembly and as large property owners in the land registers.[68] Not all rich and noble urban families

[64] *Ibid.,* Vols. IV–VI *passim.* We do not know the representatives of Turin for the sessions between 1471 and 1481.

[65] Council minutes of Feb. 1, 1471. *Ibid.,* IV, 381.

[66] Turin, Arch. Com., MSS Catasti, Ser. X, Nos. 58–61, for 1464; Nos. 64–67 for 1470.

[67] Daviso makes the same point (although without using the *catasti*) and prints lists of members habitually representing a number of the major communes ("Considerazioni," pp. 20 f.). Such lists can be easily extended to other towns and periods from Tallone's documents.

[68] Moncalieri, Arch. Com., MSS, Catasti, Ser. A, vols. 54–57 for 1463, vols. 62–65 for 1504.

provided members for the assembly. The wealthy Marchadillo and Canali of Chieri,[69] the Gastaudi and Droxio of Turin, never seem to have been represented. The vast propertied clan of the Darmelli of Moncalieri, who added *giornata* after *giornata* to their estates for almost a century, managed to break only once into the charmed circle of those wielding political power.[70]

Yet there is no doubt about the nature of communal representation in the assembly. Members were drawn from a small upper class of rich landowners and merchants, many of them from noble families, a few of them lawyers and, very occasionally, a medical man.[71] Earlier attempts of the bourgeoisie of Chivasso and other towns to exclude the feudal nobility from citizenship [72] had long since failed.[73] On rare occasions, when reform of the currency was to be discussed, the government asked communes to return members who were experts in financial and monetary questions.[74] The towns had no difficulty

[69] Chieri, Arch. Com., MSS, Catasti, Art. 143, sec. 1, vol. 42, Quarter of Albussano in 1466; vol. 53, Quarter of Albussano in 1533.

[70] Antonio Darmelli, *cantor* and canon of the church of the Blessed Maria, July, 1471. Tallone, *Parl. Sab.*, IV, 401. He owned a sizeable property amounting to 174 *giornate;* Moncalieri, Arch. Com., Catasti, Ser. A, vol. 55, fol. 29–31. One *giornata* = 100 tavoli = about 0.94 acres. Calculated from M. C. Daviso, "I più antichi catasti di Chieri," extr. from *Boll. stor.-bibl. subalp.* (1937), p. 23.

[71] E.g., Giorgio Antiochia, member for Turin from 1533 in many assemblies, and ambassador of the city to the king of France. Tallone, *Parl. Sab.*, VII, 112, 118, 245 ff. and *passim*. In the *catasto* of 1523 his property in real estate was estimated at more than 24 *libra* which places him among the 38 richest citizens. Turin, Arch. Com., MS, Catasti, Ser. X, vol. 98, fol. 170.

[72] A. Bozzola, "Appunti sulla vita economica . . . del Monferrato nei secoli XIV e XV, *Boll. stor.-bibl. subalp.*, 25 (1923), 221, n. 2.

[73] From the 1470's Pietro de Verulfi and Michael de Trecate, both nobles, were regular representatives of Chivasso at the assembly. There are probably earlier examples. Tallone, *Parl. Sab.*, V, 36, 191, etc.

[74] E.g., Cismontane council to Chivasso, July 8, 1500. Other towns received similar letters. *Ibid.*, VI, 183.

in complying with such a request, for their experts were likely to be wealthy merchants or landowners, members of the municipal council, or even the mayors (syndics) of the city who would be elected in any case.[75]

In such a situation the problem of contested elections hardly arose. Only in Ivrea, the hometown of Luigi Talliandi, were divided votes in the council at all common, and even there the majorities were usually overwhelming. For Mondovì, the town riven by fiercer feuds of Guelphs and Ghibellines than any other in Piedmont,[76] we have no records of difficulties over elections. On the other hand, members frequently refused to accept their election, and in Vercelli the council had to rule that there was no right of refusal.[77] It happened in Vercelli that of three candidates two received equal votes in the council. This problem was settled in 1496 by simply giving all three their credentials for the assembly;[78] but since this was contrary to custom,[79] a decision was taken by lot when the representatives had to return for the following session, even though one of them objected that the question ought to be decided *de jure*.[80] Just as in France the *haute-bourgeoisie*, so in the Piedmontese communes the ruling groups monopolized the administration of the towns and their representation in the three estates. At the same time, in Piedmont as in France, the individual members of this class were not eager to accept the burden of office.[81] Some nobles, as the Talliandi of Ivrea, un-

---

[75] In Sept., 1465, Pinerolo elected Pietro de Iaveno, "for this Peter is highly skilled and expert in monetary matters" (*Ibid.*, IV, 185 f.). For the assembly of 1500 (cf. previous note) most towns sent their regular members.

[76] Gabotto, *Lo Stato*, II, 465 f.

[77] Council minutes of May 4, 1487. Tallone, *Parl. Sab.*, V, 387.

[78] Minutes of May 26 and of June 3, 1496. *Ibid.*, VI, 121 f.

[79] On June 4, 1496, Pinerolo had decided to send only two "since according to custom only two are to be chosen" (*Ibid.*, pp. 122 f.).

[80] Minutes of June 24, 1496. *Ibid.*, p 130.

[81] Cf. R. Doucet, *Les Institutions de la France au XVIe siècle* (Paris, 1948), I, 375.

doubtedly regarded election as the mark of traditional respect due to their families or persons. Some lawyers might use membership of the assembly as a steppingstone for a career in ducal service,[82] a practice which became common in England in the time of Henry VIII.[83] But while in England during the sixteenth century membership of parliament came to be so highly valued that candidates more and more frequently waived their salaries, in Piedmont the representatives always insisted on full payment. Carlo de Ranzo of Vercelli even refused to go unless the town provided him with three horses.[84]

This personal reluctance of the Piedmontese patricians may be ascribed, in large measure, to the limitations of the initiative allowed to members of the assembly. Significantly, they were known as "ambassadors." They spoke not as representatives but as delegates, bound strictly by instructions received from their communes. They presented petitions prepared by other members of the council. "Thomas Croti [together with Giovanni Rostagnani] is to go to Turin," so ran the typical instructions of the council of Pinerolo in 1476, "to stay there and listen to all that is proposed; and he is always to keep the commune informed of what is done, and of what is to be done, so that he will take no action without knowledge and mandate from the commune." [85] When, a year later, Croti tried to ingratiate himself with the duke by telling his ministers that the Pinerolese were quietly accepting the taxes against which the town had protested, the council severely rebuked him, barred him from further service, and sent another ambassador posthaste to undo the damage.[86] The first session of an assembly

[82] E.g., Daniele Levini on several occasions member for Savigliano from 1465, who became civil judge and *logotenente* of Chieri. Tallone, *Parl. Sab.*, IV, 192, V, 102.

[83] K. Pickthorn, *Early Tudor Government: Henry VIII* (Cambridge, 1934), p. 132.

[84] Tallone, *Parl. Sab.*, VI, 329. Council minutes of March 17, 1517.

[85] Pinerolo council minutes, July 26, 1476. *Ibid.*, V, 142 f.

[86] Minutes of Nov. 21, 1477. *Ibid.*, pp. 223 f.

was always occupied with a statement, by the chancellor or another prominent member of the Cismontane council, of the duke's financial needs and requests for taxation, or of such policies for which the government desired the assembly's counsel and support. The delegates then returned home and were only then granted full powers to vote on the government's proposals, and only in strict accordance with the declared wishes of their own town council. Their petitions might be presented either at the first or at the second session.

Nevertheless a certain amount of freedom of action had to be granted to them. They were generally instructed "to confer about all matters with other ambassadors of the country, and to do in all matters as others of this principality did"; [87] or they were simply to vote with the majority.[88] The authorities in the communes were realists. They knew that the communes could refuse a grant only if they were virtually unanimous. The ambassadors were therefore left free to act "as to their prudence and wisdom seemed best." [89] Only rarely did a town decide to stand out against a grant "even if the rest of the country were to agree to it." [90]

In the assembly, just as in the towns, it was the dominant social group, rather than the individual, which determined policy. As Baroness Daviso has pointed out,[91] members with long parliamentary experience had ample opportunity to get to know each other, to learn to cooperate, and to develop the traditions and procedure of parliamentary action. They undoubtedly took this opportunity; yet they took it more as delegates of their particular localities and as representatives of their

[87] Instructions to the members for Moncalieri, March 20, 1469. *Ibid.*, IV, 309 f.

[88] E.g., instructions to the member Chivasso, July 15, 1469. *Ibid.*, p. 327.

[89] Instructions to the member for Ivrea, April 26, 1461. *Ibid.*, p. 91.

[90] Pinerolo council minutes, Sept. 24, 1477. *Ibid.*, V, 213.

[91] Daviso, "Considerazioni," p. 20.

class, than as members of a parliamentary institution and spokesmen of the whole country. The history of the Piedmontese assembly was therefore closely linked with the fortunes of those classes in the community whose interests it directly represented: the greater feudal magnates and the noble property owners and the bourgeois of the towns. For as long as the prosperity of these classes increased, and increased more rapidly than the prosperity of other classes in the community, there occurred a parallel increase in the power and influence of the assembly.[92] After the turn of the fifteenth century, feudal magnates and urban patriciate ceased to advance, although they maintained their relative economic position in the country. During the same period the fortunes of the assembly of the three estates again moved parallel to the economic fortunes of the upper classes; the assembly ceased to extend its political power, but was able to defend the position it had previously gained.

The latter part of the fifteenth century was undoubtedly a period of slow but marked economic advance for the towns of Piedmont. From the land registers which these towns compiled, it appears clearly that their populations were increasing— usually a fair sign of growing prosperity in that age. In Turin there were 884 property owners in 1464 [93] which meant a population of perhaps 4,000 or very slightly less,[94] excluding the

[92] This was fully appreciated by Daviso who links the "formation of the ruling class . . . which one cannot place further back than the middle of the fifteenth century. . . ," with the "flourishing of the assemblies of the Three Estates." *Ibid.*, p. 14. She did not, however, attempt to give evidence for, nor analyze, the economic and social part of this argument. It may be stated at this point that an economic history of Piedmont for the latter Middle Ages and the Renaissance period does not exist, and that it is one of the primary disiderata for the full understanding of Italian history.

[93] Turin, Arch. Com., MSS, Catasti, Ser. X, Nos. 58–61. The number of households is arrived at by adding up the number of entries.

[94] The factor used is 4.5 (as against 5 which is, perhaps, more commonly used by demographers). Such contemporary evidence as exists for deter-

clergy and those who owned no property at all.[95] By 1503 the number of inhabitants had risen to about 6,150 (1,367 householders); but in the next twenty years the population remained almost stationary, increasing to only about 6,260 (1,391 householders).[96] The trend was similar in Moncalieri. The *catasti* of that town show about 3,400 inhabitants in 1463 (759 householders),[97] 7,130 in 1504 (1,426 householders),[98] and, after that date, a slight decline to about 7,000 (1,401 householders) in 1527.[99] This is the last date before the French invasion in 1536 for which we have figures. For Chieri it has been possible to collect figures only for the fifteenth century, but they tell the same story of slow growth [100] and, undoubtedly, most other towns had similar histories.

---

mining the average number of persons in one household is not very conclusive. In 1560 Boldù estimated that Savigliano had 450 hearths (*fuochi*) and about 3,000 inhabitants, i.e., 6.7 per hearth (Albèri, *Relazioni,* ser. 2, I, 442 f). This seems rather high, and Boldù does not state his authority, although he may well have talked with the Savigliano authorities who knew from their *catasti*. There is a fifteenth century document in the Archivo Communale of Chieri (Art. 111, fasc. 3. It is in the folder for 1473; but there is no indication on the document that it really belongs to that year) which gives the number of hearths in that city as 609 and the number of inhabitants as 2,483, making a factor of 4.1. This, by contrast, seems unusually low, but is more likely to be right for the fifteenth century than the Savigliano figure.

Given the size of an average household, it is clear that an increase in the number of hearths indicates an upward trend in population. If, as seems likely, the factor increased during the period under discussion, such an increase would have accentuated the upward trend.

[95] Turin, Arch. Comm., MSS, Catasti, Ser. X, vols. 54–57.

[96] *Ibid.,* vols. 96–99.

[97] Moncalieri, Arch. Com., MSS, Catasti, Ser. A, vols. 54–57.

[98] *Ibid.,* vols. 62–65.

[99] *Ibid.,* vols. 66–70.

[100] In 1473 Chieri had 609 households (if indeed the years was 1473; cf. *supra,* n. 69; the figure seems too low), 1,398 in 1483, and 1,515 in 1496–1497. Chieri, Arch. Com., MSS, Art. 111, fasc. 3, 11–14, 42–46 bis. Only a cursory examination of the Chieri *catasti* has been possible and, since they are in good order, it is undoubtedly possible to calculate from them population figures for the 16th century.

The *catasti,* moreover, show shifts in the ownership of property within the towns. Every householder had to declare, before specially appointed commissioners, his houses inside the town, and the number of *giornate* [101] of arable, pasture, or vineyard he owned or held [102] in the surrounding country, together with certain special rights, such as the use of water from the irrigation canals. In these alphabetical registers, the noble owner of several castles and hundreds of *giornate* was entered next to the small artisan with his half acre of pasture. Only the clergy are absent, for they were exempt from the taxation based on these records. Holdings were almost invariably quite small, and even the large estates of the patricians were made up of a great number of small lots, rarely more than 30 or 40 *giornate* in extent, and usually much smaller. Each holding was evaluated in *librae, solidi,* and *denari.*[103]

Unfortunately it is not possible to obtain from these registers the market value of the property held by the inhabitants of a city at any one time, nor the changes in value over a certain period. Pounds, shillings, and pence were a purely traditional currency, used in *catasti* as early as the thirteenth century; [104] they bore no ascertainable relationship to the currency in actual use in Piedmont during the Renaissance: florins and ducats. While for any one year of the register, the values are consistent, every acre of vineyard, for instance, being given the same value as every other (unless there were very great variations in the quality of the land), the values themselves appear to have been fixed quite arbitrarily by the commissioners. Turin, Moncalieri, and Chieri each had different scales of value, and, to complicate matters further, these values varied

[101] Cf. *supra,* n. 70.

[102] There is no indication in the *catasti* of the legal nature of the proprietorship set down. It is inconceivable that all entries should have been freehold property. Most of it was probably some form of long lease, perhaps on a customary basis, and usually in métayage.

[103] These *catasti,* or registers, are in Latin and, mostly, in a good state of preservation. With a little persistence they are quite easily accessible.

[104] Daviso, "I più antichi catasti," *passim.*

in different years. Thus in Turin one *giornata* of arable land of average quality was estimated at 5 *solidi* in 1464 and at only 2 to 3 in 1523, while the figures for a *giornata* of vineyard were 20 to 5 *solidi,* respectively.[105] Since, however, the estimates are consistent for any particular year in which a *catasto* was compiled and, therefore, roughly consistent with the corresponding market values, it is possible to calculate the approximate percentage of the town's total property held by different social groups in such a year. The economic changes which these groups underwent can then be shown by a similar calculation for a later date.[106]

The graph (Figure A) and Table A show the distribution of real property in Turin for the years 1464, 1470, and 1523.[107]

[105] These values are therefore no more indicative of market values, either through a period of time or at a point of time, than are rateable values for local government taxation today.

Since the value of currency in actual use depreciated steadily throughout this period, one would have expected higher assessments in 1523 if the estimates had any direct connection with current money values. Since the reverse is the case, the valuations did not even change in the same ratio as market values. The only economic conclusion one might possibly venture is that viticulture increased, for, by comparison with arable, vineyards seems to have been less valuable in 1523 than in 1464.

In the Turin *catasti* the values of each person's holdings are added up —a great help to the investigator which he does not have in the *catasti* of Moncalieri. In the Turin registers of 1503 no values are given at all. No statistical information could therefore be obtained from them, although it might be possible to analyze the size and nature of the holdings, rather than the values, given in the *catasti*. Such a task, however, is possible only for a resident. Unfortunately, there is so far no sign that the Piedmontese historians are making a systematic attack on the *catasti*. They exist not only in Turin, Moncalieri, and Chieri, where the present author has studied them, but undoubtedly also in other towns. They could furnish much interesting material for the social and economic history of the province.

[106] It has been possible to extract sufficient statistical material for such calculation only from the registers of Turin. Turin, Arch. Com., MSS, Catasti, Ser. X, Nos. 58–61, 64–67, 95–99.

[107] I would like to acknowledge here my great debt to Mr. H. H. Montgomery of the Department of Economics of The Queen's University of Belfast, for working out the table and graph from my statistical material.

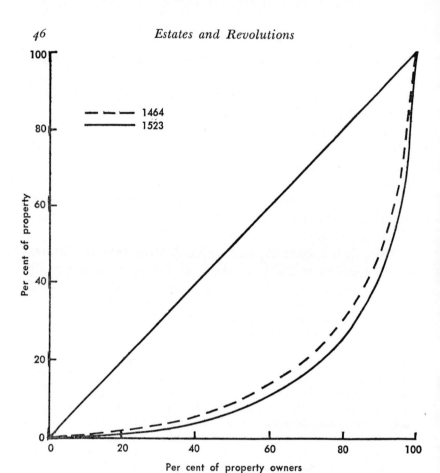

Figure A. *Distribution of Property in Turin, 1464 and 1523.* The diagonal line is the line of equal distribution of property and the areas enclosed between this diagonal and the actual curves is a measure of the inequality of distribution (inequality increased by 2 per cent over 59 years). The graph starts with the poorest section of the community, while the figures in the table indicate the richest sections; i.e., the richest 10 per cent of the population are those between 90 and 100 per cent in the graph.

It is clear that the distribution of property and, in consequence, the social structure of Turin remained fairly stable. There was, however, a definite, if small, increase in the percentage of property owned by the richest section of this community—precisely of those groups who represented the city in the three estates. Half this advance, moreover, took place between 1464 and 1470.[108] It seems probable, therefore, that the improvement in the economic position of the Turin patriciate took place between 1464 and the end of the fifteenth century.

Table A. *Distribution of Property in Turin*

| Property owners (richest, in per cent) | Percentage of total property | | |
|---|---|---|---|
| | 1464 | 1470 | 1523 |
| 1 | 13 | 17 | 21 |
| 5 | 38 | 43 | 46 |
| 10 | 53 | 56 | 60 |
| 25 | 75 | 76 | 79 |
| 50 | 91 | 92 | 92 |
| 75 | 98 | 98 | 99 |
| No. of property owners | 884 | 987 | 1393 |

The *catasti* of Moncalieri show a similar trend. They do not always give money values, but they show changes in the ownership of individual holdings.[109] Up to the end of the fifteenth century the great property owners, taken together, added more land to their estates than they lost. In the sixteenth century both big and small properties began to be more unstable. Most members of the huge Darmelli family continued to increase their possessions; but other patrician families, as the Oddano, suffered heavy losses. Up to the *catasto* of 1527 the holders of medium-sized properties did slightly better than the classes above or below them.

Until we have detailed studies of the land registers of other Piedmontese towns no definitive conclusions are possible. Yet

108 The curve for 1470 lies between the other two throughout its whole length; but for the sake of clearness it has been left out of the graph.

109 Moncalieri, Arch. Com., MSS, Catasti, Ser. A, vols. 54–57 for 1463, vols. 62–65 for 1504, and vols. 66–70 for 1527. The changes in ownership were entered after each of these dates and continued to be made until the

there are indications which suggest that the histories of Turin and Moncalieri were typical. In the second part of the fifteenth century trade increased sufficiently to make it worth while for Yolanda's government to build a canal between Ivrea and Vercelli and thus to link the Val d'Aosta with the commercial highway of the Po.[110] In Pinerolo, the one important wool town of the duchy, a number of new wool businesses sprang up.[111] In 1497 it became possible, for the first time, to farm the gabelle on salt to a Piedmontese merchant, Antonio Porta of Chivasso, who bound himself to the annual payment of the huge sum of 31,000 florins.[112] Before that date, the government had been obligated to farm this important source of revenue to Genoese and Savonese financiers.[113]

The feudal magnates undoubtedly shared in this increasing prosperity. Both personally and economically they were often closely allied to the patriciate of the communes. The counts of Crescentino were members of the Tizzoni family which habitually represented Vercelli in the assembly.[114] Pauletus Vagnoni, lord of Troffarello, Castelvecchio, and other fiefs,[115] was chosen on various occasions to represent both his native Moncalieri and Ivrea.[116] His family later concluded a marriage alliance with the Valperga, and in the sixteenth century his estates were joined to those of that powerful family.[117] The Valperga, counts of Masino, were, perhaps, the outstandingly successful family of the age. Despite the catastrophes suffered

---

compilation of the next register. Sometimes, but not always, they are dated. It is not always clear (though sometimes it is stated) when change of ownership was due to sale and when to inheritance.

[110] Daviso, *La Duchessa,* pp. 146 ff.

[111] Caffaro, "L'Arte del Lanificio," p. 515, n. 1.

[112] A.S.T., MS, Sec. 1, Inventario delle Materie Economiche: Gabella Sale Piemonte e Nizza, No. 13.

[113] *Ibid.,* Nos. 9, 11, 12.

[114] A.S.T., MS, Paesi, Inventari, 28, Vercilli, fo. 86–87.

[115] *Ibid.,* 16, Torino, fo. 62–64.

[116] Tallone, *Parl. Sab.,* IV, 214, 340.

[117] A.S.T., MS, Paesi, Inventari, 16, Torino, fo. 66.

by some of their most important members,[118] they clung tenaciously to their estates and continued adding fiefs and titles to their name.[119] The inventories and documents for the provinces of Piedmont in the state archives of Turin contain a mass of feudal contracts, wills, and lawsuits. For the latter part of the fifteenth century these appear to show a definite preponderance of acquisitions over losses by the great feudal families, especially in the western parts of Piedmont where large estates were more common than in the east.

It was inevitable that the magnates and the urban patriciate should want to play a role in the political life of the state that would match their economic advance and growing self-confidence. Their country was ruled by a dynasty that was as yet more French than Italian, more Savoyard than Piedmontese. Their dukes preferred to live on the pleasant shores of Lake Geneva rather than in the sun-baked plains of the Po valley.[120] The more important offices of state were habitually occupied by Savoyard barons. The richest benefices were held by ecclesiastics from "the other side of the mountains." [121] Yet the Piedmontese had to pay most of the taxes.[122]

The assembly of the three estates presented the most convenient instrument to redress this adverse balance. This body was the guardian of the country's privileges. Before the assembled estates every duke, on his accession, had to take an oath on the strict observance of the liberties of Piedmont. Only with the consent of the assembly could a regent carry on the government for a duke who was a minor. Every foreign treaty needed ratification by the three estates, and this necessity

---

[118] M. C. Daviso, "Filippo Senza Terra," *Rivista storica italiana,* ser. 4, 4 (Turin, 1935), 127–152. Leone, *"La Famiglia,"* pp. 353 ff.

[119] A.S.T., MS, Paesi 22, Provincia d'Ivrea, Mazzi 6, 7, 13.

[120] Daviso, "Considerazioni," p. 15.

[121] Bossi to duke of Milan, Sept. 9, 1478; Tallone, *Parl. Sab.,* V, 238.

[122] Conte di Caiazzo to same, April 2, 1490; *ibid.,* VI, 25 f; Lambert, "Registres," p. 34.

opened the door wide to parliamentary interference in foreign affairs. In return for the taxes which the assembly allowed the duke to levy in fixed proportions on towns and baronial lands,[123] it insisted on the presentation of *capitoli* which would become laws with the ducal assent. The duke could veto or ignore these *capitoli;* but, in practice, he was bound to accept the majority of these parliamentary proposals if he wanted to obtain his subsidy without trouble. The *capitoli* ranged over the whole field of administration and public law, from the dishonest practices of ducal tax commissioners to the observance of the regular instances of judicial procedure [124] or the rights of young girls not to be forced into marriage against their will.[125]

[123] The duke appointed a receiver of taxes who drew up a list of the sums to be paid by all towns and baronial territories. (These lists are printed in Tallone.) The rate was fixed by the assembly itself and each town or district then delivered its quota (cf. the preamble to the *capitoli* of the assembly of April, 1473. Tallone, *Parl. Sab.*, V, 12). But the assembly did not usually determine the type of taxation by which this quota was to be raised. The town might impose a land tax, the *talea* or *taxus*, on the basis of the *catasto* returns; but such direct taxation always proved unpopular with the propertied classes and was often difficult to collect. In consequence, the towns often had to have recourse to indirect taxation, such as gabelles on foodstuffs. Cf. M. Chiaudano, "La Finanza del Commune di Torino nel Secolo XV," *Torino,* Vol. 20, No. 10 (Oct., 1941), *passim.*

[124] Even during the French occupation, in Oct., 1539, the assembly insisted that in all criminal cases the accused should enjoy his full rights of defense, that he should be shown the indictment against him, and that he should have legal aid "as the law declares, for justice must not be denied to anyone, even the devil." The French viceroy, on this occasion, accepted this *capitolo* except for cases of *lèse-majesté.* Tallone, *Parl. Sab.*, VII, 278 ff.

[125] In so far as the *capitoli* were transformed into ducal decrees, the three estates may be regarded as exercising legislative powers; but not all *capitoli* were intended as a basis for legislation, nor did the duke require parliamentary assent for all the decrees he issued. The precise legislative powers of the assembly and of the duke were, however, never clearly defined. This lack of definition often gave rise to considerable friction between the duke and the assembly as, for instance, over the ducal orders regulating the import of salt.

It was this assembly which was the traditional meeting place and virtual monopoly of those rising classes whose ambitions, both in the economic and the political life of the state, were now moving on parallel lines.[126] Yet the ambitions of these classes were as limited as their economic advance. They wanted their share of the spoils due to the ruling classes of a feudal state, and they wanted to make certain that their ancient liberties and privileges were not overthrown, as they had been overthrown in the neighboring duchy of Milan.

Such aims might well be achieved within the framework of the traditional feudal constitution of Piedmont, the more easily so since the death of the weak duke Louis, in 1465, was followed by a long period of minorities and regencies. Yet if the collective ambitions of the parliamentary classes were limited, those of other powers in the political arena were not. The late duke's younger sons, especially the redoubtable Philip of Bresse (1443–1497), were forever intriguing for the control of the government from the vantage points of their rich appanages of Bresse, Geneva, and Pays de Vaud. Ambitious barons, such as the count de la Chambre, fought for the guardianship of a boy duke. And beyond them, more formidable because more powerful still, were the country's neighbors: the Swiss, Burgundy, and, above all, Milan and France.

All these powers were hostile to the assembly of the three estates and fundamentally opposed to any restriction of the ducal power in Piedmont. The Sforza had overthrown the Ambrosian Republic of Milan and had re-established despotic rule in their duchy. The kings of France were still struggling with their own "overmighty subjects" and had no sympathy for them in neighboring states. Louis XI even proposed to Galeazzo Maria Sforza a tripartite pact between France, Milan,

[126] Unlike the English parliament, the Piedmontese assembly was no court of law. Only on one occasion did it act as a supreme tribunal, when duke Louis of Savoy accused his son, Philip of Bresse, before the assembled estates of the murder of the chancellor Valpergo, in 1462. Even then bled assembly had a political, rather than a judicial, character. M. C. Daviso, "Filippo Senza Terra," pp. 153 ff.

and Savoy for the specific purposes of curbing the subjects of Amadeus IX, making his power as absolute as that of the king of France and enabling him to impose taxes and miltary service according to French and Milanese practice. If all three rulers agreed to give each other military support against unruly subjects, the king suggested, it would greatly increase the security of each one of them and it would be easy to dispose of the few lordlings who were the cause of all troubles.[127]

Yet this proposal for a fifteenth century "Holy Alliance" was never put into effect.[128] Whatever their political preferences, the rulers of both France and Milan found the Piedmontese assembly far too useful to wish to see it destroyed. Neither wanted to see the other's troops in Piedmont; it was both easier and safer to extend one's influence by judicious support of the various conflicting forces within the duchy. When Luigi Talliandi explained to the Milanese ambassador the powers of the assembly,[129] he advised Sforza "to select six, eight, or ten of the principal gentlemen of Piedmont, both prelates and

[127] Carlo Visconti, Milanese ambassador to Savoy, to G. M. Sforza, Lausanne, July 22, 1471; Milan, Arch. di Stato, MS, Savoia, Box 484, folder 1471, July. "Furthermore, the said Monsieur Karlo [Astardi, French ambassador to Savoy] has told me how His Majesty, the king of France, has given him to understand that he would wish to see the problems of Savoy settled: which, he hopes, can be accomplished quickly. They should wait until they had all their troops together in order to reduce this state of Savoy to the condition and form of that of France and that of Your Serene Highness [i.e., the duke of Milan]. The duke and duchess [of Savoy] should then be better able to manage their subjects, keep them on a rather tighter rein and maintain the free archers, as is the custom in France; and it seems that the nobles should be obliged to serve in time of war: for, since His Majesty, Your Excellency and the house of Savoy are at present united and allied, this would greatly enhance the security and stability of the state of each one of you, for you could each help the other with your troops. And he says that it seems to the king that this can easily be done; for it will only be necessary to knock down three or four lordlings who are the cause of all these commotions and novelties. . . ."

[128] The Milanese ambassador gave a polite but evasive answer. *Ibid.*

[129] Cf. *supra,* n. 7.

laymen, and to give them honours and subventions and to treat them well," for the three estates would always listen to them and in this way the country could be controlled.[130] Such advice was hardly necessary: all of Piedmont's neighbors had long since followed precisely this policy. In 1468 the Venetian ambassador, Antonio Dandolo, wrote: "In the duchess's council, according to what the duke's physician told me, the majority are adherents either of the duke of Burgundy or of the king of France, for they have castles and estates within his jurisdiction; and others again [are adherents] of Milan." [131] The chancellor Jacopo di Valperga admitted that he had been placed in his high office through the influence of France "for the purpose of subjecting Savoy to His Majesty so that it would always be in his power to come to Italy [i.e., invade Italy] whenever he pleased." [132] When Yolanda's Venetian alliance was to be ratified by the assembly—for even on such matters the duke had no power to commit the state on his own authority—both Venice and Milan were lavish with bribes, the one to procure acceptance, the other rejection.[133] So unreliable was the Piedmontese nobility that the regent Yolanda had to follow suit and bribe her own magnates with pensions and offices.[134]

Thus the assembly was used by those who cared nothing for it and who yet increased its power every time they invoked its aid for their own purposes. This was the condition of both the strength and weakness of the three estates. It explains the assembly's remarkable forays in the direction of parliamentary control over the government and, at the same time, its repeated failures to persist in such offensives. Only once were the three

[130] Tallone, *Parl. Sab.*, V, 180.

[131] Dandolo to doge of Venice, Turin, Oct. 30, 1468. Milan, Arch. di Stato, MS, Savoia, Box 483, folder 1468, October.

[132] Daviso, "Filippo Senza Terra," p. 147.

[133] Sforza to Antonio di Romagnano, Nov. 15, 1568; Tallone, *Parl. Sab.*, IV, 280. Dandolo to doge, Feb. 18, 1569; *ibid.*, pp. 301 f. Antonio Bracelli to Sforza, May 7, 1570; *ibid.*, pp. 351 f.

[134] Lambert, "Registres," p. 40. Jacques Lambert was Yolanda's "conseiller et maistre des requestes" (p. 64) and thus in a position to know.

estates faced with a situation in which they were called upon to act on their own in the name of the whole country. The tragicomedy of their failure revealed the fundamental weakness of the assembly.

On June 22, 1476, the armies of Charles the Bold of Burgundy and of his ally Yolanda of Savoy were annihilated by the Swiss at Morat. Yolanda immediately began to negotiate with Charles's archenemy, her brother Louis XI of France. Charles acted quickly. On June 28 his men ambushed the duchess and her son and carried her off to Burgundy. But Luigi Talliandi and other Piedmontese gentlemen in Burgundian service showed sufficient patriotism and presence of mind to hide the boy duke from the kidnapers and convey him safely back to Savoy. Without him, Burgundy had no hold over Savoy.[135] This was a golden opportunity for Louis XI to intervene as protector of his young nephew. He concluded an armistice for him with the Swiss,[136] summoned the estates of Savoy and induced them to confer on him the wardship of the young duke Philibert and to hand over to him the fortresses of Chambéry and Montmélian.[137] It would not do, however, to intervene as openly in Piedmont. Louis therefore proposed to support Philibert's paternal uncle, Philip of Bresse.[138]

In Turin, Yolanda's Cismontane council were unwilling to accept such intervention. They had sworn loyalty to the regent;

[135] Daviso, *La Duchessa,* pp. 225 ff. F. Gingins La Sarra, *Dépêches des Ambassadeurs Milanais sur les campagnes de Charles-le-Hardi* (Paris-Geneva, 1858), Vol. I, *passim.*

[136] Louis XI was not unhappy to see his too-independent sister defeated, but he could not allow the Swiss to destroy her state. He had made this quite clear already a year earlier: Jean Irmy, citizen of Bâle, to Sforza, Feb. 20, 1475: "I have heard that the king of France has written to Berne after Madame of Savoy was defeated by the Bernese . . . and that he would be content that she should have some punishment, but that His Majesty will not on any account have her destroyed; and if they should wish to destroy her, he would give her aid and succor with all his power." Gingins La Sarra, *Dépêches,* I, 45.

[137] Daviso, *La Duchessa,* pp. 249 ff.

[138] Treaty of Roanne, July 22, 1476. Tallone, *Parl. Sab.,* V, 137 ff.

they feared for their offices, and even for their heads, if Philip and his party should take over the government: honor and self-interest both counseled resistance. First in an assembly of notables, and then in a regular meeting of the three estates, they declared "that they would in no way permit [Yolanda] to hand over part or the whole of the state to others, and that they would take over themselves all authority in the state" to preserve it for her as regent.[139] It was a virtual declaration of the sovereignty of the assembly. Brave words were spoken about the defense of the country against all foreign intervention, whatever the alleged legal claims of outsiders might be. The assembly agreed that troops should be raised to defend the Piedmontese passes. Members of the council and envoys from the assembly were sent to Milan and to France to ask for support and to prevent Philip's intervention. In Turin, the Milanese ambassadors did their best to stiffen Piedmontese resistance.[140]

Yet the Cismontane council was in a desperate position. Sforza gave fair words, but could he be trusted? In his turn, the duke of Milan was unwilling to commit himself against France unless he could be certain that the Piedmontese would not weaken. The reports from his ambassadors were not reassuring. Although the council insisted that what concerned all should be decided by all,[141] opinion both in the country and in the assembly was divided. Philip of Bresse could count on the inevitable group of discontented barons and on the *populari,* the smaller towns and lesser nobility who had suffered from the heavy taxation of Yolanda's government and held that she had let herself be dominated by selfish and greedy advisers.[142] Philip fomented the discord by making promises of offices.

---

[139] *Ibid.,* p. 110. Also quoted in Daviso, "Considerazione," p. 23.

[140] The whole episode from the reports of the Milanese ambassadors, Pietrasanta and Bianco, June to Aug., 1476. Tallone, *Parl. Sab.,* V, 109–180.

[141] Bianco to Sforza, July 18, 1476; *ibid.,* p. 129.

[142] Same to same, July 22, 1476; *ibid.,* pp. 136 f.

Even some of the members of the council now began to waver. An August 15 the three estates once more determined unanimously to resist Philip. But it was only a romantic gesture. Five days later Philip marched into Turin, and everyone, except the most heavily compromised members of the council, went out to welcome him. The council and the three estates had failed utterly to uphold their own and Yolanda's authority. Philip, indeed, preferred to go carefully. "Although it was neither necessary nor honest, after the election of such governments, to consult the subjects," his French advisers declared, "yet it had seemed proper to monsignor the governor [i.e., Philip] to do so, in order to justify his action to everyone and to declare to the whole country, why and for what reasons, with what intentions, and with whose support he had come to govern." [143] But when the bishop of Turin tried to explain the council's loyalty to the regent, Philip cut him off harshly with the words: "I will do my duty and I just want to see who says anything to the contrary." [144] There was no further opposition, and even Sforza could only vent his rage in a few border raids.

Despite this defeat of the assembly's pretensions, the situation had not fundamentally altered. Yolanda came to terms with her brother and returned after a few months. Deprived of French support, Philip had to retire to Bresse.[145] After her death in 1478, renewed ducal minorities gave plenty of scope to all the old forces for playing their accustomed parts. The assembly fully maintained its position. They passed *capitoli* on administrative reforms,[146] scaled down the government's ever-increasing demands for taxation, while yet supporting Charles I's war against Saluzzo,[147] and successfully dug in their heels over that duke's attempt to obtain grants for a standing

---

[143] Same to same, Aug. 20, 1476; *ibid.*, pp. 166 f.

[144] *Ibid.*, p. 167.      [145] Daviso, *La Duchessa*, pp. 264 ff.

[146] Tallone, *Parl. Sab.*, V, 256 ff., 316 f., 350 ff., 396 ff., 437 ff.

[147] *Ibid.*, pp. 341, 345, 350 ff., 389 f., 396 ff.

army.[148] All this could be done on the basis of "privileges" without any attempt to broaden the scope of parliamentary action.

But the old jealousies between Piedmontese and Savoyards persisted. The defeat of 1476 had only intensified the desire of the Piedmontese upper classes to drive the Savoyards from their commanding and lucrative positions in the state.[149] The driving force for action might again come from ambitious nobles or princes of the blood; but the action itself took place in the assembly and with the full support of the classes represented in it. The most far-reaching of these attempts occurred in 1481. Louis XI had appointed the count de la Chambre as governor of the young duke Philibert. This Savoyard noble aroused the fierce enmity of the Piedmontese by his misgovernment. The duke's uncles moreover felt slighted at being debarred from power. At the instigation of one of them, Gian Lodovico di Savoia, bishop of Geneva, the assembly now proceeded to elect six councilors, supernumary to the Cismontane council, to advise the duke on all important questions. The Milanese ambassador, reporting this move, had no doubt that Gian Lodovico and Philip of Bresse hoped in this way to obtain control over the country.[150] The six councilors included the two bishops of Turin and Vercelli, Claudio di Racconigi, governor of Vercelli, and Matteo Confalonieri, another powerful baron who had been one of the leading members of the Cismontane council in the crisis of 1476. It was clearly both a victory for the Piedmontese party, and a remarkable advance in parliamentary interference with the government.

Perhaps this latter point was not fully appreciated. In any

[148] G. A. Aquilano, Milanese ambassador, to duke of Milan, May 10, 1487; *ibid.,* pp. 389 f.

[149] E.g., Antonio di Romagnano to duke of Milan, Sept. 7, 1487; *ibid.,* pp. 236 f. Bossi to same, Sept. 8, 1478; *ibid.,* pp. 237 f.

[150] G. P. Martinengo to Gian Galeazzo Sforza, Dec. 10, 1481. *Ibid.,* p. 294.

case, the intrigue came to an end with the death, a few months later, of the weak Philibert, and the accession of the vigorous Charles I.[151] But when the latter died, in 1490, leaving only a very young son and the prospect of a renewed regency, the implications of the action of 1481 had become fully apparent. The French States-General of Tours, in 1484, had revealed the surprising possibilities of parliamentary control over appointments to a council of regency, and the consequent dangers to independent monarchical rule.

The assembly of Pinerolo of 1490 was the last occasion on which the three estates attempted a major offensive. The action had been carefully prepared before the first session took place, on April 6. The Piedmontese were willing to accept the young dowager duchess, Bianca of Montferrat, as guardian of her son Charles II (Carlo Giovanni Amedeo) [152] in return for the confirmation of the country's liberties, a Piedmontese as well as a Savoyard governor for the young duke, and a number of the principal offices of state. They demanded especially equal representation with the Savoyards in the ducal council, the marshal's baton of Piedmont, and the governorship of Vercelli.[153] On these points the parliamentary classes were united; but, as usual, they were not the only contestants in the arena. Bianca's chief adviser, the archbishop of Auch, the youngest of the sons of duke Louis, was held to favor the Savoyards; his brothers, Philip of Bresse and the count of the Genevese, were, as usual, eager to intervene; France pursued her traditional policy of supporting the Savoyards, even though she did not interfere directly; Milan was in a more ambiguous position. Bianca, as an Italian, was more likely to resist French influence

[151] Daviso characterizes the reign of Charles I as "a renewed reaction of the Savoyard element," "Considerazioni," p. 30.

[152] Some Piedmontese historians do not accept Carlo Giovanni Amadeo as Charles II but reserve this title for the next Charles who reigned from 1504 to 1553.

[153] Caiazzo to duke of Milan, April 2, 1490. Tallone, *Parl. Sab.*, VI, 25 f. Just as for the events of 1476, the reports of the Milanese ambassadors are again the best authority. *Ibid.*, pp. 11–63.

than any of the young duke's great-uncles; hence her guardianship must be supported as must be the pretensions of the Piedmontese to high positions of political power, provided this could be done without openly antagonizing the Savoyards and thus driving them even more securely into the arms of France.[154] At the same time, Lodovico il Moro was fully aware of the dangers of such a policy which inevitably involved support of a representative assembly against monarchical power. Bianca must temporize with the assembly, so his ambassador was to advise her; for "according to the custom of the country, many resolutions will be passed which will appear contrary to the aims which Her Grace should pursue in order to maintain for herself the control over the government"; yet if she bided her time, all the actions of the three states would be no more "than a shadow without form and substance," as had been proved in the case of the regent of France six years earlier.[155] Bianca and her advisers followed these counsels with consummate skill.

On the first day of the session, all ambassadors, including those of France and Milan, addressed the assembly [156]—a procedure unthinkable in a contemporary English parliament, and a characteristic demonstration of the international character of the domestic politics of Piedmont. The next day, the ambassador of the count of the Genevese proposed the election by the assembly of six councilors in equal numbers from "each side of the mountains" and from each of the three estates.[157] Once again a member of the ducal family was using the assembly to limit ducal power for the sake of his own ambitions.[158] One day later, on April 8, the assembly presented its

---

[154] Same to same, April 5, 1490. *Ibid.*, p. 28.

[155] Gian Galeazzo Sforza [Lodovico il Moro ?] to Caiazzo, March 25, 1490. *Ibid.*, pp. 12 f.

[156] Caiazzo to Sforza, April 6, 1490. *Ibid.*, pp. 29 ff.

[157] Same to same, April 7, 1490. *Ibid.*, pp. 32 f.

[158] *Ibid.* The count's ambassador explicitly stated his master's claim to a share in the government.

*capitoli* with all the Piedmontese demands, including those of the count of the Genevese. The most startling proposal, however, was the article demanding that, during the period of the minority, the three estates should have the right to assemble at least every two years without awaiting a summons from the government.[159] This went further than anything proposed by the States-General of Tours.[160] Throughout the fifteenth century the assembly had been summoned almost every year and frequently several times within the twelve months. It was not, therefore, more frequent assemblies that the parliamentarians of 1490 wanted, but the autonomy of the three estates and the consequent guarantee of their continued influence over the government through the six councilors appointed by them.

It is unlikely that Luigi Talliandi, Amedeo di Valperga, and the other leaders of the assembly had any intention of establishing parliamentary government in Piedmont.[161] Such ideas belonged to the seventeenth, rather than the fifteenth, century. Their aim was, undoubtedly, to establish as firmly as possible the control of the Piedmontese upper classes over the government of their country.[162] But the constitutional implications

---

[159] *Ibid.*, pp. 34–40.     [160] Daviso, "Considerazioni," p. 33.

[161] Gabotto, *Lo Stato Sabaudo,* II, 424, who seems to have thought so.

[162] After the death of Charles the Bold of Burgundy, his daughter Mary was forced to concede to the States-General of her Netherland provinces the right to assemble without summons by the sovereign. This was article 13 of the famous *Grand Privilège* of 1477. Mary's husband, the archduke Maximilian, was able to prevent this privilege from being exercised in practice. But on May 12, 1488, when Maximilian was a prisoner in Bruges, the estates of Flanders, Brabant, and Hainault passed a resolution that was strikingly similar, both to the *Grand Privilège* of 1477 and to the resolution of the assembly of Pinerolo of 1490: "And in order that all the matters mentioned above should be better handled, for the greatest good and profit of our lord and our provinces, and to get rid of any novelty which might be introduced to their prejudice, we have advised and concluded . . . that from henceforth the estates of all the said provinces should assemble once a year . . . during the period of the minority of our honored lord [Philip the Handsome]; and to this place all the prov-

of their demands were clear to all. The regent and her advisers could never accept such fundamental limitations of the traditional rights of the crown. They accepted all *capitoli* on purely administrative matters, made more or less vague promises about the appointment of Piedmontese nobles to offices of state, but rejected outright the demand for the six councilors and for autonomous assemblies.[163]

The assembly now despatched Talliandi to the French court, in the unlikely hope of obtaining support from that quarter and, at the same time, continued negotiating with the government. After a week Talliandi had not yet returned,[164] and members, finding their expenses mounting, were anxious to go home. As a last throw, before dispersing, they appointed a committee of six to continue pressing for the acceptance of the rejected demands.[165] But this was a virtual admission of defeat. After a session of only ten days, the assembly was complaining of "immense sweat and labors" and "intolerable expenses" [166] —and committed suicide. The committee was no substitute for the organized will of the country represented in the assembly.

---

inces must send their deputies without being commanded to do so. The deputies shall have power to receive all manner of complaints and grievances concerning the common affairs of these provinces . . . " (H. Pirenne, "Le Rôle Constitutionnel des Etats Généraux des Pays-Bas en 1477 et en 1488," *Mélanges Paul Frédéricq* [Brussels, 1904], pp. 277 ff).

Luigi Talliandi had been in Burgundian service in 1476. He probably had Burgundian friends and it is therefore not impossible that he knew of the *Grand Privilège* and of the resolution of 1488.

[163] Answers appended to each *capitolo*. Tallone, *Parl. Sab.*, VI, 34-40.

[164] Christoforo di Bollate to duke of Milan, April 15, 1490. *Ibid.*, p. 51.

[165] April 16, 1490. *Ibid.*, pp. 52 f. The membership of the committee is significant: Giorgio de Provanis, prior of the monastery of Novalesa, and member of a family prominent in public service, was the only ecclesiastic; Amedeo di Valperga and Brianzo di Romagnano were representatives of the high nobility of Piedmont; Luigi Talliandi and Vasco di Solario, both from Ivrea, belonged to the noble urban patriciate, and Antonio Plantaporri was a lawyer from Chieri.

[166] Cf. *supra*, n. 165.

The Milanese realized immediately that the government had won a resounding victory,[167] and the regent was quick to follow up her advantage. She sent special commissioners to the towns to demand whether they supported the assembly's action in despatching Talliandi to France and in setting up the committee, both of which she declared to be illegal.[168] Having to face the ducal wrath on their own, some towns began to waver. A sufficient number, however, appear to have stood by their representatives, and the duchess preferred not to take any direct action against the committee.[169] In another assembly, in October, 1490, she implicitly recognized the committee by demanding that the three estates pay its expenses of some 3,300 florins.[170]

The assembly had been defeated in its attempt to obtain direct control over the appointment of the duke's ministers and in its efforts to establish a legal existence independent of the ducal will. Yet the primary purpose for which these constitutional efforts had been made was nevertheless attained. In the political maneuvering which followed the crisis of 1490 the Piedmontese won most of their objectives. Claudio di Racconigi was reinstated as marshal of Piedmont and as governor of Vercelli; Amedeo di Romagnano followed the Savoyard Champion as chancellor; and Piedmontese influence steadily

[167] Sforza to Bollate, April 20, 1490. *Ibid.*, p. 55.

[168] Instruction to the commissioners, May 27, 1490. *Ibid.*, p. 60 ff.

[169] This seems the most likely explanation of what happened. We have the answers of only Moncalieri, Chivasso, and Vigone. Chivasso disowned its representatives, Moncalieri temporized, and Vigone remained firm. *Ibid.*, pp. 63 ff.

[170] Edict of Oct. 8, 1490. *Ibid.*, pp. 83 f. Perhaps this was also an astute reminder to the assembly that independent action was expensive and had to be paid for. Daviso is undoubtedly right in rejecting Tallone's theory (*Parl. Sab.*, I, clxxxvi) that the committee represented the six councilors whom the assembly had wanted to elect ("Considerazioni," p. 35). This is perfectly clear both from the resolution appointing the six and from the whole balance of forces at the time.

increased at the court which from that time onward remained almost permanently at Turin.[171]

Piedmontese historians have seen in the events of 1490 a turning point in the history of the three estates, and from the failure of that year they have traced the progressive decadence of the institution. Such an interpretation provided an excellent justification for the subsequent absolutism of the House of Savoy. The argument, however, is too facile.

The constitutional offensives of the three estates up to 1490 had been motivated less by a desire to put into practice a theory of parliamentary government than by the ambitions of powerful persons and states, both inside and outside the principality. With the death of the remaining sons of Louis I, and with the end of the regencies, in 1496, there disappeared the old opportunities for dynastic intrigue and political opposition by the princes of the blood. Milan soon lost its independence, and the French and the Habsburgs found it easier to influence the court of the Savoy monarchy than the assemblies of the three estates.

The internal driving force of the three estates had been the political ambitions of the Piedmontese upper classes. After 1490 these ambitions were at least partially satisfied by the entry of the Piedmontese into offices and benefices previously reserved for the Savoyards. At the turn of the century, the economic advance of the rich landowning classes, both in town and country, began to slow down, and with it the incentive for further political conquests. There was no longer any compelling reason why the assembly should be made to encroach further on monarchical authority: that it had ever attempted to do so had been the almost incidental result of a number of converging lines of force. It was therefore perfectly natural that on one occasion, in 1512, the assembly declined to advise the duke on foreign affairs, remarking that he had a good council

[171] Daviso, "Considerazioni," pp. 36 f.

who were better able to do so.[172] Similar opinions had been
voiced in the fifteenth century,[173] and in 1512 the assembly may
well have felt that it would be a mistake to become a party to
the duke's agreement to pay the alleged debts of the House of
Savoy to the Swiss. Over a number of years, the Swiss had been
claiming enormous sums, totaling more than 800,000 florins,
on the basis of forged documents provided for them by a former ducal secretary, Dufour.[174] Fear of invasion by the redoubtable Swiss pikemen made the three estates willing to
grant part of this sum in taxes; but they would take no responsibility for Charles III's incompetent diplomacy. The assembly had, indeed, long since realized that if they did not pay
for the government's legitimate needs, someone else would,
to the detriment of their own influence; [175] but they fought
hard and successfully to keep down taxation. Two years after
their defeat of 1490 they reduced the government's demand
for 232,000 florins to 108,000. To most Piedmontese this success
must have appeared to bring much more substantial benefits
than the dubious advantage of having the assembly appoint a
number of the duke's councilors, to the greater glory of but a
few leading families. In the 46 years between 1490 and the
French invasion the assembly voted fifteen grants. These varied
considerably in size, according to the needs of the government,
and in some years the tax burden was undoubtedly heavy.
But in other years taxes were light, and there was only a slight
upward trend over the period as a whole, the annual average

[172] Tallone, *Parl. Sab.*, VI, 276 ff. This has been regarded as an abdica-
tion.

[173] E.g., on March 24, 1469, Cuneo instructed its representative not to
vote on the Venetian alliance since this was the duke's own affair. Cuneo
had not been consulted on previous alliances; so why should they now accept responsibility? *Ibid.*, IV, 314.

[174] *Ibid.*, VI, 264 f. A good account of the Dufour case can be found in
M. Bruchet, *Marguerite d'Autriche* (Lille, 1927), pp. 88 ff.

[175] In 1476 Matteo di Confalonieri warned the assembly: "If we do not
help her [Yolanda], others will, and then we will be treated as we deserve."
Tallone, *Parl. Sab.*, V, 72 f.

### Table B. *Parliamentary Grants 1492–1535*

| Year | Total grant (fl.) | For no. of years | Per annum (fl.) |
|------|-------------------|------------------|------------------|
| 1492 | 108,600 | 2 (1492–1493) * | 54,300 |
| 1496 | 150,000 | 2 (1496–1497) | 75,000 |
| 1499 | 222,100 | 3 (1499–1501) | 74,034 (74,033 for second two years) |
| 1503 | 259,200 | 2 (1503–1504) | 129,600 |
| 1505 | 196,900 | 3 (1505–1507) | 65,634 (65,633 for second two years) |
| 1509 | 215,400 | 3 (1509–1511) | 71,800 |
| 1511 | 100,000 | 2 (1511–1512) | 50,000 |
| 1513 | 45,000 | 1 (1513) * | 45,000 |
| 1514 | 233,300 | 3 (1514–1516) | 77,767 (77,766 in 1516) |
| 1518 | 245,500 | 3 (1518–1520) | 81,834 (81,833 for second two years) |
| 1522 | 276,100 | 3 (1522–1524) | 92,034 (92,033 for second two years) |
| 1526 | 75,000 | 1 | 75,000 |
| 1528 | 24,000 | 1 | 24,000 |
| 1530 | 201,100 | 3 (1530–1532) | 67,034 (67,033 for second two years) |
| 1533 | 334,000 | 3 (1533–1535) | 111,334 (111,333 for second two years) |
| Total | 2,686,200 | 44 years | |

Average per annum 61,050 fl.

\* The sum demanded in 1492 was 232,000 fl; in 1513, 250,000 fl.

over the first half being just under 60,000 florins, and for the second half just over 60,000. [176]

[176] The highest grant was in 1503: fl. 259,000, payable over two years. In 1533 there was another high grant of fl. 334,000, payable over three years. All figures from *ibid.*, VI, 105 ff., 139, 164 f., 205, 219, 242 f., 290 f., 373 ff., 421 ff.; VII, 33 ff., 68 ff., 126 ff. For further details of parliamentary grants during this period see Table B.

The distribution of the tax burden among the different classes and localities represented in the assembly appears to have remained constant. Between 1492 and 1533 the 17 towns of the "principatus" (the original

In defense of its own and of the country's liberties the assembly was as successful after the crisis of 1490 as it had been before. If, as has been suggested,[177] the government really attempted to weaken the three estates by summoning the assembly only at rare intervals, such a policy was soon given up. The monarchy was not yet strong enough to dispense with the support of the Piedmontese upper classes; for its own resources had in no way increased and the Swiss blackmail, carried on for more than twenty years, was a perennial source of weakness. On the one occasion when the monarchy attempted to upset the balance of power, it met with a complete rebuff. In 1515 Charles III proposed the creation of a permanent military force.[178] Discussions dragged on for two years. The communes were evidently afraid that the duke might use the troops against them and not against foreign enemies; for in the assembly of March, 1517, the government felt the need of a specific denial of any such intentions.[179] Whatever these really

principality of Piedmont) who habitually sent members to the assembly paid between them from 22 to 24 per cent of each subsidy; the 37 baronial districts paid 10 to 11 per cent; and the three cities of Chieri, Mondovì and Cuneo paid 15 to 17 per cent; (*ibid.*, VI, 107–117, 432–436; VII, 139–143). It is not possible to compare the percentages paid by the other towns and baronial districts at different times because they are not always grouped in the same way in the lists of quotas (cf. *supra*, n. 123; but it is safe to assume that their percentages also remained roughly constant.

[177] Tallone, I, clxxxviii, overstates this point. Bianca summoned another assembly only a few months after the one at Pinerolo, and another one in 1492. Then there was an interval of 4 years—the only period when the biennial meetings proposed in 1490 did not take place. After that there were sessions almost every year—much more frequently than in contemporary England. In any case, it was not the demand for periodicity that was important in 1490, and against which the government reacted, but the demand for autonomous assemblies.

[178] Assembly of Chieri, March 7, 1515; *ibid.*, VI, 326. Similar unsuccessful proposals had been made in 1451 and 1487.

[179] The representatives of Vercelli reported "that His Excellency demanded these troops for the benefit of the country and that he did not intend to use them to raise money nor to involve the country in any expense, but only for the benefit of the community and the country . . ."

were, the three estates could not overlook what was happening in France and remained firm in their refusal.[180]

In the first third of the sixteenth century the three estates undoubtedly maintained their constitutional position. As an institution they were perhaps more effective in the political life of their country than the English parliament was in England. They were certainly more powerful than the parliament of Sicily or the almost defunct States-General of France. They even made some tentative procedural advances toward the practice of insisting on the redress of grievances before supply [181] and toward the use of parliamentary committees.[182]

Yet there were some fundamental weaknesses in the position of the three estates. Piedmont remained wide open to the influence of its more powerful neighbors. While, in the fifteenth century, such influence had tended to favor the growth of parliamentary power, in the sixteenth it became increasingly more probable that it would be hostile to the assembly; for

_____

(*ibid.*, p. 333). It was a sign of the much greater political stability of Sicily in the sixteenth century that in the long debates over the Sicilian cavalry neither side ever suggested that this force might be used to make the government independent of parliament. Cf. Koenigsberger, *The Practice of Empire*, chap. 7.

180 On this point Daviso quotes Commines' opinion about the danger of a standing army to the liberties of a country ("Considerazioni," pp. 39 f.).

181 Council minutes of Chivasso, referring to the assembly of Dec., 1514; Tallone, *Parl. Sab.*, VI, 313 f.: "The grants were offered and then a demand was made that the petitions be accepted; and since the most illustrious duke made objections to some of them, the country [i.e., the assembly] did not proceed to the remaining business, that is the grants to the councilors, so that these latter, through hope of such grants, should be favorably inclined toward the country." By refusing to make its customary grants to the treasurer-general and other ministers the assembly evidently attempted to put pressure on the council for a more favorable consideration of their bills.

182 The assembly of Turin, Oct. 4, 1533, elected "three, four, or more honest and learned men" who were to discuss proposed decrees on legal procedure. *Ibid.*, VII, 122.

almost everywhere in Europe the monarchies were freeing
themselves from their medieval restraints. Just as serious was
the absence, inside Piedmont, of a driving force which could
use the assembly for the attainment of its social and political
ambitions in the way in which the English gentry were to use
parliament in the reigns of Elizabeth and the Stuarts. The
social dynamic of the Piedmontese aristocracy and communes
had now spent its limited force, and there was nothing to take
its place.

From about 1530 there began to appear rifts in the once-
united front of communes and feudal aristocracy—rifts which
were even more serious than the constant feuds of Guelfs and
Ghibellines. Like most medieval countries, Piedmont had allowed the free importation of foodstuffs and had restricted
exports, both in order to keep down prices. In 1490, for instance, the assembly had petitioned against any interference
with such imports.[183] In 1530, however, the assembly reversed
its policy and requested the removal of restrictions from the
export of grain and rice.[184] A few months later the question
was discussed again, and one of the ministers informed the
duke that the rich wanted free exports and the poor did not; [185]
the large producers, landed aristocracy and wealthier communes, were exporting at the expense of the consumers.[186] The
duke, himself a big landowner, accepted this policy of free exports after some hesitation.[187]

At the same time the communes became increasingly restless
at the heavy demands made by the government for the defense
of the country. In October, 1530, the duchess, acting as regent
in the duke's absence, reported that the nobles were disposed
to grant further aids, but that the representatives of the towns

---

[183] *Ibid.,* VI, 38.        [184] *Ibid.,* VII, 59 ff.

[185] Gioffredo Passerio to Charles III, Oct. 21, 1530. *Ibid.,* p. 92.

[186] Instructions to the representatives of Vercelli, Sept. 27, 1533. *Ibid.,*
p. 117.

[187] Beatrice of Portugal to Charles III, Oct. 25, 1535. *Ibid.,* pp. 156 f.

refused.[188] This division between communes and nobles now became the dominating pattern of the assemblies before the French invasion. Tempers began to rise. In December, 1532, the council arrested the representatives of Moncalieri when they opposed the government.[189] It was not the first time the government had arrested members of the assembly; [190] but it had not happened for a long time, and now it was possible only because Moncalieri had voted against the other towns.

In 1533 the duke obtained the handsome grant of 334,000 florins, payable over three years.[191] But two years later when, under the threat of Swiss and French invasion, the government came back for more money, the division in the assembly became an open breach. The towns, led by Vercelli, refused any further grant. The nobles were "much inclined and willing to serve you," the duchess wrote to her husband,[192] and they assembled in force with their retainers. Nevertheless, both they and the ducal council advised against an open rupture with the towns.[193] For the nobles joined the communes in grumbling about the government's disregard of their privileges and the rapacity of ducal officials. "And I assure you," the regent concluded her letter, "there were some who spoke in a most disagreeable way."

There was no grant in that year,[194] and eight months later

[188] Same to Same, Oct. 25, 1530; *ibid.*, p. 93.

[189] Moncalieri council minutes, Dec. 8, 1532: "And because a reply was given which did not please the most illustrious lord, our duke, nor conformed to the replies of the other communes, he arrested the deputies and would not release them until he had a more agreeable reply from their commune . . ." (*ibid.*, p. 106).

[190] E.g., the member for Vercelli in 1464. *Ibid.*, IV, 168.

[191] *Ibid.*, VII, 126 ff.

[192] Beatrice to Charles III, Oct. 23, 1535. *Ibid.*, p. 153.

[193] Same to same, Oct. 25, 1535. *Ibid.*, pp. 156 f.

[194] There is no document in Tallone's collection to support his statement (I, cclxxxiii) that the assembly of 1535 granted a subsidy of 100,000 florins.

the French occupied the whole of Savoy and about two thirds of Piedmont without meeting any serious resistance. Spanish and imperial troops, from Milan, marched into the remaining third, ostensibly in the name of the duke; but for the next 23 years Piedmont ceased to exist as an independent state.

The assemblies of the three estates continued to function in both parts of Piedmont. After the first two or three years the French did their best to govern the country well. They were evidently anxious to avoid the mistakes which had cost them their dominion over Naples and Milan.[195] The king swore to observe all Piedmontese privileges, and the Piedmontese, in their turn, took the oath of fealty to France without undue scruples about their loyalty to the House of Savoy.[196] The Venetian ambassador to France remarked that although Charles III had enjoyed a certain degree of popularity because taxation had been light, yet his government was considered corrupt, and, in Piedmont even more than in Savoy, there were many who spoke evil of him.[197] When the worst results of the invasion had been forgotten, French rule became genuinely popular.[198] The viceroys continued to summon the three estates and forwarded their *capitoli* to the king, generally with favorable comments. It was no more the policy of the French monarchy to abolish the three estates of Piedmont than it was its aim to do away with the provincial assemblies in France. Piedmont had simply become another province of the kingdom.

[195] For the French administration of Piedmont, cf. L. Romier, "Les institutions françaises en Piémont sous Henri II," *Revue Historique,* vol. 106 (Paris, 1911).

[196] Tallone, "Ivrea e il Piemonte," p. 58.

[197] Matteo Dandolo, "Relazione di Francia, 1547," Albèri, *Relazioni,* ser. 1, II, 183.

[198] The viceroy Brissac to Henry II, on the occasion of a Piedmontese embassy to the king, April 30, 1551: "I could not let them go without testifying to Your Majesty the affection, obedience, and loyalty to your service which I have found in these your subjects . . ." (Tallone, *Parl. Sab.,* VII, 384 f.).

For this very reason, however, the three estates could no longer claim a genuine partnership in sovereignty. They represented the provincial autonomy of Piedmont; but not by one whit could they influence the policy of the monarchy. They could petition for a diminution of the tax burden (and the king might grant their request, seeing the poverty of the country or fearing insurrection and depopulation); [199] but no longer could they resist the arbitrary imposition of taxes, nor their collection at the point of the pike.

The introduction of the *eletti* did not substantially alter this situation. They were a committee of three or four members of the assembly charged with representing the three estates during the intervals between sessions and with defending the country's privileges. This institution was modeled on the *commissions intermédiaires* of the French provincial estates and, more especially perhaps, on the *procureurs du pays* of Provence.[200] Just as the *deputazione* of the Sicilian parliament, so the *eletti* of Piedmont performed the useful function of keeping the government in touch with the desires of the country and of warning against avoidable indiscretions; but they never emerged as rivals to the government. Nevertheless, it was important that parliamentary habits were kept alive during the French occupation.[201] The Piedmontese could still make their voices heard, and the French government was generally willing to listen to them. This fact goes far to explain the ready acceptance of French rule by an Italian-speaking population. Only the old grievance of their exclusion from the higher offices and ecclesiastical benefices was revived; [202] but if peace should return,

[199] E.g., Guillaume du Bellay to Cardinal du Bellay, July 5, 1538. *Ibid.*, pp. 340 f.

[200] *Ibid.*, p. 319 and *passim*. For the French institutions, cf. Doucet, *Les institutions*, I, 344 f.

[201] In the deliberations of the assembly of 1540 the old medieval slogan of representative government appeared once more: "What concerns all should be approved by all" (Tallone, *Parl. Sab.*, VII, p. 306).

[202] Instructions to the assembly's envoys to the king, March 12, 1550; *ibid.*, p. 358.

there was a chance that the French court might view Piedmontese claims more favorably.

The nominally independent part of Piedmont had fared worse. Unlike the French, the Spaniards felt no need to win the good will of the Piedmontese. Charles V himself said that his troops had done things of which the Moors and Turks would have been ashamed.[203] The governor of Milan, Ferrante Gonzaga, even suggested the flooding of the whole Piedmontese plain to serve as a screen for Lombardy against the French.[204] The three estates continued to meet; but with the country heavily garrisoned and virtually ruled by Spanish military commanders, their activities were confined to little more than the granting of money. Much time was spent in wrangling about contributions. All the pent-up bitterness against the clergy's privileges now exploded, and they were blamed—quite unjustly—for the country's unpreparedness to meet the invasion.[205] Yet all tried to emulate them. Giorgio di Valperga produced letters from the imperial commanders exempting him and the other magnates from further taxation. The delegates from Ivrea, Bugella, and Santhià declared that they would rather sell their own sons than pay for the fortifications of Vercelli.[206] In the end the three estates did what they could,[207] but their morale remained low.

In 1554 the lieutenant-governor wrote to the new duke, Emmanuel Philibert, that it was no use asking the three estates for further grants; they were too poor.[208] After one more attempt in October of that year, Emmanuel Philibert thereupon

[203] Tallone, "Un Vercellese illustre del sec. XVI," *Boll. stor.-bibl. subalp.* (1900), p. 155, n. 1.

[204] E. Armstrong, "Tuscany and Savoy," *Cambridge Modern History*, III, 400.

[205] Assembly of Aug., 1536; Tallone, *Parl. Sab.*, VII, 162.

[206] Vercelli council minutes, March 9, 1541; *ibid.*, pp. 194 f.

[207] Assemblies of 1547, 1548, 1549. *Ibid.*, pp. 205–212.

[208] Giovanni Amedeo di Valperga, count of Masino, to Emmanuel Philibert, Feb. 16, 1554; *ibid.*, p. 217.

ceased altogether to summon the three estates until his restoration to all his states.[209]

When, in later years, Emmanuel Philibert told the Venetian ambassadors that he had conquered his country with the sword and was therefore under no obligation to observe its right to representation,[210] he was finding an excuse for a policy of absolutism begun in 1554—three years before his victory of St. Quentin over the French could justify his theory of conquest by enabling him to stake his claim for his hereditary dominions at the peace of Cateau-Cambrésis. The whole country welcomed him enthusiastically. With the return of the House of Savoy there would be peace, an end to the extortions of the French and Spanish soldiery, low taxes, freedom of trade, and, for the upper classes, the spoils of government which foreigners had monopolized for almost a generation.[211] The assembly of the three estates met in June, 1560, and loyally voted what it was asked for, a huge salt tax of 36 ducats per *carrata,* designed to bring in 190,000 ducats. In return they did not even obtain the usual promise of the confirmation of their privileges.[212]

This was the last assembly. For Emmanuel Philibert it was only an interlude, a chance snatched by this astute politician in a favorable situation and not to be repeated; for the temper of this "khaki parliament" was not likely to recur. Brought up in the courts and traditions of Charles V and Philip II, the

[209] Armstrong, "Tuscany and Savoy," p. 409. "The Estates of Piedmont . . . had almost ceased to exist during the French occupation; and he [Emmanuel Philibert] made no effort to revive them. . . ." In fact, the three estates continued to function in the French sector of Piedmont throughout the occupation, while in the sector under his own rule Emmanuel Philibert himself ceased to summon them.

[210] G. Correr, "Relazione di Savoia, 1566," Albèri, *Relazioni,* ser. 2, V, 12; G. F. Morosini, "Relazione di Savoi, 1570," *ibid.,* II, 123.

[211] Boldù, "Relazione, 1561," p. 441.

[212] Count della Trinità to Emmanuel Philibert, June 17, 1560. Tallone, *Parl. Sab.,* VII, 220 ff. Only Cuneo objected (*ibid.,* p. 222), but without success.

duke was determined to be the absolute ruler of his country.[213]
He had shown his true temper as early as 1552, when he captured the little town of Bra and hanged all the Piedmontese
who had helped to defend it against him. It was not an act of
passionate revenge, for Emmanuel Philibert was not blood-
thirsty; [214] rather was it a demonstration of cold-blooded ruthlessness, and as such it was appreciated at the imperial court.[215]
With his parliamentary grant of 1560 he could maintain his
army of 24,000 of whom 8,000 were veterans of the French
wars.[216] With such a force he could impose his will on the
country and levy taxes without further recourse to the three
estates. Within a year, enthusiasm had changed to fierce hostility, and the people began to look back with affection to the
French occupation [217] during which, as one Venetian ambassador put it, the men did good business on the money spent
by the occupation troops, and the women enjoyed the great
liberty introduced by the French.[218]

Yet, to the duke the idea of cooperating with the three estates
seemed impossible. The larger section of the country had willingly accepted allegiance to the king of France. Even after 1560
the majority of the nobles were openly in the pay of either
France or Spain, and sometimes of both. There was a desperate
shortage of able and experienced men to advise the duke and
to administer the state; for few Piedmontese had filled high office in the previous twenty-five years.[219] The duke was forced
to distribute honors and offices indifferently; for he could not
afford to favor the few loyalists against the many who had ac-

[213] Boldù, "Relazione," p. 432.

[214] Lippomano, *Discorso,* p. 381. Cf. also his treatment of the Vaudois
Protestants; Armstrong, "Tuscany and Savoy," p. 404. On the other hand
it is quite impossible to accept Albèri's characterization of him as "this
splendid historical figure, Emmanuel Philibert" (*Introduction to Morosini's Relation,* ser. 2, II, 114).

[215] Tallone, "Ivrea e il Piemonte," p. 60.

[216] Boldù, "Relazione," pp. 436 f.                    [217] *Ibid.,* pp. 439 f.

[218] Correr, "Relazione," p. 12.

[219] *Ibid.,* p. 18; Boldù, "Relazione," pp. 432 ff.

cepted the French. Thus, while the former were disappointed in their hopes, the latter still did not change their opinions.[220] On whom could Emmanuel Philibert rely but on himself?

The old Piedmontese ruling class had disintegrated. Already in 1538, representatives in the assembly had claimed that they would be hanged if it was not found that in two years of French occupation a third of the population had died of hunger or committed suicide in despair, and that a quarter of all landed property had been thrown on the market because the owners had been unable to pay the taxes imposed by the invaders.[221] The *catasti* of Moncalieri certainly show a quite unusually large turnover of holdings during that period. Many properties disappeared altogether, in others, only one or two small holdings were left. While a number of medium owners added to their properties, and while the place of some small holders was taken by others, many of the old aristocratic families were ruined, and many holdings remained deserted.[222]

It was the same all over Piedmont.[223] The communes were ruined, the nobility impoverished, and their estates mortgaged.[224] Riven by the old family feuds of Guelfs and Ghibellines, divided into pro-French and pro-Spanish factions, they were no longer capable of presenting a united front in defense of the country's privileges. Of all the political parties in Piedmont the duke alone had a clearly thought-out policy, and he

[220] *Ibid.*, p. 440.

[221] Guillaume du Bellay to Cardinal du Bellay, July 5, 1538; Tallone, *Parl. Sab.*, VII, 240 f.

[222] Moncalieri, Arch. Com., MS, Ser. A, vols. 66–70.

[223] On this point both the Venetian ambassadors and the government itself were agreed. Cf. the preamble of an edict of 1561: "The long war has caused infinite damage to the people . . . the flight of many inhabitants, artisans, and peasants to other states and far-off countries, in order to escape from the cruel blows of war and the unbearable military burdens. . . . The land and the fields have remained uncultivated, and our states are deprived of crafts and industries" (quoted in A. Garino Canina, "La Finanza del Piemonte," p. 515).

[224] Boldù, "Relazione," p. 439.

pursued it with supreme skill and relentless determination. A hundred years earlier he might have enlisted the support of an assembly which had emerged not without credit from its long struggle to preserve the country from the worst effects of foreign domination. But to Emmanuel Philibert, contemporary and early companion of Philip II of Spain, these achievements could not weigh against Piedmontese disloyalty to the Savoyard dynasty. Political support must from now take the form of personal loyalty to the ruler.

To this end the duke used his patronage on a scale hitherto unknown in Piedmont. Well over 70 major offices, benefices, and fiefs were given to the Piedmontese nobility in the one year of 1560 alone, with many more to commoners.[225] The duke's court officials were appointed at a third of their official salaries and served only four months each year, so as to give as many as possible the honor of attending the duke's person. In this way the court of Turin was as large as that of the greatest kingdoms in Christendom.[226] Where no offices existed, nor could be created, the duke bestowed honorary ranks and titles.[227] It was the classic policy of creating a court nobility and binding it to the person of the sovereign.

At the same time the monarchy made no serious attempt to interfere with the nobles' position on their own domains. Emmanuel Philibert issued a number of edicts liberating the serfs; but he made little effort to enforce them. The serfs who were numerous especially in Savoy had to wait for their genuine liberation until the eighteenth century.[228] As in France, and even more in Brandenburg-Prussia, the absolutism of the monarchy was only achieved by renouncing effective interference with the nobles' control over their own fiefs.[229]

[225] A.S.T., MS, Sec. Ia, Protocolli, vol. 223 bis, Atti ricevuti da Segretarii e Notaj Ducali nell'anno 1560. More than 300 folios of such appointments.

[226] Sigismondo Cavalli, "Relazione della Corte di Savoja, 1564," Albèri, *Relazioni,* ser. 2, pp. 26 ff.

[227] *Ibid.* [228] P. Egidi, *Emanuele Filiberto* (Turin, 1928), II, 96 ff.

[229] A typical case is the judgment given on the Valpergas' claim to the lordship over the little town of Borgomasino. The ducal court upheld

From the point of view of the monarchy, Emmanuel Philibert's policy was entirely successful. The country grumbled,[230] but was both morally and materially incapable of resisting. The penalties for this failure were very heavy. Charles III's average revenue had been between 70,000 and 90,000 ducats. Emmanuel Philibert's was about half a million, often much higher and only rarely lower.[231] Even allowing for the devaluation of money in the second half of the sixteenth century, this revenue represented a very heavy burden of taxation for such a poor country. The salt gabelle was so high that the peasants virtually gave up eating salt and used it only for their animals. Their very beds were requisitioned when they could not pay.[232] Shortly before his death Emmanuel Philibert excused his policy to the Spanish ambassador by saying that he wanted to give his son a chance to win popularity by reducing taxation in his accession.[233] Whether this was true or not, Charles Emmanuel failed to take this opportunity. All the duke's careful attention

---

their claims to jurisdiction in first and second instance, forced the inhabitants to register their property with their lords and concluded: "Moreover, we order and decree that the aforesaid men of Borgomasino, and every one of them, from now onward shall use all modesty and reverence towards the said count [Valperga di Masino] both in word and deed, as befits subjects towards their lord . . ." A.S.T., MS, Paesi, Provincia d'Ivrea, Mazzo 3, No. 5; Borgomasino, No. 2.

[230] On this the unanimous testimony of the Venetian ambassadors.

[231] Estimates of the Venetian ambassadors—unfortunately Garino Canina's tables of the duke's revenues do not inspire as much confidence as one would wish ("La Finanza del Piemonte," p. 521). This author starts his essay with the calculation that 3 lira at 104 *grossi* give a value of 33-2/3 *grossi* per lira! All subsequent calculations are based on this curious arithmetic. He also makes the remarkable statement that before 1559 there were no registers in Piedmont such as Domesday Book or the Sicilian censuses. But the *catasti* of the communes had been compiled from the thirteenth century onwards, and every archivist in Piedmont knows of their existence.

[232] Boldù, "Relazione," pp. 445 ff. Also the appeal of the inhabitants of Val di Ponte, c. 1560, A.S.T., MS, Paesi, Provincia d'Ivrea, Mazzo 11, No. 8; Pont e Valle, No. 6.

[233] "Relacion del Conde Pedro Antonio Lunato sobre la muerte del Duque de Savoya." British Museum, MS, Add. 28,451, fo. 327.

to the growth of industrial production in Piedmont [234] could not make up for the stifling taxation and the exactions of his standing army. Throughout the reign the Venetian ambassadors speak of deserted farmlands and almost universal poverty and apathy. The population declined steadily,[235] and in 1601 Simon Contarini remarked that even the biggest cities of Piedmont could not compare with the least of Venetia and Lombardy.[236] The country's industries remained insufficient to supply its needs, and the people continued to work for the merest subsistence.[237] Not for nothing was the Savoyard monarchy hated by its subjects throughout the reigns of Emmanuel Philibert and Charles Emmanuel.[238]

It was impossible that the assembly of the three estates of Piedmont could have survived the French occupation for long. With the old ruling classes shattered by war and foreign domination, and with no new rising group to take their place, the monarchy was left without effective opposition and, inevitably, turned the balance of power in its favor. Modern Italian historians, with the afterknowledge of the unification of Italy in the nineteenth century, have seen in the despotism of Emmanuel Philibert the first great step toward national unity and freedom. Yet there was no inevitablity in the final emergence of Piedmont as the leader of the national movement, even though

[234] Egidi, *Emanuel Filiberto,* II, 99–131.

[235] G. Prato, "Censimenti e Popolazione in Piemonte nei secoli XVI, XVII, e XVIII," *Rivista Italiana di Sociologia,* 10, Fasc. 3 and 4 (Turin, 1906), 334 f.

[236] Albèri, *Relazioni,* ser. 2, V, 264.          [237] *Ibid.,* pp. 265 f.

[238] Armstrong, "Tuscany and Savoy," p. 409. "Meanwhile, the resources of Piedmont were developed; and its prosperity perhaps increased in as high a ratio as its burdens." This judgment of Emmanuel Philibert's reign is not borne out by the accounts of the Venetian ambassadors who were, moreover, generally sympathetic to the duke. It is significant that the short period of Savoyard rule in Sicily, from 1714 to 1720, was more unpopular than any that island had experienced since the French occupation of the thirteenth century.

the House of Savoy can claim the credit for keeping their state independent. For all their shortcomings and selfishness, the three estates had preserved the country from the exploitation of rapacious princes and maintained the conditions for material progress. Two and a half centuries of despotism and of political and economic stagnation were a heavy price for the final *risorgimento*—a price which is perhaps not even yet fully paid.

### The House of Savoy [239]

Louis, 1449–1465
Amadeus IX, 1465–1472
Philibert I, 1472–1482
Charles I, 1482–1490 [240]
Charles II, 1490–1496
Philip II, 1496–1497 [241]
  (Philip of Bresse)
Philibert II, 1497–1504
Charles III, 1504–1553 [242]
Emmanuel Philibert, 1553–1580

Charles Emmanuel, 1580–1630

Regency of Yolanda of France, wife of Adameus IX, unofficial, 1465–1472, official, 1472–1478

Regency of Bianca of Montferrat, wife of Charles I, 1490–1496

[239] Reigning dukes are sons of the preceding, unless otherwise stated.
[240] Brother of preceding.      [241] Son of Louis.
[242] Brother of preceding.

# CHAPTER 2

# The Parliament of Sicily
# and the Spanish Empire

THERE WAS A bon mot current in Italy during the six-teenth century: in Sicily the Spaniards nibble, in Naples they eat, and in Milan they devour. It may be that it was really the other way round about Naples and Milan, that the Spaniards just ate in Milan but devoured in Naples. But the saying was certainly correct about Sicily: the Spaniards got relatively much less money out of it than out of their other Italian dominions. It is usually agreed that this was due to the strength and effec-tiveness of the Sicilian parliament. At a certain level of his-torical analysis this opinion is certainly correct. In the early seventeenth century, Sicilian enthusiasts claimed, as Professor Titone discovered, that only two parliaments still preserved their rights and powers, those of England and of Sicily.[1] Clearly, these enthusiasts knew nothing about the States-Gen-eral of the United Provinces of the Netherlands, nor of the Polish Diet, the Swedish Riksdag, or of several of the German Landtage. But then, why should they have known about the distant north of Europe? For us, it is more important to know whether they were correct about Sicily itself. The question is, how important and how powerful really was the Parliament of Sicily during the period of Spanish rule, especially in the six-teenth and early seventeenth centuries?

I shall attempt to answer this question in terms of the role which parliament played in the political life of the island, and, for the purposes of this communication, I shall largely ignore its legislative powers and other, more formal, roles. At the out-

[1] V. Titone, *La Sicilia spagnuola* (Palermo, 1948), p. 41.

set I had better say that I do not think there is a simple, straightforward answer to my question. The reason for this difficulty is itself quite simple: after the beginning of the fifteenth century, that is, after the age of the restoration of the Sicilian monarchy by Martin I and Martin II, the parliament of Sicily as such was never again involved in a struggle for ultimate political power in Sicily—at any rate until the end of the Spanish rule. It is, however, not obvious why this should have been so.

From Ruggiero Moscati's excellent book [2] we know the compromises which the two Martins had to make with the various privileged orders and corporations of the island. Nevertheless, they restored the crown very effectively as the ultimate political authority in the country. Parliament emerged from the two reigns with its defensive powers fully intact but without the will to challenge the crown on fundamental issues. It showed this clearly, on the one hand by its stubborn and effective resistance to the financial demands of the count of Prades and, on the other, by its relatively tame acceptance of viceregal rule. If the Sicilian privileged classes had regarded this as a fundamental issue, they would undoubtedly have pressed their demands for a king of their own at the moment when it would have been most effective, during the civil war in Catalonia, in the 1460's. As the Irish in their relations with England, they would have seen in Aragon's difficulties their own opportunity. But this was precisely what the Sicilians and their parliament did not do.

By the beginning of the sixteenth century, everyone seems to have taken it for granted that a struggle over ultimate political power would not arise again. The viceroy Medinaceli wrote to his successor: "In this kingdom Your Serenity will find the same loyalty toward the king, our lord, as in Castile." [3]

---

[2] R. Moscati, *Per una storia della Sicilia nell'età dei Martini* (Messina, 1954).

[3] *Collección de Documentos Inéditos para la Historia de España,* XXVIII, 361.

Even the generally very hostile Castilian, Pedro Velázquez, writing a memorandum on the government and defense of the kingdom in the 1570's, says: "that the evil nature of the natives of this kingdom, the close links which the nobles keep with each other and also with the commoners, sharing out offices among themselves, and the lengths to which their passions go, make them difficult to govern." That it would be better if all officials in Sicily were foreigners—by which he means Spaniards—but that this was not possible "as the safety of the state consists in the subjects, or the greater part of them, being content with its government." [4] In other words, Velázquez repeats the popular and platitudinous contemporary views about the supposedly bad character of the Sicilians which made them difficult to rule, but he suggests, at least by implication, that they are content with their government, i.e., that they are perfectly loyal unless they should be outrageously provoked by not being allowed to hold any offices in their own country; and there was never any question of that.

The question of ultimate power, then, is clear enough; but it still left open a wide field for power struggles between the viceroys and parliament over finance and other political matters. But just how important were these power struggles?

To answer this question, historians of Sicily (and I myself included) have tended to rely heavily on Scipio di Castro's *Avvertimenti al Signor Marc'Antonio Colonna, quando andò Vice Re de Sicilia*.[5] There was good reason for this. Castro was obviously very well informed and he was one of the most intelligent and acute commentators on Sicilian politics during this period. I will briefly recall his main arguments.

[4] "En lo que toca a las cosas del stado y guerra de Reyno de Sicilia . . . "(British Museum, MS, Add. 28, 396, fo. 218r).

[5] *Thesoro Politico* (Milan, 1601), Pt. 2, pp. 459–463. There are many MS copies, of varying accuracy, in different European libraries. Definitive edition is by A. Saitta, Rome, Edizione di Storia e Letteratura, 1950. Saitta's contention that the *Avvertimenti* were not actually addressed to Colonna but were of a more general character does not affect the argument of this paper.

Castro starts by immediately, and very skillfully, setting the tone for his comments: "Parliament has great power to trouble an inept viceroy." Six difficulties can arise for the viceroy:

(1) a complete rejection of his demands—which means, of course, the financial demands which he places before parliament, usually every three years;

(2) that parliament offers much less than it is asked for;

(3) & (4) that parliament attaches damaging conditions to its grants, i.e., damaging to the viceroy or his friends;

(5) that parliament sends its own representative to the court in Spain; and

(6) that independent and opposition-minded persons are chosen as deputies.

Such troubles, says Castro, usually originate with the *braccio ecclesiastico,* the house of prelates, because they are rich, independent of the viceroy, especially when they are Spaniards, usually quarreling with the viceroy over the *monarchia* (the claim of the kings of Sicily to be permanent papal legates in the kingdom) and because they really have to pay the donatives while the nobles let their vassals pay the taxes. The towns, because they also have to pay themselves, often follow the prelates. Castro advises five methods of dealing with the prelates:

(1) quarrel with them as little as possible and make friends with some of them;

(2) make the demands look so reasonable that a rejection would look very bad;

(3) summon parliament in an awkward season, so that the prelates will send proxies who can be managed more easily;

(4) always let the treasurer of the realm hold the votes of the vacant sees;

(5) arrange that there is always present some prelate who is dependent on the viceroy, because of a lawsuit or something similar.

To manage the *bracco demaniale,* the towns, the viceroy should:

(1) win the vote of the *pretore* of Palermo who usually depends on the viceroy;

(2) see that his own officials hold all the proxy votes and draw up a balance of votes before the session to make sure he has a majority.

Now the first two difficulties—complete rejection by parliament of the demand for a donative or its serious reduction—had not happened for a hundred years when Castro wrote, the last case being that of the count of Prades in 1478. It was to happen once more, in 1591, but in a pattern unforeseen by Castro: a refusal of the grant by the nobles—not at all, as Castro had feared, by the prelates and towns. The prelates and towns, in fact, supported the viceroy against the nobility. I have not myself found any case of a serious reduction—a lower offer than the demand. The rest of Castro's points, however, were valid enough. Parliaments did attach conditions to their grants of donatives; they did send their own representatives to Spain and, no doubt (although this is difficult to prove either way), the towns sometimes sent opposition-minded deputies.

Nevertheless, if one takes Castro's comments on parliament together, they do appear overdramatic. No doubt, this was what he intended, for he was writing a cautionary tale for the new viceroy, Colonna. Moreover, it is quite clear that Castro was concerned with the personal position of the viceroy and not with the relations between parliament and the crown as such. About the conditions which parliament attaches to its donatives he writes that they can be prejudicial to the viceroy's reputation, or a restraint on his power—the viceroy's, not the crown's, that is!—or damaging to his friends. Castro knew, of course, that the king could accept or reject these conditions and *capitoli* as he wished. The parliament of Sicily had lost the power of insisting on the redress of grievances before supply, i.e., the acceptance of its *capitoli* before the grant of the donative, if indeed it ever had this power. No representative assembly which did not win this point ever won its struggle with the monarchy, I believe. Castro was not talking about this at all, but about the position of the viceroy at the court of Madrid; i.e., he was talking about court politics, not about constitutional struggles. Even so, it is surprising how rarely the viceroys mention parliament in their correspondence with Madrid. The one who did it more often than any of the others was the duke of Terranova—strictly speaking not a viceroy at all, but president of the kingdom. It may well be that Terranova, as a Sicilian baron himself, was more concerned with maintaining the powers of parliament than the Spanish or Italian viceroys. For instance, in 1574 he suggested to the king that revenues could be increased by new taxes on salt, cheese, sugar, and tunny fish, but that it would be necessary to obtain the consent of parliament which, however, he thought could be done.[6] The Council of Italy commented coolly on this suggestion that it was quite unnecessary to consult parliament and would create a bad precedent.[7]

Even Terranova, in his correspondence with Madrid, never suggests that he has any serious trouble in his dealings with parliament. He once mentions difficulties with the prelates which, he says, he has overcome with a mixture of "subtlety" and "rigor." [8] This seems to have been the case Castro knew about and it rather looks as if he generalized from this one case. All this contrasts most strikingly with the correspondence of Margaret of Parma, Philip II's governor general of the Netherlands, who hardly wrote a single letter without complaining of the difficulties she had with the estates of Brabant and the other provinces.

Castro's practical advice on how to handle parliament was undoubtedly sound. It was exactly the sort of advice a good political manager would follow. But, again, the impression he

[6] Terranova to Philip II, June 12, 1574; Simancas, *Secreterías Provinciales*, leg. 981.

[7] Consulta of Aug. 20, 1574, *ibid.*

[8] Terranova to Philip II, Oct. 2, 1574; C. d'Aragona, *Corrispondenza particolare* (Palermo, 1879), p. 434.

gives is overdramatic. Viceroys frequently asked the king to send personal letters to important personages and the council of Italy even drafted a standard formula for such letters. But I have found no documentary evidence that any viceroy ever followed Castro's suggestion of summoning parliament during the bad season so that prelates and nobles would send proxies (*procuratori*). It was hardly necessary. Very few barons and prelates ever attended parliament in person and it was customary that royal officials held many of the *procure*. In 1594 parliament complained to the king about this practice. Philip II referred the complaint back to the viceroy who, naturally, preferred to leave matters as they were. Castro's advice really means that any viceroy who is a reasonably good politician can manage parliament quite effectively and that only the neglect of some fairly elementary precautions would lead to trouble.

My theory that Castro was deliberately overdramatizing the viceroy's difficulties with parliament is supported by an analysis of all the other memoranda which were written on the government of Sicily, either by the outgoing viceroys themselves or by an official in the government for the benefit of an incoming viceroy—as Castro's *Avvertimenti* were written for Marc'Antonio Colonna. Some of these have been published, but the majority seem to exist only in manuscript form, mostly in the British Museum, although sometimes also in Spanish archives.

The earliest seems to be the *Relazione delle cose di Sicilia* by Ferrante Gonzaga, in 1546.[9] He does not mention parliament at all. Neither does Juan de Vega in his letter to Philip II, written probably in 1557, in which he gives some very dramatic details about the difficulties of being a viceroy of Sicily.[10] The duke of Medinaceli in his 60 pages of *Advertencias a D. García de Toledo,* in 1565, is equally silent on parliament.[11] I have not found any memoranda from the viceroyal-

[9] F. C. Carreri, ed., in *Documenti per servire alla Storia di Sicilia,* Società Siciliana per la Storia Patria, ser. 4, vol. 4 (Palermo, 1896).

[10] In *Papiers d'Etat du Cardinal de Granvelle,* C. Weiss, ed. (Paris, 1844), V, 144–166.

[11] In *Colección de Documentos Inéditos,* vol. XXVIII.

ties of Toledo, Pescara, and Terranova, unless the memorandum by Pedro Velázquez of 1574, which I quoted earlier, belongs to this genre, although I do not think so. Velázquez, however, at least mentions the *deputazione,* the committee of the three *bracci* which represented parliament between sessions and which, as we now know from Giuseppe Schichilone, had only received its definite constitution between 1567–1570.[12] Velázquez compared it, with characteristically Castilian distaste for Aragonese and Catalan institutions, to the fraternities of knights and hidalgos in Saragossa and to the *deputación* in Barcelona; he accused its members of corruption, which was quite likely; and he complained that it claimed to maintain the *capituli* and privileges of the kingdom "as if there were a difference between the service of His Majesty and the general good of the kingdom."[13] When the king referred this view to Terranova, the president reassured him that his right to appoint the members of the *deputazione* gave him complete control over this institution.[14] A few years later, the viceroy Colonna agreed with him.[15]

The next memorandum is that by Castro and it is followed by two further ones which again do not mention parliament at all. They are the *Relacion de las Cosas del Reyno de Sicilia,* by Pedro de Cisneros,[16] written for Alvadeliste, and *Los avertimientos del doctor Fortunato sobre el govierno de Sicilia*[17] written for Olivares. Now their silence is remarkable. Cisneros was Colonna's secretary and would almost certainly have known Castro's *Avvertimenti.* They circulated widely in manuscript copies long before they were published in the *Thesoro*

[12] G. Schichilone, "Origine e Ordinamento della Deputazione del Regno di Sicilia," *Archivio Storico per la Sicilia Orientale,* ser. 4, vol. 3 (1950).

[13] British Museum, MS, Add. 28, 396, fos. 218v–219r.

[14] Terranova to Philip II, Jan. 25, 1575; C. d'Aragona, *Corrispondenza,* pp. 115 ff.

[15] British Museum, MS, Add. 28, 400, fos. 192–193. A memorandum probably written by one of Colonna's officials and on his orders. Cf. Koenigsberger, *The Practice of Empire* (Ithaca, 1969), pp. 159 f.

[16] British Museum, MS, Add. 28, 396, fos. 333–354.

[17] *Ibid.,* fos. 399–458.

*Politico* in 1601. The conclusion seems inescapable: in all of Colonna's many bitter fights, against the Inquisition and the factions, both in Sicily and at the court of Madrid, parliament never played the role which Castro had warned that it might.

Fortunato's silence on parliament is even more surprising, for he wrote after the attempt by the barons to refuse a donative, in 1591. One can only guess at his reasons. It seems likely that he regarded the so-called revolt of the *braccio militare,* the house of nobles, not as a parliamentary opposition at all.

In government circles it was thought that the barons had been instigated by the inquisitor Páramo,[18] by the leader of the organization which everyone in the sixteenth century, including Castro, regarded as, by far, the most formidable and dangerous opponent of the viceroys. From Medinaceli onwards, none of the authors of memoranda on the government of Sicily ever left out the Inquisition and, next to finance, defense, and patronage, it was the most common topic in the viceregal correspondence with Madrid—very much in contrast to parliament. As far as the viceroys' relations with parliament were concerned, the abortive revolt of the *braccio militare,* in 1591, may well have been reassuring. The prelates and towns, the two *bracci* whom, Castro had said, the viceroy should fear most, had remained unshakably loyal; and the resistance of the barons had collapsed as soon as the viceroy showed some firmness of purpose.

The next one of our memoranda on the government of Sicily was written by the viceroy Olivares in 1595. He does discuss parliament and his discussion reads as one would imagine Castro's to have read if Castro had not been so intent to dramatize all conceivable dangers for the viceroy. "At times, there have not lacked rumors that matters were not as they should be, which usually happens when there is a crowd," Olivares writes; but he continues that there are many who are zealous in the service of the king and that one should arrange for them to have the *procure* to prevent trouble. Nevertheless, one

[18] Koenigsberger, *The Practice of Empire,* p. 156.

should not drive them too hard and support their reasonable petitions to the king who would not deny them if they did no harm.[19] Of the *deputazione* Olivares writes that, sometimes in the past, they have transgressed the limits of their authority and produced some disquiet in the kingdom by acting from private interests. But, he concludes, "nothing of this has happened in my time." [20] I strongly suspect that he simply took the point from Velázquez's memorandum of twenty years before.

Pedro Celestre, writing in 1611 for the duke of Osuna, gives a detailed and accurate description of the composition and functions of parliament and the *deputazione,* but does not suggest that there is ever any opposition.[21] On the contrary. The *deputazione* is obliged to refer everything to the viceroy, he says, and nothing is done without the viceroy's approval; but the viceroys always treat the deputation with great respect and oblige the kingdom in all that can justly be done.[22]

Antonio de Amico, writing in 1632, used practically the same words, probably because he simply copied from Celestre; but he added that it was well known how badly the deputation performed its duties.[23]

My last memorandum was written by Francisco Bustamante, in 1640.[24] He strikes a distinctly more pessimistic note about both parliament and the deputation. But there is also a distinct air of unreality about his memorandum and one has the impression that Bustamante had not had any practical experience of government for a number of years before 1640. He simply copied Olivares' memorandum about difficulties arising when

[19] "Cosas del Govierno y Estado Universal del Reyno de Sicilia hecho por la Excelencia del Conde de Olivares." British Museum, MS, Add. 14, 009, fo. 365v.

[20] *Ibid.,* fo. 380v.

[21] "Idea del Govierno del Reyno de Sicilia," British Museum, MS, Add. 24, 130, fos. 26v–31v.

[22] *Ibid.,* fo. 31v.

[23] "Noticias del Govierno del Reyno de Sicilia," British Museum, MS, Add. 28, 466, fos. 141r–142v.

[24] A printed copy in British Museum, MS, Add. 14, 009, fos. 406r–413v.

there are a considerable number of people,[25] and his strictures on the deputation closely follow those of Velázquez and reiterate the well-known, and undoubtedly true, complaint that its members were corrupt.

The pattern which has emerged from this discussion is clear enough. No one, except Castro, regarded the parliament of Sicily as a really serious political problem. The reason was twofold: first, there was the well-known loyalty of the Sicilians to the crown; second, there was the equally well-known ability of the viceroys to manage parliament, by attaching the leaders of the *bracci* to themselves, by keeping the proxy votes in the hands of their own officials, and by controlling the appointment of the members of the deputation.

Nevertheless, I do not think Castro's views can be simply dismissed, even if, as I have suggested, he overdramatized the situation. I think Castro wanted to suggest the potential danger which parliament might still represent to the viceroys. Spanish rule in Sicily rested essentially on consent—the consent of the privileged orders and corporations of the island. Their local privileges had hardly been touched, even by Philip II's administrative reorganization of the government of the island. In the seventeenth century the nobility even obtained, as of right, the ability to buy local jurisdiction, the *mero e misto imperio*. If they no longer controlled the central government, they could and did have great influence over it, at all levels. If they did not like a particular viceroy, they could and did get rid of him. This was the easier as the Spanish system of government itself tended to build up alternative centers of authority to its viceroys. In Sicily the most important of these was the Inquisition, but it must not be forgotten that the viceroy's own ministers were appointed not by himself but by the imperial government in Spain.

All this meant that political struggles in Sicily were concerned with personalities and not with questions of ultimate power. Ultimate power ceased to be a live issue as soon as the

[25] *Ibid.*, fo. 413r.

kingdom came to be ruled by viceroys and accepted this form of government. It was the same in Catalonia and Aragon. In the 1460's John II fought a deadly civil war for ultimate political power in Catalonia with Barcelona and the Catalan estates. Barcelona and the Catalon corts emerged from this struggle with practically all their privileges intact. But since, very soon afterwards, the monarchy effectively transferred itself to Castile, Catalonia became an outlying province in which the problem of ultimate power was simply shelved. As long as the central monarchy made no very pressing demands, this state of affairs could continue for a very long time. And the monarchy did not make such demands because it was not worth its while. Catalonia was poor and it was not worth stirring up trouble for the comparatively small extra sums of money which might be squeezed out of the country. In Joan Regla's book on Catalonia under Philip II, the corts is hardly mentioned at all.[26] Yet the country maintained all its privileges and autonomies. But when, in the seventeenth century, the Count-Duke Olivares reversed this policy, the Spanish monarchy came to be faced with a fight for ultimate power as deadly as that which John II had had to wage nearly 200 years before.

The situation in Aragon was essentially similar. Here, too, the struggle for ultimate power was simply shelved until the rather fortuitous events which led to Philip II's invasion of the kingdom in 1591. The Aragonese cortes as such had had nothing to do with these events, but their former powers were broken nevertheless.

It was a very different story in Castile. Here, at the very center of the Spanish Empire, the refusal of the majority of the cortes to grant a royal request for money, in 1520, was not, and could not be, limited to a struggle over an unpopular regent: it became a struggle for ultimate political power between the monarchy and the cortes. The monarchy won and the cortes ceased to be a serious political problem for the crown.

But what of the Netherlands? By 1555, when Charles V ab-

[26] J. Regla, *Felip II i Catalunya* (Barcelona, 1956).

dicated, they had become an outlying dominion of the Spanish
Empire, just as Catalonia and Sicily. Why then was there a
power struggle between the monarchy and the estates? The
answer is complex. In the first place, the Netherlands were
much richer than Catalonia or Sicily. The question of taxation
was therefore almost as important for the monarchy as it was
in Castile. Secondly, there was during the regency of Margaret
of Parma, 1559–1567, a struggle for power within the Netherlands itself, regardless of the ultimate authority of the king in
Madrid. It was a struggle between the Netherlands government
on the one hand and the high nobility on the other. At one
point, when the seigneurs had forced the dismissal of Cardinal
Granvelle, it almost looked as if a Sicilian political pattern
would prevail. But the insoluble religious problem, together
with the social tensions of the time, produced the rebellion
which led eventually to the complete overthrow of royal power
in the northern part of the Netherlands.

It did not happen in Sicily. The monarchy never pressed its
financial and political demands unduly. The viceroys were
most anxious that it should not. Again and again they pointed
to the poverty of the kingdom. One should not even think of
increasing the donatives, for the greatest troubles would follow,
wrote Olivares,[27] and this was a typical argument. But the problem of ultimate power might still arise in Sicily, and then parliament might once more take the center of the stage. After
all, the nobles and prelates might all come in person; the towns
might all send their most Cato-like deputies (as Castro had
said), and, at least legally, they might still make an issue of
insisting on the grant of their *capitoli* before voting the donative. It looks to me as if Castro had such a possibility in mind.
We know that it did not happen and that it was not very likely
to happen; that, indeed, as traditions hardened, it became progressively less likely. But this was not as obvious to Castro in
1577 when he wrote his *Avvertimenti* as it is to us who know
the subsequent history of Sicily; and the example of Catalonia

[27] "Cosas del Govierno," fo. 365v–366r.

should make us doubly cautious. The parliament of Sicily fought no major battles; yet its very existence (like that of a "fleet in being" that never fires its guns but yet preserves its country from defeat) safeguarded the privileges of the island. And if these privileges, like all similar privileges during the *ancien régime,* benefited only a comparatively small section of the population, every Sicilian benefited from relatively low taxes. In the end it remained true that in Sicily the Spaniards nibbled, but that elsewhere in Italy they ate and devoured.

# CHAPTER 3

# English Merchants in Naples and Sicily in the Seventeenth Century[1]

LONG BEFORE the struggle between Elizabethan England and Philip II's Spain flared up into open war, there was an increasingly bitter struggle for the trade of the Spanish colonies and dominions. During the sixteenth century English trade broke away from the traditional medieval channels and

---

[1] The main sources for the history of the English merchants in Naples and Sicily are the "State Papers, Naples and Sicily (S.P.)" and the "Foreign Entry Books," in the Public Record Office. The former consist of letters by English consuls and merchants in Naples, Messina, and Palermo to successive secretaries of state, while the latter comprise the letter-books of the secretaries for the southern department, being copies of outgoing letters to the consuls and of royal letters to the viceroys. The Port Books, which are also in the Public Record Office, contain useful particulars of ships bound for Naples and Sicily and their cargoes; but as they usually give only the port of destination and not the ports of call, statistics of the trade and its development cannot be compiled from them, for it is impossible to tell which of the ships, listed for various other Mediterranean destinations, called also at south Italian ports, and what cargo they discharged there. Much scattered information can be found in the "State Papers, Spanish," in the manuscript collections of the British Museum (B.M.) and the Bodleian Library, in the published *Calendars of State Papers (C.S.P.), Venetian,* and in other printed sources. There are a few more consular letters in the *Bath MSS Collection,* listed on page 248 of the *Fourth Report on the Historical Manuscript Commission.* These are not, at the moment, available for study, but it is unlikely that they contain much new material. The absence of an "Italian Company" means that there are no company records for Italy like the Turkey Papers of the Levant Company for Constantinople and Aleppo, which give a full and continuous account both of the commercial and diplomatic activities of

new companies were established to trade regularly with places where formerly only an occasional English merchantman had made its appearance. There were rivals everywhere. Spaniards, Portuguese, and Venetians claimed the monopoly of the trade of certain areas, and the Dutch, who were newcomers like the English, were keen and hostile competitors for the trade of the decaying older empires. Sixteenth-century trade was therefore closely related to and often indistinguishable from intermittent naval warfare and piracy; and nearly everywhere the greatest rival was still Spain.

The most important and most successful new fields of expansion for English trade were, on the one hand, America and the East Indies and, on the other, the Near East and the Mediterranean. In America and, to a lesser extent, in India there were expanding markets for goods which the English merchants could supply, chiefly, manufactures, certain materials, slaves, and fish; requirements which the imperial powers, Spain, Portugal, and the decaying Mogul Empire, could not satisfy. In return Britain offered markets for the colonial goods which Spain and Portugal could not themselves absorb.

In the Levant and even more in the central Mediterranean conditions of trade were radically different. Here there were old-established static markets and organized export industries for currants, oil, silk, and wine. The volume of trade remained constant and limited, and any expansion of English trade meant a diminution of the trade of Spain or Venice or of their dependencies. For the Ottoman and Venetian empires and the Italian dependencies of Spain were not colonies of the American and Indian type but states or constituent parts of empires with rights and individuality of their own.

Successful expansion of English trade in the Mediterranean

---

the company's agents. Although these sources leave considerable gaps, especially in the second quarter of the seventeenth century, they nevertheless provide a comprehensive picture of the development of English trade in Naples and Sicily, as well as an interesting commentary on seventeenth-century commercial practices and Anglo-Spanish relations.

was therefore dependent on two main factors: commercial efficiency greater than that of the older trading powers together with the provision of a better market, and political backing of the English merchants by a government strong enough to secure them against armed attacks by their rivals or restrictions imposed on them by the governments of the countries in which they traded. This meant that the expansion of English trade in the Mediterranean was directly dependent on naval power and, as this increased in the course of the seventeenth century, so trade increased and the position of the English merchants became more secure.[2] As southern Italy was both economically poorer and politically more self-conscious than the countries of the eastern Mediterranean, and as Spain and the Barbary pirates were less influenced by considerations of commerce than were Venice and the Porte, the influence of political and naval factors in the development of English trade in the central Mediterranean was much greater than it was in the Levant. All traffic between the east and the west Mediterranean must pass through this area and it was, moreover, the vital link on which depended the communications of the Spanish Empire in Europe. These strategic considerations gave the south Italian trade a political importance out of proportion to its purely economic value. In the latter part of the seventeenth century, before the establishment of permanent Mediterranean bases, the admiralty and the British Mediterranean squadron came to rely on the British consuls in Naples and Sicily for information and active assistance. The consuls thus played a vital if unspectacular part in the defeat of Louis XIV.

Neither merchants nor statesmen at the beginning of the seventeenth century were fully aware of these factors. As long as there was no permanent Mediterranean squadron, the political importance of the merchants in Naples and Sicily was limited to providing material for the anti-Spanish agitation in

[2] For the development of British naval power in the Mediterranean see J. S. Corbett, *England in the Mediterranean*, 2 vols. (London, 1904).

Parliament.[3] The diplomatic support which the merchants received was due not so much to a realization of the value of their trade or their strategic position as to a general policy of government support of English merchants against Spain. The strategic position of the English merchants in Naples and Sicily was only slowly appreciated, and it was not until the last quarter of the seventeenth century that British policy logically developed to the next stage in the control of the Mediterranean—the occupation of permanent naval bases at Tangier, Gibraltar, Minorca, and finally Malta.

While diplomatic and naval support for the English merchants in southern Italy was only gradually developing, their commercial superiority over their Italian and Spanish rivals was marked from the very beginning of their activities. In the last decade of the sixteenth century, Moryson wrote in his *Itinerary:*

The Italians, the old conquerors of the world are at this day so effeminate and so inamored of their Paradise of Italy, as nothing but desperate fortune can make them undertake voyages by Sea or Land. . . .[4]

and he went on to particularize:

I observed English Shipps going forth from Venice with Italian Shipps to have sayled into Syria and returned to Venice twice, before the Italian Shipps made one retorne, whereof two reasons may be given, one that the Italians pay their Marriners by the day, how long soever the voyage lasteth, which makes them upon the least storme putt into harbors, whence only few wyndes can bring them out, whereas the English are payed by the voyage, and so beate out stormes at Sea, and are ready to take the first wynde any thing favourable unto them. The other that Italian Shipps are heavy in sayling, and great of burthen, and the Governors and Mariners not very expert, nor bold, and so are less fitt in that narrow Sea full of

[3] Cf. the case of the *Trial* below.

[4] F. Moryson, *Itinerary: Shakespeare's Europe*, C. Hughes, ed. (London, 1903), p. 135.

Ilands, to beate out stormes at Sea, whereas the English Shipps are swift in sayling. . . .[5]

Added to these advantages there was an excellent market for Mediterranean goods in England and plenty of capital and enterprise to finance even risky commercial undertakings. In the earlier part of the century English enterprise left enough room for the French and the Dutch and later, especially during the Messinese war,[6] the English had the advantage of being neutral in fighting which involved their two most dangerous rivals, and nearly succeeded in driving both the Dutch and the French completely out of the Mediterranean carrying trade.

After the peace with Spain of 1604 English merchants could settle for the first time in the Spanish dominions of Italy. Naples, Messina, and Palermo were at first primarily ports of call for ships proceeding to or coming from Venice and the Levant, ports where part of a ship's cargo might be discharged or taken aboard, rather than ports of destination. The central Mediterranean trade was at no time sufficiently important to warrant the establishment of a special company, even assuming that the Levant Company would have submitted to a breach of its monopoly position in the Mediterranean. As centers of distribution of goods from both east and west, the south Italian ports were inferior to Leghorn which was nearer to England and had been a free port since 1593.[7] For this reason much of its trade was re-export to Naples and elsewhere, often by English merchants. The merchant in Naples or Sicily might want only part of the cargo of a ship from England and payment of the high Neapolitan duties would not have to be made on the whole cargo. Much of the Leghorn trade, as the Venetian secretary pointed out, was the sale of stolen goods bought cheaply from pirates; and for such shady practices Leghorn, with its large international trading community, was much better placed than any port in a Spanish dominion.

    [5] *Ibid.*, p. 136.      [6] See below.

    [7] *C.P.S., Venetian*, XX, p. 222. A. C. Wood, *A History of the Levant Company* (Oxford, 1935), p. 64.

Starting as casual traders in English cloth, fish, and metals, and in Italian silks, oil, and wines, and still given to some of the piratical habits of the previous century, the English gradually established permanent and respectable merchant communities in the big Neapolitan and Sicilian ports. Consuls were appointed, and a slowly increasing body of rights and privileges was wrung from grudging Spanish viceroys in proportion to the increase of the economic importance of these communities and of British sea power. Only temporarily checked by two short wars with Spain in 1625 and 1655, the English merchants far outstripped the import, export, and carrying trade of all other nations. Up to the year 1702 their economic and political status continued to improve in spite of native and foreign competition, official Spanish obstruction, and even of several attempts to prohibit their trade altogether.

After so many years of bitterly-fought naval and trade war, it was not to be expected that relations with the local Spanish authorities would immediately become smooth and cordial after 1604. The governments, both in Madrid and in London, were anxious to build up normal commercial intercourse. Philip III wrote repeatedly to his viceroys urging them to favor the English.[8] In particular he commanded that in cases pending for contraband, the ships and goods should be restored to their owners if they deposited caution money for their appearance before the court dealing with the case.[9] James I, for his part, resisted strong pressure from parliament to make reprisals or declare war when the Spaniards did not observe the terms of the peace.[10]

Nevertheless, conflicts continued, due to minor piracies [11] or ignorance of Spanish laws on the part of the English, and to distrust, reprisals, and more often plain rapacity on the part of

[8] E.g., quoted by Resoute in a letter to Salisbury, March 10, 1606, in S.P., 93/1, 13.

[9] *C.S.P., Venetian*, X, 319.     [10] *Ibid., passim.*

[11] E.g., the complaints of the Genoese Cigala, S.P., 93/1, 6; and of the Algerians, in Rymer, *Foedera* (London, 1732), XIX, 2.

the Spaniards. In 1604 there occurred an incident which was to play a principal part in determining Anglo-Spanish relations for the next seven years. A ship, the *Trial,* belonging to the London merchants John Eldred and Richard Hall, and carrying a cargo worth 200,000 crowns,[12] was captured by the galleys of the viceroy of Sicily, the duke of Feria. William Resoute, the merchants' agent in Palermo, wrote that Eldred and Hall had confessed quite openly that they had pillaged a small abandoned ship but that they had been willing to restore the property to its rightful owners.[13] Nevertheless the Sicilian courts declared the ship a pirate, confiscated its cargo and imprisoned the crew. Following the merchants' appeal to the Privy Council, Sir Charles Cornwallis, the British ambassador in Madrid, took up the case with the Spanish government. It soon appeared that it was typical of many others and would become a test case. The Spanish legal system, according to which in cases of conviction the goods of the accused were divided in equal proportions between the crown, the judge, and the informer, gave no chance of acquittal in an inferior court.[14] It was always possible to bribe witnesses with part of the booty and appeals to superior courts took years and were very costly. Moreover, Feria had powerful friends at the court of Madrid and the Spanish government did not take English threats of reprisal very seriously.[15]

The owners of the *Trial,* despairing of obtaining help from the pro-Spanish Privy Council, now appealed to parliament, which debated the case in March, 1607. The Spaniards had tried to make members of the crew confess to piracy, and the account of the torture and death of three of their number produced a profound effect.[16] Parliament promised a large subsidy

[12] *C.S.P., Venetian,* X, 482.

[13] Resoute to Salisbury, 1606, S.P., 93/1, 13.

[14] Cornwallis to Salisbury, Oct., 1605, *Memorials of Affairs of State . . . Original Papers of Sir Ralph Winwood* (London, 1725), II, 155 ff.

[15] *Ibid.; C.S.P., Venetian,* X, 396.

[16] *C.S.P., Venetian,* X, 396 ff.; *Journals of the House of Commons,* I, 341 f., 373 f., 1044 ff.

in case of a breach with Spain and clamored for the issuing of letters of marque.[17] It took all Salisbury's skill to avert a crisis and explain that nothing would be gained by the granting of letters of marque since the Spaniards would immediately retaliate by confiscating all English property in Spanish dominions.[18] But the government promised to do its best for the merchants. A special agent, George Rookes, was dispatched to Sicily,[19] and Cornwallis renewed his efforts in Madrid. Yet the Spaniards were desperately slow, even in their own most important cases; Cornwallis wrote that they were hoping for trouble for the British government in Scotland and Ireland, and Salisbury, who received a pension from Spain,[20] was not as firm as Cornwallis thought necessary. "Of the Merchants' Causes I grow almost wearye, and pitty you I protest that [you] are indeed made rather a factor than an Ambassador. . . ." [21] he wrote to Cornwallis in 1607.[22]

In December, 1609, the Council of Italy, the supreme court of appeal for Italian cases, finally pronounced in favor of Eldred and Hall.[23] This altered nothing, for the new duke of Feria, heir to the deceased viceroy, simply refused to restore the confiscated property, and the discussion continued. In August, 1610, Cornwallis's successor, Cottington, was finally ordered to present an ultimatum: he would be recalled and let-

---

[17] *C.S.P., Venetian,* X, 485 ff.

[18] S. R. Gardiner, *History of England from the Accession of James I* (London, 1863), I, 340.

[19] "The Instructions given to George Rookes goeinge into Sicilie, 1604," B.M., MS, Cotton, Julius E., II. This is a manuscript copy with no signature of the minister concerned. The date of the heading, not repeated in the text, does not seem to be correct. The *Trial* was captured in the autumn of 1604 and the judgment of the Sicilian court was not given until 1605. The British government is more likely to have sent a special agent after the debate in parliament, i.e., 1607 or later, than before the usual diplomatic means had been tried.

[20] Gardiner, *op. cit.,* II, appendix.     [21] Winwood, *op. cit.,* II, 343.

[22] Cornwallis, during his term of office, had dealt with nineteen mercantile cases; S.P. 94/16, 290.

[23] S.P., 94/16, 242.

ters of marque would be issued if there was not an immediate and favorable consideration of the merchants' cases. At the same time Eldred and Hall, "not without permission of the Council," fitted out two ships for reprisals. When the Spanish ambassador demanded the restitution of a prize they had taken, the council delayed the case long enough for the merchants to sell their prize in Flanders.[24] This helped. A whole series of orders to courts dealing with British mercantile cases was issued by Philip III and the duke of Lerma, his chief minister,[25] and at least some of the cases were settled. But the duke of Feria was at that time in Paris as Spanish ambassador, and the consideration of his case had to await his return.

There is no indication in the correspondence of the British ambassadors that Feria ever returned the confiscated property, although the *Trial* itself was restored to its owners. The last available reference to the case indicates that in April, 1611, it was not yet settled.

The case of the *Trial* shows clearly the difficulties and hazards which the British merchants in the Mediterranean had to face in the early years of the seventeenth century and the political repercussions involved. Sir John Digby, the new ambassador in Madrid, proposed to go to the root of the trouble by suggesting to the Spanish government that special commissions should be appointed to hear appeals from local courts, that no goods should be confiscated until such appeals had been heard, and that British consuls should be appointed in all ports where British merchants traded.[26] These proposals were not entirely new.[27] Cottington had demanded the appointment of special commissions in his note of 1610; the stay of execution of judgements given by local courts had been proposed by Philip III himself,[28] and Cornwallis had often complained of the inadequacy of such consuls as there were. In Messina the merchants

---

[24] *C.S.P., Venetian*, XII, 74.    [25] S.P., 94/17, 215 ff.; 94/18, 47.
[26] Gardiner, *op. cit.*, II, 79 ff.; S.P., 94/18, 153 ff.
[27] As Gardiner (II, 79 ff.) seems to imply.    [28] S.P., 93/1, 13.

had, in 1606, proposed to the viceroy the appointment of an Italian as consul, and Resoute complained to Salisbury that a foreigner and especially a Catholic was no fit person to represent the merchants and to "seale with the Armor of His Royal Majestie of England." [29] At about the same time certain English Jesuits in Naples had induced the Neapolitan government to confer a "kind of consulship" on an Irishman called Walle. It was part of Rookes' mission to depose Walle and elect a new consul.[30] Digby's proposals were not immediately accepted by the Spanish government [31] and, with the proposed Spanish marriages and the growing crisis of German protestantism, the merchants' cases from about 1611 onwards ceased to be the main issue in Anglo-Spanish relations.[32] The British government, however, no longer acquiesced in the appointment of its consuls by Spanish viceroys and began to exercise strict control over their election.

In these uncertain conditions trade with the Spanish dominions in Italy was not at first very considerable. The Port Books for 1615, for instance, mention only four ships bound for Naples and none bound for any Sicilian port, but this leaves out of account those ships which were bound for other ports and only disposed part of their cargo in Naples and Sicily as also the large quantities of goods which were taken by barges from Leghorn to Naples. Cargoes were varied, though probably not as much as those destined for the Barbary coast: [33] cloth, especially the variety called perpetuana, was the chief article of export to Naples, with fish and iron coming next in importance.[34]

[29] S.P., 93/1, 19.     [30] Instructions given to George Rookes.

[31] Gardiner, *op. cit.*, II, 79 ff.

[32] Correspondence of Digby, S.P., 94/17, 19.

[33] The *Dragon* of London, sailing for Barbary, had a cargo which included brown fustian, Polonia clothing, narrow Normandy canvas, pewter, green copps, opium, tiles, narrow satin, Holland cloth, broadcloth, a chest of thirty fowling pieces, quicksilver, 25 Turkey sword blades, two dozen spectacles with cases. From Exch. K.R. Port Books, 19/8, of March 22 and April 4, 1615.

[34] E.g., the *Desire*, *C.S.P., Venetian*, XIV, 82.

Although there are no systematic accounts of English commercial activities, any political crisis in Italy produced a great increase of correspondence between southern Italy and England which throws considerable light on the life and activities of the English merchants. The most important Italian crisis during James I's reign was the duke of Osuna's conspiracy against Venice.[35] England was nominally neutral, but the government allowed Venice to buy and equip ships in England. Osuna tried to do the same through private English merchants whom he supplied with money, and for some time during the year 1617 the Venetian ambassadors in capitals of western Europe were frantically trying to prevent Osuna's agent, Alexander Rose, from carrying out these designs. Rose's role seems, however, to have been ambiguous; for his ship, the *Royal Merchant,* would not trust the viceroy sufficiently to go into Naples, and stood off until the Neapolitan galleys appeared, when it fled back to Messina. Osuna had forcibly detained several English ships in Naples for use against Venice,[36] and Rose may have feared that Osuna might evade payment for the ship by forcible seizure. The seizure of neutral ships by belligerents for their own use, the right of angary, was to be one of the main points at issue between the governments of Naples and Sicily and the English merchants throughout the seventeenth century.

Buckingham's unsuccessful expedition to Cadiz and the war with Spain led to the first complete interruption of English trade in the central Mediterranean since 1604. An English proclamation of April 19, 1626, explained a previous proclamation prohibiting trade with Spain as meaning that English merchants were allowed to trade in or with Spain and Spanish dominions, provided they did not expose their ships to capture in Spanish ports and provided also they did not trade in contraband.[37]

[35] For a short English account, see Corbett, *op. cit.,* chap. 5.
[36] E.g., the *William* and *Ralph* and the *Delight, S.P.,* 93/1, 76.
[37] *Acts of the Privy Council of England, 1625–1626* (London, 1934), p. 441.

The English clearly wanted to make the best of both war and trade. In Naples their merchants were imprisoned for one day only, but their goods were confiscated in reprisal for the damage done at Cadiz. At the same time it was not the English merchants alone who suffered. On December 30, 1625, the Venetian secretary in Naples wrote: "No business is being transacted in this city, as there is little credit and no money, and they are terrified of the English; the provisions for defence are worth very little." [38]

In the peace treaty of 1630 [39] it was agreed that the merchants of either country should not be "troubled for the sake of their religion" (Article 19) and that in case of another war they would be given six months grace to wind up their affairs (Article 23). In 1634 Charles I wrote to the viceroy of Naples thanking him for favoring British merchants and helping them to re-establish their trade. [40]

In the period following the peace, the English began to take over a large part of the carrying trade between the Levant and Sicily, and between the Italian ports. This was done by merchants of the Levant Company who were primarily engaged in trade with Turkey and the Venetian possessions in Greece, rather than by merchants resident in the two kingdoms. [41]

Owing to the ineffectiveness of English foreign policy during the period of Charles I's personal government, the English merchants in Naples and Sicily had little diplomatic backing in their relations with the Spanish authorities. In September, 1640, a French fleet, appearing off the Bay of Naples, came upon the two English ships *Northumberland* and *Bristol Merchant,* whom they forced to yield after firing a few shots. Apart from an inconclusive gunnery duel with some Spanish shore batteries this was their only exploit. "They have done no harme," says the anonymous English letter describing the events, "but to the English whose ships were taken, and they

---

[38] *Ibid.,* p. 264.     [39] S.P., 108/465.

[40] B.M., Add. MSS, 38, 669, fo. 31b.

[41] *C.S.P., Venetian,* XII, 36 and *passim,* also references in the succeeding volumes.

infinitely abus'd heer, as intelligencers with the French whome those ships came purposely heer to meet and victuall as the Vicekinge and from him the people report, so that wee do not walke the streets but with danger and fears. . . ." [42]

Late in year 1640, or early in 1641, the merchants in Naples sent a letter to the king and parliament complaining of the treatment they received at the hands of the Naples government, especially since the appearance of the French fleet. They claimed that in the last few years they had been "wrested out of their estate to the value of 120,000 crowns," mainly by fraudulent shopkeepers who bought their goods, went bankrupt, took refuge with the Church, and then bought their freedom with bribes from the courts of justice and returned to their shops with a "salva guardia." Complaints to the viceroy were delayed or rejected. The letter ends by painting a probably exaggerated but very vivid picture of the conditions under which the English colony in Naples lived and worked:

. . . unto this Add the badd payment or never which wee receive from the kinge of Spaine his ministers when they ceaze [seize] upon our Comodities as lead fish or the like for the use of his Navye. The stayinge of our shipps Contrary to your Majesty's royall Articcles of peace, the demands and exactions for the king's necessities as from the natives the Contempt of your Capitulations inforcinge our commodities from places adioyneinge and good marketts, to the Citie where Customs are excessive and payments sildom or never. Imprisonment without cause, often by quite inferior officers, infringinge our libertie, wronge our Creditt, throwing disgrace upon our Comerce and our reputations.

In April, 1641, Charles I wrote to Sir Arthur Hopton, the ambassador in Madrid, to demand the release of English men and goods in Bari,[43] but this seems to have been the only action taken and the merchants could expect little support from the home government at a time when English naval influence in the Mediterranean was nonexistent. The question of defaulting debtors became a recurring complaint and was not satisfactorily settled until 1668. Yet despite their difficulties the

[42] S.P., 93/1, 123.        [43] S.P., 104/170, III.

merchants in Naples and Sicily must have considered their trade sufficiently profitable to remain there, and there are indications that both their position and the value of their trade improved. This was especially so during the Commonwealth period when Charles Longland, the British consul, practically transformed Leghorn into a British base.[44] The commercial connection between Leghorn and southern Italy was sufficiently close, and the British Mediterranean squadron sufficiently respected, for the British communities there to attain a diplomatic importance which they had not possessed earlier in the century. But an attempt by the merchants in Naples to have the case of a Dutch prize decided not by the viceroy's courts but by the British parliament led to the arrest of the captains who had captured the Dutch ship. They were released on the intervention of the English consul but the Dutch ship remained in the hands of the Spaniards.[45]

It was characteristic of seventeenth-century commercial practice that Cromwell's raid on Santo Domingo in April and May, 1655, did not immediately disturb Anglo-Spanish relations in the Mediterranean. In June of that year the protector himself bought six stud horses from Naples which were taken to England in the *Success*. But the Venetian resident in Naples who reported this transaction also reported that the English were preparing to abandon Naples.[46] In October, 1655, the Neapolitan government raided the houses of the English merchants. They found only 30,000 ducats worth of cloth which had just arrived and which the English had not yet been able to remove with their other goods.[47] In January, 1656, one English merchant asked for permission to trade freely in Naples, offering 200,000 ducats worth of goods to the customs every year.[48] The request was not granted, but it gives an indication of the value which the English attached to the Naples trade, and of their well-grounded fear of being displaced by the Dutch.

Just as after Buckingham's Spanish war, the English mer-

---

[44] Corbett, *op. cit.*, I, 244.          [45] *C.S.P., Venetian*, XXIX, 15 ff.

[46] *C.S.P., Venetian*, XXX, 67.          [47] War was declared in Feb., 1656.

[48] *C.S.P., Venetian*, XXX, 162.

chants lost little time in re-establishing themselves as soon as peace was concluded. In 1660 the Venetian resident in England reported the import of French, Spanish, and Neapolitan wine, "of which they [the English] consume an incredible amount." [49] In 1664 the south Italian trade had sufficiently recovered for the English merchants to ask for the appointment of several consuls and for a clearer definition of their duties and authority. Francis Brown, who had been consul before 1649 and had been deposed by the Commonwealth government for royalist sympathies, was reappointed and given authority over all other consuls in the kingdom, notably the consul in Gallipoli, on the "heel" of Italy.[50] The appointments were made by royal patent on recommendation by local merchants. With the appointment of Brown and, after his death in 1671, of George Davies, we have for the first time a regular series of consular letters which give a fairly complete picture of the British community in Naples, although its trading activities are never described in anything but general terms. There are unfortunately no such purely business reports to London offices as we have for the Turkey trade of the Levant Company.

British trade in the south Italian ports had now completely changed its character since the early days of the century when it was carried on by a few individual ships and merchants at irregular intervals. It is worth quoting at some length an official relation made by Consul Davies for the English government in 1675:

As touching the trade of this Kingdome . . . it consumes as much English Woollen goods, fish of all sorts, Pepper, Tin and Lead nigh as Italy does besides, and our Shipps make returns in Silk and Oyle chiefly for England, and in Corne and Wine for other Parts, whereof this Kingdom is very abundant. I believe 60 Ships a year, one year with another, lade for England, and as many more for

[49] Fr. Giavarina to the senate, Aug. 6, 1660, in *C.S.P.*, *Venetian*, XXXII, 179.

[50] Kent to Williamson, April and May, 1664, S.P., 93/1, 143 ff. Kent was later English consul in Florence and minister in Rome.

other Parts. The Customs are extreme high, about 12 or 13 per Cent on goods imported, and 8 or 9 per Cent on goods exported, but on fish, as Pilchards, Herrings and Newfoundland fish it is 30 or 40 per Cents, according to the abundance or scarcity at the Market.[51] . . . There is no nation drives one quarter of the trade here that our Nation doth, which makes these people love them beyond others. . . .[52]

This relation was written at a time when the Spanish armies and ships besieging Messina provided an unusually good market for English goods and when the carrying trade between Italian ports was interrupted for all except English ships. The legal position of English merchants in Naples and Sicily had greatly improved since the beginning of the century, yet there were still sharp conflicts with the local Spanish authorities who were often quite impervious to official orders from Madrid or even to their own commercial advantage. In 1674 Davies wrote that the English "enjoy all the emunities or rather more than any nation besides but would at change of every viceking bee diminished if not look[ed] after in which I am as vigilant as I can. . . ."[53] In 1668 Francis Brown had obtained a viceregal order to the effect that all debts by Neapolitan shopkeepers to the English merchants had to be met, notwithstanding any "salva guardia" or moratorium they might have obtained. Even more important was the "delegacion," the right to have all matters tried before one of the chief ministers of state and not in the ordinary courts, a right which the English claimed from "time out of minde" but which the Spanish authorities tried to abolish as late as 1691. This was an advance on Digby's proposal for a commission to hear appeals, and it is significant that this privilege was established, not by an agreement between the British and Spanish governments, but by the efforts of the merchants on the spot when British naval power in the

---

[51] This compares unfavorably with an average duty of 6⅓ per cent on imports and exports in Messina in 1642. "Observations on the Messina Trade for Customs," B.M., Stowe MSS, 759, fo. 61.

[52] S.P., 93/2, 56.    [53] S.P., 93/1, 253.

Mediterranean had become strong enough to make their claims effective. The actual value of this privilege depended on the particular minister of state who exercised this jurisdiction, and the English were lucky in having, during the critical period of the Messinese war, the Regente Galeota, the second minister of the kingdom, who, according to Davies, favored them so much that the natives were "fearfull of going to law on that score, not spareing to say that the Regente Galeota is absolutely partiall for the English." In view of this fact it seems extremely doubtful whether the English were as popular with the Neapolitans as Davies claimed. If all ministers appointed to the "delegacion" were not as biased as Galeota, it is still reasonable to suspect that there were means of inclining them favorably to the English, for this is one of the few subjects about which there were never any complaints from Davies. The local courts, on the other hand, were very jealous and when in 1686 the consul's servants were involved in a street brawl with some *sbirri,* they tried their best to procure convictions before the inevitable complaint to the viceroy and the intervention of the "delegate."

The improvement of the British position in Naples was due in no small measure to the personal efforts of Consul George Davies, a man who worked hard to maintain the dignity of his office and who, perhaps because of his own personal conceit, thoroughly understood how to manage Spanish grandees. When the Spanish governor of Gallipoli struck the English consul, Charles Bruton, because Bruton's partner had struck a "native" porter who had dropped some goods into the sea, Davies indignantly claimed that "His Majesties Consuls ought to be esteemed as much as the Residents of these petty states of Italy." [54] Davies was not, however, well served in his appointments and later complained bitterly about Bruton's fraudulent and blackmailing activities [55] bringing the position of British consuls into disrepute. By 1681 Davies had won his point with regard to the petty Italian states. In June of that year, Captain

[54] Davies to Williamson, Jan. 19, 1677, in S.P., 93/2, 188.
[55] S.P., 93/2, 281.

Wren, of the warship *Kingfisher,* demanded that two Genoese ships, lying in Naples, should hand over five English sailors said to be aboard. The Genoese captain denied this, and when Wren met two of them in the street and had them taken aboard the *Kingfisher,* he retaliated by kidnaping two English sailors and unsuccessfully tried to attack Wren himself. Davies brought the matter before the viceroy and, after some further attempted evasions, the Genoese captain was compelled to yield. The viceroy, so Davies wrote approvingly, threatened the Genoese captain with prison, "asking whether they were not ashamed to be so false, whether the small state of Genova could anyways pretend to have satisfaction given them as is due to soe Greate a Prince as his majestie of Greate Britaine", [56] an interesting example of the seventeenth-century view of the rights of large and small states. In the last resort the consul could always ask for a direct royal letter to the viceroy, and such letters the viceroy could not usually afford to disregard without getting into serious trouble with his own government. But as the English merchants could obtain such letters only for special reasons, the local Spanish authorities could often go a long way in their policy of obstruction without having to concern themselves with serious diplomatic consequences. [57]

The viceroys were subject to more immediate and therefore often more effective pressure than that exerted by the British navy and British diplomatic influence in Madrid. In 1668 the improverished landowning nobility of Naples tried to induce the government to prohibit the import of all foreign woolen goods, following a papal prohibition of the import of Naples silk into Roman territory. They claimed that they could make good the inevitable loss of the export trade of silk and oil to England from increased sales of home-produced goods. So drastic a measure required the consent of Madrid and, although the viceroy supported it, nothing seems to have come of the matter. Consul Brown regarded it as a breach of the peace capitula-

[56] S.P., 93/2, 303.

[57] Between 1674 and 1679, i.e., during the Messinese war, there were ten royal letters to the viceroys of Naples and Sicily.

tions between Spain and England, which it undoubtedly was.[58] Nevertheless, the protectionist party remained very strong in the viceroy's Collateral Council. The Neapolitans made determined attempts to break what seems to have amounted to an English monopoly in the overseas cloth, silk, and oil trade, especially at the beginning of the Messinese war in the early sixteen-seventies. In 1675 Davies wrote: "We used to have eight or ten houses in this factory, but now only three, the natives being of late crept into the trade, causing goods to come directly from England for their owne account," that Naples woven silks were no longer fashionable in England so that they now sent mainly raw silk to be worked up there and that the Neapolitans had begun to manufacture their own cloth and bags which, though not of the same quality as English cloth, decreased its sales.[59] In 1689 the viceroy considered the native cloth industry sufficiently developed to contemplate once more the prohibition of the import of English woolen manufactures and other goods. Davies took the matter seriously enough to submit a long pamphlet detailing the advantages which accrued to the kingdom from the English trade and warning against the consequences of its prohibition.[60] He pointed out that the four commercial houses of the English in Naples (they had increased by one since 1675) paid the royal treasury 90,000 ducats per annum apart from another 215,000 in excise and market dues.[61] Their exports of oil, silk, wine, and grain were of greater value than their imports. They were therefore bringing money into the country. Half their exports were paid for in bills of exchange and a third in letters of credit on Genoa, Venice, and Leghorn. They also leased the export duties of Apulian oil and soap and the revenue derived from silk which amounted to 80,000 ducats a year. Most important

[58] S.P., 93/1, 206.     [59] S.P., 93/2, 68.

[60] "Raggioni per le Mercanzie, che s'immettono dall' Inghilterra in questo Regno di Napoli," printed by Davies without date or author. There is a copy in S.P., 93/3.

[61] That is, if the latter part of this sentence is the correct interpretation of the obscure phrase "oltre doc. quindecimila al gran' à rotolo, e piazza maggiore."

of all, they kept down the rate of bills of exchange by the increase of trade they had produced and by their good credit in Italy. If imports were now prohibited they could not export or pay interest on their leases "which would be the total ruin of the Royal Treasury and its revenues." Neapolitan oil could never be sold for cash because it was used for the manufacture of cloth. If the English manufacturers could not sell cloth in Naples they would manufacture less and therefore need less oil for which, in any case, they were not dependent on Naples; they were only loading it here because it did not pay them to have their ships return empty. France did not want Neapolitan cloth or other goods, and all French imports would have to be paid for in cash. And, again most important, the low rate on bills of exchange, on which the whole credit system of the Neapolitan economy depended could not possibly be maintained if English goods were excluded.

Whether the Neapolitan government was impressed by the consul's arguments or whether directives came from Madrid, where the Spanish government may well have been concerned about the political repercussions of such a move during a war with France, nothing more was heard of the scheme and it remained the last frontal attack on English trade during the seventeenth century.

While the consular letters of the last third of the seventeenth century give a fairly clear picture of the development of English trade, the bulk of Davies's correspondence with Secretary of State Williamson is concerned mainly with politics and their effect on English merchants and shipping in the central Mediterranean. From about 1674 to 1679 we have a nearly complete set of weekly letters. The setting for this stream of information was the revolt of the city of Messina from Spain, and French intervention in Sicily during the Dutch war of Louis XIV.[62] In 1674 the Messinese had expelled the Spaniards and the

---

[62] The standard modern account is E. Laloy, *La Révolte de Messine: L'expédition de Sicile et la politique française en Italie,* 3 vols. (Paris, 1929–1931). There is an excellent short English account, especially of the naval war, in Corbett, *op. cit.,* II, chap. 23.

Spanish party of the Merli and asked for annexation by France because they could not resist Spain singlehanded. Louis XIV seized this favorable opportunity of reviving Mazarin's old policy of overthrowing the Spanish Empire in Europe by the conquest of its Italian dominions. With the French established in Sicily, Spain would be cut off from her north Italian provinces and from the Austrian Habsburgs, and France would once and for all dominate the central and western Mediterranean. Late in 1674 the French admiral Valbelle, with a small squadron, broke through the Spanish blockade and in February, 1675, Vivonne, the captain-general of the French fleet, arrived off Messina and compelled the Spaniards to retire to Naples. It was, however, more difficult to keep open regular lines of communication with France, and when later in the year 1675 the redoubtable de Ruyter arrived with a Dutch squadron, the French were in imminent danger of being cut off in Messina while their land offensive against Palermo and the rest of Sicily was making no progress. In the battle of Stromboli, in December of that year, de Ruyter defeated a superior French fleet which nevertheless succeeded in reaching Messina by sailing right round Sicily and entering the Straits of Messina from the south. After the Dutch squadron had withdrawn from the Mediterranean in August, 1676, the position became a stalemate, with the Spaniards unable to maintain an effective blockade and the French not strong enough to conquer the whole of Sicily.

England had withdrawn from the Dutch war in 1674, and during the Messinese war the English merchants were therefore neutrals. The situation was highly favorable to them: the Spanish navy and armies at Naples and Milazzo needed supplies, and while the French at Messina cut off all Spanish trade through the Faro (the Straits of Messina), English ships had a virtual monopoly of the carrying trade of the Levant, Naples, and Leghorn and, even more important, of the local corn and oil trade from Apulia which supplied the town of Naples itself. The position, however, had its difficulties, for English, Spanish, and French conceptions of neutral rights and duties differed considerably and depended less on formal ideas of international law than on political and economic advantages and necessities. The English had, with some reservations, adopted the French doctrine of *robe* by which enemy goods in a neutral ship, or neutral goods in an enemy ship, rendered both ship and goods liable to confiscation as contraband.[63] The French, however, did not apply this doctrine on this occasion, even against English ships carrying goods from one Spanish port to another. Although English captains who had put into Messina claimed that they had been forced to do so by French warships, the French claimed no general right to pre-empt their cargoes and were themselves very indignant when the grand master of Malta detained English ships and forced them to sell their cargoes to prevent these from going to Messina.[64] If the French did use force to take English ships into Messina, their victims had no strong objections.[65] Samuel Stanier, the English consul in Messina, successfully insisted on full payment for all goods, and for this reason the French let all cargoes except corn pass and only rarely insisted on the sale of oil.[66] English captains were often only too glad to sell their cargoes at the inflated prices of the beleaguered city, despite a proclamation by the British government forbidding all trade with Messina.[67]

The Spaniards, not unnaturally, resented this, for it made

[63] R. Pares, *Colonial Blockade and Neutral Rights* (Oxford, 1938), pp. 165–167.

[64] Louvois (?) to M. le Baillif d'Hautefeuille, Dec. 3; 1674, B.M., Harleian MSS, 4516, fo. 9.

[65] Vallavoire (?) to Colbert, from Messina, Jan. 1, 1676. "Besides, we have induced the English and the Venetian consuls to request their ships to bring us corn, promising them payment for what will be consumed here" (*ibid.*, 4617, fo. 249).

[66] S.P., 93/2, *passim*. Letters of Samuel Stanier to Williamson. Stanier wrote several times of English captains being forced to sell their cargoes in Messina and does not mention the agreement quoted in note 65 above.

[67] "The King's Declaration against assisting the King of Spaine's Subjects in Rebellion," March 28, 1676. S.P., 104/185, 39.

nonsense of their blockade. "The Spaniards here are very much concerned at the English shipping flocking dayly into Messina," wrote Davies in 1676, "which they wrongly believe are all laden with provitions, whereas (except four or five shipps that were carried in by force by the ffrench men of warr) they are only a company of greedy masters that passing by bound for other places, putt in there to sell their owne ships provitions and buy more at [the] next port at smaller rates." The Spaniards were not prepared to make such subtle distinctions and their galleys lay in wait for English ships coming out of Messina and arrested them as prizes, claiming that they carried contraband to the French. Davies and Gifford, the English consul in the Spanish part of Sicily, had the greatest difficulty in obtaining their release. De los Torgas, who was Spanish viceroy in Naples until 1675, roundly declared that the English were all French spies,[68] and even his successor, de los Vélez, who was much more favorably inclined towards the English, could not always help Davies to obtain the immediate release of English ships from the Spanish admirals who had captured them, especially as the charge of voluntary trading with the French was often justified.[69]

The Spaniards made several attempts to prevent supplies from reaching Messina by imposing restrictions on the carrying trade.[70] But these attempts did not last long, both because of strong British representations backed by the close vicinity of Sir John Narborough's squadron, and because of the grave economic loss entailed. A temporary oil embargo in 1675 lost the treasury 100,000 crowns in customs receipts.

The greatest cause of friction with the Spanish authorities, however, was the exercise of the right of angary by the Spaniards.[71] According to the English view, a belligerent might, in case of urgent necessity, detain a neutral ship and use it for his

[68] S.P., 93/2, 52.

[69] E.g., the case of the *George* and the *Industry*, April, 1676. S.P., 93/2, 123 ff.

[70] S.P., 93/2, 60.        [71] Cf. above.

own purposes, provided that full compensation was paid for the loss of time.[72] The Spaniards interpreted it as a right to detain English ships in harbor for indefinite periods, just in case they might be needed, and for these delays they did not pay at all or only quite inadequate sums. Spanish warships also captured English ships on the pretext that they were carrying contraband or goods belonging to Jews which were also regarded as contraband. Often enough they were justified in their suspicions, but equally often no reasons at all were given for the detention of English ships which were released as much as four weeks later without any charge or action against them. Davies's and Stanier's letters are full of complaints against this practice and of requests for special royal letters to the viceroys, or for a demonstration by one or two of Narborough's frigates. The vacillating policy of the Spaniards rarely led to positive results, for most of the captured ships were eventually released without having been used or having had their cargo confiscated, while Spanish trade suffered as much harm as the English merchants. This was due to the divergent interests of the Spanish naval and civil authorities. The admirals were interested only in making the blockade of Messina effective; the viceroys were too much dependent on export and import revenues to be able to support them wholeheartedly.

Friction was further increased by the Spanish habit of enticing sailors from English ships into service on their warships. All protests against this were in vain, for the Spaniards offered high pay and good conditions, and Spanish captains went so far as to demand the clothes and back pay of deserters from the captains of the English merchant ships. In 1676 Davies finally obtained a viceregal order against this abuse after English deserters with Spanish help had reboarded their ship in order to collect their clothes and had had a regular fight with the remaining crew.[73]

[72] Davies to Williamson, Oct. 30, 1674, S.P., 93/1, 247.
[73] S.P., 93/2, 145.

In strong contrast to relations with the Spaniards, relations with the French in Messina were very much easier, mainly because the English had it all their own way. From the first the French paid well for the cargoes of ships they had forced into Messina, and although Stanier was very uneasy about the general effects of this on English trade which was, after all, mainly with Spanish ports, the French commander in chief claimed with some justification that "The King would bee pleased his subjects and ships were detained here to supply their necessity, so long as he (Vivonne) endeavoured to make them depart satisfyed." [74] The French claimed that they could seize enemy goods bound for enemy ports, but Stanier maintained that they were not entitled even to go aboard an English ship. The matter was settled in the case of the *Merchant Bonaventura* when Vivonne personally intervened and excused the French intendant who had made the claim as being new to his job.[75]

The reason for this contrast between French and Spanish practice was that Louis XIV could on no account afford a breach with England. In a memoir addressed to Charles II on September 17, 1676, he emphasized the great advantages England was gaining from his war with Holland, complained that Dutch vessels carried English papers, and reminded Charles of an order in council of July 21, 1675, that vessels flying the English flag should be English built and that their master and two-thirds of the crew should be English. But he went on to assure Charles that any ship acquired by the English since 1673, in whatever port it might have been built and of which the master and some part of the crew were English, would be recognized, "so as not to deprive the English of the advantage of buying Dutch ships." [76] If Louis had hoped that these con-

[74] Stanier to Williamson, May 23, 1676, S.P., 93/2, 134.

[75] S.P., 93/2, 142.

[76] J. B. Colbert, *Lettres, Instructions, et Mémoires* (Paris, 1864) III, 1, n. 440. The reference is quoted by Corbett, *op. cit.*, II, 99.

cessions would result in the cessation of the English carrying contraband for the Dutch and Spanish, he was mistaken, for in October, 1677, Colbert wrote to Barillon, the French ambassador in England, that vessels which did not even carry English papers carried contraband in Sicilian waters under the English flag and that "it is hard to suffer this and to see English ships trading with, and transporting troops and all sorts of contraband merchandise to all the Italian states under the authority of the king of Spain." [77]

The British government had also become alarmed at the possible effects of this practice and in 1675 and 1676 the secretary of state, Henry Coventry, had written strongly worded letters to all Mediterranean consuls forbidding the issuing of papers to non-British ships.[78] However good relations with France might be during the war, the English could not be interested in seeing them firmly established in Sicily for, as Consul Davies realized, "it would be of badd Consiquence for trading to the Levant and these parts of Italie, on occation of the least disguste with ffrance." [79] Moreover, French commercial competition was already making itself felt, even during the war; while the import of French woolen goods was prohibited, "yet [they] come in abundance being winkt at by the Governors of the Custome house who have farmed the Customes." [80]

Pepys' friend, Richard Gibson, wrote notes for the admiralty [81] emphasizing the commerical and strategic importance of Sicily and pointing out that with Sicily in French hands "wee shall be debarred of our Trade to Turkey . . . and to Messina for Silkes, and of our Galipoly, Zant, Venice and Naples Trade," and that we should lose markets for one-third

---

[77] Colbert, *op cit.*, III, 1, n. 440.      [78] S.P., 104/185, 25 and 28.
[79] S.P., 93/2, 177.
[80] Davies, "Relation of Naples," 1675, S.P., 93/2, 68.
[81] "Mr. Gibson's Notes touching the importance of Sicily," Bodleian MSS, Rawlinson, A 185. (Undated, probably written about 1676.)

of our manufactures. The anonymous author of another paper on this subject [82] even went so far as to suggest that Sicily was more important than Flanders whose value consisted only in preventing the king of France from being master of Holland. This was a gross exaggeration and was not likely to be taken seriously by the government. But Gibson also suggested that for assistance in the reconquest of Sicily, Spain might be induced to hand over Minorca to Britain for a naval base. In 1676 Sir Thomas Clutterbuck was sent as a special agent for commercial and naval affairs to southern Italy [83] and in the offensive and defensive alliance of April, 1678, between Britain, Spain, and the emperor, Spain was to hand over to Britain the port and castle of Mahon in Minorca.[84] Nothing came of the alliance, for Charles II was simultaneously negotiating with France, but the future course of British Mediterranean strategy, the acquisition of bases east of Tangier, was now clearly indicated.

When the French finally evacuated Sicily in February, 1678, and left Messina to the tender mercy of the Spaniards, the attitude of Britain was one of the main reasons for their decision. Since 1675 Narborough had established his base in Malta, dangerously close to the French lines of communication.[85] The English had acquired a reputation for firing the first shot without declaration of war, and once it had become apparent that Sicily could be conquered only by an effort which France was not then in a position to make, Louis XIV considered it wise to evacuate the island before the scales of naval power in the Mediterranean were turned against him.

The Spaniards were not grateful, and indeed, from their point of view, the English had behaved in a most unneutral

[82] Perhaps also Gibson (*ibid.*).      [83] S.P., 104/185, 36.

[84] S.P., 104/180, cf. C. L. Grose, "The Anglo-Dutch Alliance of 1678" (*English Historical Review*, XXXIX, 368 ff.).

[85] Corbett, *op. cit.*, II, 99 ff. Also letters by Narborough in the Navy Board papers, Public Record Office, Adam. 106/312.

manner, virtually providing a second line of communications for the French in Messina. Stanier knew what to expect and left Messina with the French. His partners, John Cutting and Thomas Beal, who took over his effects in Messina, were promptly imprisoned by the returning Spaniards. The same happened to Davies in Naples a little later, and the Spaniards tried unsuccessfully to prove that Davies had given Stanier notice of sailings of English ships from Apulian ports so that the French could intercept them.[86] The Committee of Trade and Plantations, to whom Cutting's and Beal's petition for relief was referred, advised that Mr. Secretary Coventry prepare a letter for His Majesty's signature to the viceroy of Sicily pointing out that his action was "contrary to the freedom of trade and good correspondence of both nations." [87] Davies was released after two days, and Charles II wrote a very indignant letter to the viceroy.[88] The British government regarded Davies as a most useful man and, in 1679, was in a position to uphold the dignity of its representatives.[89]

The Messinese war and the Treaty of Nijmegen mark a turning point in the history of British trade in Naples and Sicily. The advantages of neutrality had given the English merchants a lead in the carrying trade of the central Mediterranean which put them far ahead of the other nations.[90] The Dutch, fighting for their lives, had sold to Britain many ships of their merchant fleet and could no longer maintain a permanent naval squadron in the Mediterranean. France, Britain's most dangerous rival and competitor, had been defeated in Sicily, and the Spaniards were too much weakened by the war and the Messinese revolt to be able to afford a diplomatic breach with

[86] Cutting and Beal to Nicholas Meade in London, March 24, 1679, S.P., 93/2, 291.

[87] Report of the Committee of Trade and Plantations, May 22, 1679, S.P., 93/2, 292.

[88] S.P., 104/186, 45.    [89] S.P., 104/185, 163.

[90] Cf. Davies' description of the trade in 1689, above.

Britain. Spanish viceroys and naval commanders could still obstruct British trade in southern Italy but could no longer seriously challenge the British position except by open war.

The correspondence of the consuls became increasingly concerned with the movements of both merchant and war ships. This was a new feature of consular reports in times of peace and shows that Britain's naval interest in the Mediterranean had developed beyond the occasional dispatch of a squadron to carry out particular tasks within the Straits. In the war of the League of Augsburg there were no such dramatic events in the central Mediterranean as the French Messina expedition of 1674–1678. Consequently the consular letters of the time were mainly detailed reports of close cooperation with the British Mediterranean squadron.

By the end of the century the English merchants had firmly established themselves and their trade in Naples and Sicily. They were still distrusted and disliked by the Spanish authorities, but it was a far cry from the activities of the early Jacobean merchant-pirates to the position occupied by Sir George Davies—he had been created a baronet in 1686—and his colleagues in Palermo, Messina, Trapani, and Gallipoli at the outbreak of the War of the Spanish Succession. At least in peace time the Spaniards could no longer do without the merchants. So sure were the latter of their position that even after war had broken out Davies wrote to Nottingham that while in all other Spanish dominions British merchants had had to leave, in Naples they would be allowed to stay for another six months. But two months later, in October, 1702, Davies wrote his last letter from Leghorn: the English, Dutch, and Germans had been given a fortnight in which to leave, and as this had allowed them no time to wind up their affairs, most of their debts remained uncollected and were duly sequestered by the Neapolitan government—a striking contrast to the carefully planned departure of the English in 1655. In the old feud the Spaniards had in the end scored a victory, even if this was shortlived. Davies himself stayed in Leghorn waiting hopefully for an early conclusion of the war, but he never returned to Naples.[91]

The last word was with the British navy. Its control of the sea enabled Britain's ally Austria to overthrow the Spanish dominion in Naples and Sicily. This was a success which France, lacking control of the sea, had failed to achieve in all its long wars with Spain during the previous two hundred years. The growth of British naval predominance was largely due to factors operating outside the Mediterranean, yet the merchants in southern Italy had a share in this development. During the war of the League of Augsburg and during the first months of the war of Spanish Succession they did their best to make up for the absence of British naval bases in the Mediterranean, furnishing information and arranging for supplies and repairs to British warships.[92] Their own position was, however, too insecure to provide a permanent alternative to fortified naval bases under full British control. To establish these was the task of British Mediterranean policy in the eighteenth century.

## *English counsuls in Naples and Sicily*

### Naples
Walle. Deposed *c.* 1607.

Alexander Hebrun, *c.* 1607–?. He was proposed by the English government, but his appointment is not certain.

Francis Brown. Before 1649. Acting consul since 1660. Appointment 1668–1671.

(Sir) George Davies. 1672–1702.

Daniel Gould. 1706–1708.

### Gallipoli
William Locke. 1664–?

Charles Bruton. *c.* 1675–1678.

Henry Chillingworth. 1678–?

[91] Davies died in 1705.
[92] Secretary Vernon to all Mediterranean consuls, Dec. 12, 1701, writing in appreciation of their work. S.P., 104/198.

Messina

Martin Wilkinson. Acting consul since *c.* 1664. Appointment 1671–1674.

Samuel Stanier. 1674–1678.

Charles Balle. 1679–*c.* 1688.

Thomas Chamberlain. 1688–1702.

Palermo

Henry Gifford. *c.* 1675.

Trapani

Francesco Bono. Acting consul since 1650. Appointment 1664–?

# CHAPTER 4

# The States-General of the Netherlands before the Revolt

PARLIAMENTS AND representative assemblies, the basis of modern democratic institutions, have had an unbroken history in only two countries of Europe; yet, in the later Middle Ages, they played important parts in the political life of nearly every European country outside the Italian and Swiss city-states. In some kingdoms, as in Sicily, they survived up to the eighteenth century as respectable guardians of ancient privileges without, however, seriously rivaling the powers of the monarchy. Elsewhere, they either disappeared altogether, like the States-General of France, or they lost all real power and influence, like the Cortes of Castile or the *Landtag* of Prussia. Only the English Parliament, the States-General of the Netherlands (and perhaps, though with some serious interruptions, the *Riksdag* of Sweden) established themselves permanently as equal, or superior, partners of the monarchy in the control of ultimate power in the state. Of these the States-General of the Netherlands maintained itself only in the seven northern provinces of the Burgundian dominions; but there its victory was so decisive that, at least formally, it displaced the monarchy altogether.

These events are well-known; they have generally been studied as aspects of the revolt of the Netherlands in the latter part of the sixteenth century. Not so well-known is the history of the States-General before the great revolt. Although, from the time of Gachard, Belgian historians and archivists have made sporadic attempts to collect material for such a history,[1] it has not yet been written.[2] Yet this history is essential to the full understanding of later events; for the States-General of the Netherlands played a most important role for more than a century before the days of Calvinism, the Sea Beggars and William the Silent. Most of the claims put forward by the States-General during the revolt against Philip II had precedents during the previous hundred years. Twice, in 1477 and in 1488, the States-General became the instrument of revolutionary movements, claiming powers and performing actions which were traditonally reserved to the monarchy. If its successes were short-lived, on these occasions, it remained a potential center of opposition to the monarchy, an alternative focus of power in the state; and while its members might, for long years, remain almost unaware of this, it was never entirely forgotten—least of all by the monarchy.

This chapter attempts no more than to discuss some of the more important aspects of the relations between monarchy and States-General before the revolt against Philip II. This it is hoped, will be followed in due course by a fuller account of the subject, as part of a projected comparative study of European representative assemblies during the period of their decisive struggles with the monarchies.

The States-General of the Burgundian provinces *de par deçà,* later to be called the Netherlands, had no definite date of birth. Each of the provinces which the House of Bur-

---

[1] One volume has been published: J. Cuvelier, *Actes des Etats Généraux des Anciens Pays-Bas,* I (1427–1477), in *Commission Royale d'Histoire, Recueil des Actes des Etats Généraux* (Brussels, 1948).

Mme Renée De Bock-Doehaerd has very kindly allowed me access to the transcripts of documents from provincial archives, collected by Gachard and his successors. To her, and to the rest of the staff of the Archives Générales du Royaume, and of the Bibliothèque Royale, of Brussels, I would like to express my thanks for their great helpfulness during my two visits to these archives.

[2] Exception should be made for the small book of J. Gilissen, *Le Régime Représentatif avant 1790 en Belgique* (Brussels, 1952).

gundy added successively to its possessions had its own provincial estates with its own well-established powers and traditions.[3] In 1430, Philip the Good summoned the estates of
Brabant, Flanders, and Holland to a joint assembly at Malines
in order to discuss the high price of English wool, a question
in which all three provinces were vitally interested.[4] Following repeated requests by the towns of Brabant, Flanders, Holland, and Zealand, the duke summoned another joint assembly
of the towns of these provinces at Ghent, in 1434, to discuss
English competition in the cloth industry.[5] There followed
further assemblies to which varying groups of provinces were
summoned to deal with problems of trade, the reform of
the coinage, or other matters which concerned more than one
of the provinces under the duke's rule.[6] In the history of these
assemblies there is no evidence that Philip the Good deliberately set out to create a States-General as a new institution designed to give greater unity to his dominions. The joint assemblies were summoned because it suited all parties concerned to discuss specific common problems in this way, and these
problems were nearly all questions of economic policy. At no
time during his reign did Philip ask these joint assemblies for
financial help—he did, of course, ask for *aides,* or *beden,* from
the separate provincial assemblies—and not until 1464 did an
important political question appear on the agenda. Only thir-
teen years later, at the death of Charles the Bold in 1477, the
States-General acted not only as a recognized and self-conscious

[3] Some of them, notably the estates of Holland and Hainault, already
possessed a tradition of cooperation which continued for a time as a
special relationship, even after the States-General had become a recognized institution. P. A. Meilink, "Berichten uit de Staten Generaal van
October–December 1482 te Aalst," in *Bijdragen en Mededeelingen van
het Historisch Genootschap . . . te Utrecht,* 57 (1936), 322, n. 2.

[4] J. Cuvelier, *Actes,* I, 8 ff. It is somewhat doubtful whether the assembly of the estates of Hainault, Flanders, and Picardie, of 1427, which was
to discuss Philip the Good's claim to the succession of Hainault, may be
regarded as a forerunner of the States-General. *Ibid.,* pp. 1 ff.

[5] *Ibid.,* pp. 12 ff.     [6] *Ibid.,* pp. 17–52.

institution but as the claimant to the ultimate control of political authority in the Burgundian dominions.[7]

For much of the rest of the fifteenth century, however, the States-General preserved many of the characteristics of a largely functional and *ad hoc* institution. Right through the sixteenth century it remained primarily an assembly of the delegates of provincial estates, reflecting the varying composition and interests of these latter bodies and especially their particularism. Thus Flanders, the richest and most powerful of the provinces, was generally represented in its provincial estates by its "four members," the cities of Ghent, Bruges, Ypres, and the *Franc* of Bruges, the important country district of western Flanders where political control was largely in the hands of the lower nobility.[8] In Holland the voice of the "six large towns," Dordrecht, Amsterdam, Haarlem, Leiden, Delft, and Gouda, was equally overwhelming. The nobles had only one vote against their six, and the clergy had long since ceased to attend the Holland assemblies altogether.[9] In Brabant, Artois, and Hainault all three estates were represented but, especially in matters of taxation, the consent of the towns was most important for the government, and most difficult to obtain; for the towns, unlike the nobility, could not shift the burden of taxation onto other shoulders. In Hainault this meant, in practice, the towns of Mons and Valenciennes,[10] and in Brabant al-

[7] From this point of view it is possible to accept Pirenne's view of the assembly of 1463–1464 as representing the beginning of the States-General, although Pirenne does not appear to have known of the earlier joint provincial assemblies. *Histoire de Belgique* (Brussels, 1907), III, 191.

[8] The *Franc* as the "fourth member" of Flanders had been created by the medieval counts of Flanders to counterbalance the overwhelming influence of the great towns. Cf. J. Dhondt, "Les Origines des Etats de Flandre," in *Anciens Pays et Assemblées d'états; Sect. Belge de la Commission Internat pour l'Histoire des Assemblées d'états* (Louvain, 1950), I, 45.

[9] R. Fruin, *Geschiedenis der Staatsinstellingen in Nederland,* T. Colenbrander, ed. (The Hague, 1922), p. 79 ff.

[10] Valenciennes, at times, claimed representation at the States-General on her own account, apart from Hainault.

ways the four "capitals," Brussels, Louvain, Antwerp and Bois-le-Duc.[11]

The representatives who attended the meetings of the provincial estates were, in fact, little more than delegates of the towns who sent them to the assemblies, who paid their salaries and expenses, and whose instructions they had strictly to follow. The nobles and prelates could either attend in person or also send representatives. The powers of the representatives at the meetings of the States-General were similarly limited: in consequence no clear-cut distinction can be made between the history of the States-General and the history of the provincial estates. Many of the problems which had faced the dukes in their dealings with the estates of their separate provinces therefore reappeared immediately in the States-General. Successive governments tried hard to induce the provincial estates to grant their representatives to the States-General full powers so that agreements on taxation and other matters might be reached quickly. But the estates clung stubbornly to the system of limiting their delegates' powers. The delegates themselves—burgomasters, aldermen, or pensionaries (i.e., salaried law officers) of the towns—saw no cause to diminish the powers of their town councils. Moreover, this very limitation could prove very useful in defensive tactics against the financial demands of the crown which could often be delayed for weeks and months by the obligation to refer back to the provincial estates and, beyond them, to the towns. In the assembly of May, 1476, Charles the Bold's chancellor, Hugonet, driven to

[11] This is not the place to discuss the organization of the provincial estates in detail. Cf. C. Hirschauer, *Les Etats d'Artois de leurs origines à l'occupation française, 1340–1640* (Paris-Brussels, 1923), I, *passim*; L. Devillers, "Participation des états de Hainaut aux assemblées des Etats généraux des Pays Bas (1438–1790)," in *Bulletin de la Commission Royale d'Histoire*, 74 (Brussels, 1905), 27 ff; J. Craeybeckx, "Aperçu sur l'histoire des impôts en Flandre et au Brabant au cours du XVI<sup>e</sup> siècle," in *Revue du Nord*, 29 (1947); F. Rachfahl, *Wilhelm von Oranien* (Halle, 1906), I, 527 ff; F. H. J. Lemminck, *Het Ontstaan van den Staten van Zeeland* (Roosendaal, 1951).

exasperation by the stone-walling tactics of the delegates, finally asked sarcastically whether their authority was also limited
in the number of times they might drink during their journey.
"This remark was not taken well by the estates," one of the
delegates wrote afterwards, "and they said to the chancellor:
go on, go on, you can say what you like; but we will make the
reply we have to make." [12]

The meetings of the States-General therefore had the appearance of a congress of delegates from quasi-autonomous
powers, rather than that of an institution representing the
country as a whole. During the fifteenth century it was never
definitely established which particular provinces should attend,
and membership varied a great deal. Gradually, however, con-
ventions for membership hardened. When, in 1534, Charles
V's government proposed a defensive union and a standing
army for the provinces, the States-General objected that these
proposals were unacceptable while some of the provinces who
would have to be part of the union never attended the assemblies.[13] The provinces which were now regularly summoned
were Holland, Zealand, Flanders, Brabant, Malines, Namur,
Lille-Douai-Orchies, Artois, Tournai-Tournaisis, and Hainault
with Valenciennes.[14]

The two problems, that of the membership of the States-
General and that of the powers of the delegates, were both
aspects of a more fundamental problem: the divergence of interests between ruler and subject. It was the aim of successive
Burgundian and Habsburg rulers of the Netherlands to weld

[12] Cuvelier, *Actes*, p. 256.

[13] States-General of Malines, July, 1535. Brussels, Archives Générales du
Royaume, *Papiers de l'Etat et de l'Audience*, 1228, fo. 35. The provinces
in question were Friesland, Utrecht, Overyssel, Pays d'Outremeuse, Luxem-
bourg, and Chiny, as well as a few small lordships under the Burgundian
crown.

[14] L. P. Gachard, *Lettre à MM. les Questeurs de la Chambre des Rep-
résentants . . . concernant les anciennes Assemblées nationales de la
Belgique* (Brussels, 1841), p. 8.

their dominions together into a greater political unity and to provide them with more efficient and powerful government. Against these centralizing policies prelates, nobles, towns, and provinces set their traditional privileges and autonomies. Heavy and steadily increasing demands for money by the government, on the one hand, and unwillingness of the subject to pay, on the other hand, were the key to this relationship. At the same time, neither side pursued its policy consistently; all were fundamentally interested in carrying on the government of the country as peacefully and as harmoniously as possible. The right of the "natural prince" to govern was never seriously questioned until traditional loyalties had become frayed by years of bitter civil and religious war, in the second half of the sixteenth century. Thus, contrary to all reason and experience, the citizens of Ghent preserved a blind and pathetic trust in the emperor when they rebelled against his governor-general in 1537–1540.[15] On the other side, the rulers never made a frontal attack on the liberties of the country. It was a matter of pride or, at least, an effective propaganda point, that the Netherlanders lived in greater freedom than the subjects of the king of France, and that their prince did not arbitrarily impose taxes on them.[16] Despite Charles V's occasional reluctance to summon the States-General, no serious attempt was made to dispense with it altogether until the reign of Philip II and even then no less an autocrat than the duke of Alva tried to have his proposed taxes approved by the assembly.[17]

Nevertheless, the relationship between crown and estates was ultimately a question of power. The claims of both sides had finally to be resolved by the victory of one or the other

---

[15] Ghent, Archives de L'Etat, MS, *Varia*, No. 265, *passim*. J. de Jongh, *Maria van Hongarije* (Amsterdam, 1951), II, 108 ff.

[16] E.g., discourse by Hugonet to the States-General of Bruges, Jan., 1473, J. Cuvelier, *Actes*, p. 185. Mary of Hungary's proposals to the States-General of Jan., 1552; Brussels, Arch. Gén., *Pap. d'Etat*, 1228, fo. 161 ff.

[17] Craeybeckx, "Aperçu," p. 98.

and, until that happened—as it happened sooner or later everywhere in Europe—there was bound to be a shifting balance of power. This became apparent at the very beginning of the career of the States-General in the dispute over its claim to assemble independently of a ducal summons. On December 15, 1463, Philip the Good had declared his intention of going on a crusade. Only shortly before, his bad relations with his son had issued in an open breach. This situation induced Brussels and the towns of Holland, at the end of December, to propose a meeting of the delegates of their own provinces, as well as those of Flanders, Zealand, Artois, and Hainault. Both Philip and his son, the count of Charolais,[18] answered this proposal by summonses of their own. There ensued a fortnight's confusion, with delegates hurrying to different meeting places, until, on January 9, 1464, all assembled at Bruges.[19] Philip was furious. "We are marvelling greatly," he wrote to the towns, "how the inhabitants of our towns of Holland dare to be so presumptuous as to assemble on their own authority and to desire our subjects to assemble, seeing that it is by no means up to them to do this in our province of Holland, nor in Flanders, nor anywhere else; but that this right belongs only to us, as your prince and lord, and to no one else." [20] The estates, having achieved their main object in the reconciliation of the duke and his son, were unwilling to start a quarrel on a point of principle at that precise moment and asked Philip's forgiveness.

This dispute, however, was bound to recur. If the estates could establish the right of assembly without ducal summons, then their independent authority was assured. Nevertheless, they were rarely willing to quarrel with the government over this point unless they had other reasons for quarrel as well. In the general revolt against the political system of Charles the Bold, in the early months of 1477, the States-General claimed the right of independent assembly, as article 13 of the

18 The later Charles the Bold.     19 Cuvelier, *Actes,* p. 53 ff.
20 Philip to the towns, Dec. 31, 1463. *Ibid.,* p. 72.

famous *grand privilège* forced on Charles's daughter Mary.[21] During the first regency of Maximilian of Austria, after the death of Mary of Burgundy in 1482, the estates of Flanders continued to press this claim at times of crisis. Willem Zoete, the pensionary of Ghent, declared that "all our provinces are privileged, by express privileges, to assemble at all times as they may choose, to conclude confederations and alliances for the advantage and good order of the provinces, and to make certain that they suffer no let or hindrance in the exercise of their rights, privileges and liberties; and all this without having to ask the consent of the prince." [22] But, from the time of Philip the Fair until the revolt, there is little evidence of the estates maintaining their claim to independent assembly. During the first half of the sixteenth century, both provincial estates and States-General were summoned with sufficient frequency to satisfy the provinces and to make such a claim seem rather academic.[23] For the government, however, the question remained one of vital importance and it was clearly recognized as such, since the prince must at all costs maintain that the existence of the States-General depended on his will. Maximilian consistently upheld this view, even though he had

[21] H. Pirenne, "Le Rôle Constitutionnel des Etats Généraux des Pays-Bas en 1477 et en 1488," in *Mélanges Paul Frédéricq* (Brussels, 1904), p. 277 ff. The point was also incorporated in the separate privileges granted to the different provinces at that time; e.g., in the privileges of Holland, Zealand, and Friesland it forms paragraph 15. *Handvesten ende Privilegien van Vrouwe Maria aengaende Hollandt, Zeelandt, ende Vrieslandt . . .* (The Hague, 1662), p. 9.

[22] Declaration of Willem Zoete, April 28, 1488; I. L. A. Diegerick, *Correspondance des Magistrats d'Ypres députés à Gand et à Bruges pendant les Troubles de Flandre sous Maximilien* etc. (Bruges, 1853), Annex G, p. xl f.

[23] In Holland the estates met independently in the so-called "little dagvaarten" to discuss questions of trade and finance. But, perhaps because they did not discuss questions of high policy, the government does not seem to have objected. H. Terdenge, "Zur Geschichte der holländischen Steuern im 15. und 16. Jahrhundert," in *Vierteljahrschrift für Sozial- und Wirtschaftsgeschichte,* 18 (1925), 163 ff.

signed the provincial privileges of 1477 which included the right of independent assembly.[24] Mary of Hungary held that the confederation of the prelates of Brabant, in 1544, was illegal precisely because she denied such a claim.[25]

Much less clear-cut was the attitude of both States-General and government towards the problem of joint debates and discussions between the various delegations. The provinces and estates represented by these delegations were deeply jealous of their autonomy and, in general, insisted on reference back, rather than on discussions with other delegations. In practice, however, common discussions between the representatives of at least two or three provinces were unavoidable if agreement was to be reached at all, especially on the government's demands for *aides*. The deputies of the smaller provinces were often instructed to follow the lead of Flanders and Brabant and to discuss a common policy with the deputies of these provinces.[26] The attitude of the government was also ambivalent. Common discussions meant more rapid decisions on the government's proposals, and this was convenient. Moreover, if an important delegation had been persuaded to give a favorable vote, that would set a good example to the others. On the other hand, the resistance of Flanders or Brabant to a grant might equally well persuade others to resist too. This was one of Mary of Hungary's constant worries. On January 4, 1536, for instance, she wrote to her brother: "I hope that with the other provinces the difficulties will not be too great, unless indeed they follow the example of Brabant; for there are always those who will

24 J. Molinet, *Chroniques*, G. Doutrepont, ed. (Brussels, 1935), I, p. 618.

25 P. Gorissen, "De Prelaten van Brabant onder Karel V (1515–1544)," in *Anciens Pays* (Louvain, 1953), VI, 118 ff.

26 E.g., at the States-General of April, 1482, when the question of the guardianship of Maximilian's children was discussed, the representatives of Namur declared that they would vote with Brabant, Hainault, and Holland, "which was practically a condition; for in all assemblies of estates they had always agreed on a common policy" (*Relation de Jeannet de la Ruyelle*, L. P. Gachard, ed., *Bul. Com. R. Hist.*, ser. 3 (Brussels, 1860), 325.

put it into other peoples' heads that promises made to them in the past have not been kept; this is causing me great difficulties." [27] Already in 1473 Charles the Bold had prohibited common discussions.[28] Charles V was so afraid that those who opposed his policy might find in the States-General an opportunity to organize that, on one occasion at least, he preferred not to assemble the States-General at all. "You have done well," he wrote to Margaret of Austria in 1519, "to have told the estates of Brabant that a general assembly of the estates of our provinces is not at present necessary. We wish and desire you expressly not to consent to the meeting of the said general assembly, so that no league or confederation may be formed to the detriment of our pre-eminence, nor cause resistance to our officers." [29] This decision remained an isolated incident.

But at the beginning of Philip II's reign, when the political system of the Netherlands was beginning to break down, government policy began to oscillate violently between the two approaches to the problem of common discussions. The strain of the seemingly unending French wars, economic depression and famine prices, the quarrels between the estates and the higher nobility over the latters' claim to exemption from payment of the *aides*—all these combined to make the subject more unwilling than ever to grant the king's financial demands. Finally, the government despaired of coming to terms with either the States-General or with the estates of Brabant and, in September, 1556, sent high government officials to the Brabant towns to negotiate with each separately for an *aide*.[30] But this attempt at bypassing the estates altogether met with no success and, a year later, the policy was completely reversed. In November, 1557, the deputies appeared at the States-Gen-

---

[27] Mary to Charles V, Brussels, Arch. Gén., *Pap. d'Etat,* 49, fo. 4.

[28] Cuvelier, *Actes,* p. 215.

[29] Charles V to Margaret, April 9, 1519. Van den Bergh, *Gedenkstukken tot Opheldering der Nederlandsche Geschiedenis* (Utrecht, 1894), III, 219.

[30] K. J. W. Verhofstad, *De Regering der Nederlanden in de jaren 1555–1559* (Nijmegen, 1937), p. 96.

eral, for once with full powers, and the government decided to allow them to meet in joint session to discuss the financial position.[31] The result was indeed a compromise on the *aide* demanded, but it was coupled with a long list of grievances and petitions on matters of high policy.[32] Thereafter Granvelle, and probably Philip II as well, became convinced that the States-General could no longer be trusted.

It was over taxation that the interests of crown and States-General were most clearly opposed. Throughout this period it was generally accepted that the prince had a right to expect financial help for the defense of the country. When, however, wars continued for years on end, when defense, turning into aggression, demanded ever greater sacrifices, the loyal subjects not only resisted the demands for money but began to question the conduct of the government's foreign policy: when Charles the Bold's wars which had demanded such heavy sacrifices ended in the catastrophe of Morat and the duke's death at Nancy, the Netherlanders rose in revolt and the States-General claimed for itself the control of foreign policy.[33] But neither by its tradition nor its constitution was the States-General fitted to carry on the tasks of government; its control over foreign policy broke down within a few months.[34] The conflict with the government, however, continued. Minorities and regencies gave the estates their chance. Charles the Bold, the "natural lord" of the Netherlands, had been able to propound a theory of the divine right of princes. "Since his subjects had not wanted to be governed by him as children are governed by their father," so runs the report of one of his characteristically forceful speeches, "therefore they could be disinherited, as the son could be disinherited of his father's property for his misdeeds; and

[31] Brussels, Arch, Gén., Manuscrits divers, 327, fos. 39–56.

[32] Verhofstad, *De Regering*, p. 119.

[33] J. Cuvelier, *Actes*, p. 270–334.

[34] E.g., I. Strubbe, "Staatsinrichting en Krijgswezen," in *Algemene Geschiedenis der Nederlanden* (Utrecht, 1952), IV, 125 f.

that, from thenceforth, they would be governed and live under him as subjects of their lord who held his lordship by the grace of God, his creator, and from no one else; and that he would remain prince as long as it pleased God, in despite of the beards of all those who did not like it." [35] Against this, Maximilian of Austria, the husband of Charles' daughter, might claim as a natural right to act as the regent for his son, but in fact he owed his position to the consent of the estates. Nor would the estates allow him to forget this. Those of Flanders tried to force him to keep the unfavorable peace of Arras (1482) with France, even at the cost of civil war. In this they had the sympathy of some of the other provinces, notably of Brabant. When in 1488 the burghers of Bruges took Maximilian captive, the States-General was much more anxious to mediate between him and the Flemings than to rescue their ruler from ignominious imprisonment by his son's subjects.[36]

Not until 1576 did the States-General make similarly determined forays into a sphere of government normally reserved to the prince; but the fundamental problems persisted through the sixteenth century. During the reign of Charles V there was only one open revolt, that of Ghent, 1537 to 1540, and that was more in the nature of a taxpaying strike than of revolutions such as those of 1477 or 1488. But the interminable, destructive, and apparently senseless wars with Guelders, and the increasingly expensive and dangerous wars with France, produced an intermittent, but gradually swelling, rumble of dissatisfaction with the emperor's foreign policy. Twice, in 1512 and in 1522, Margaret of Austria feared the imminent out-

[35] Report of an address by Charles the Bold to the estate of Flanders, July 12, 1475. L. P. Gachard, *Collection de Documents Inédits concernant l'Histoire de la Belgique* (Brussels, 1833), I, p. 257.

[36] L. P. Gachard, "Lettres inédites de Maximilien, duc d'Autriche . . . sur les affaires des Pays-Bas de 1478 à 1508," in *Bul. Com. R. Hist., l.c.,* ser. 2, vol. 2 (1851), *passim.* Kervyn de Lettenhove, *Histoire de Flandre* (Brussels, 1850) vol. V, *passim,* and especially the documents printed in this volume.

break of rebellion.[37] Complaints continued that the Netherlands were made to conquer Italy for the emperor and Denmark for the count palatine.[38] The joint session of the States-
General, in November, 1557, was particularly outspoken on
these points.[39]

More effective than their intervention in foreign policy were
the attempts of the provincial estates and, later, of the States-
General in its turn, to control the collection and expenditure
of the taxes they voted. Since, as everywhere else in Europe,
there was at that time a chronic shortage of efficient and reasonably honest civil servants, successive governments were not in
principle opposed to a development which relieved them of the
onerous and unpopular task of collecting taxes. More and more
the estates insisted on such control before they would grant any
*aides* at all. In 1513, Margaret herself suggested that the States-
General should appoint its own commissioners to supervise the

---

[37] Margaret to Maximilian, Nov., 1512: "And the provinces are in such
a bad mood, and the common people use such evil language, that I am
very much afraid a calamity will overtake us if we do not find some
means. . . ." This passage appears only in the draft of the letter and
was erased by the advice of Margaret's secretary, Marnix. It is all the more
significant for that. A. Walther, "Hubert Kreiten, Der Briefwechsel Kaiser
Maximilians I. mit seiner Tochter Margareta," in *Göttingische Gelehrte
Anzeigen*, 170 (1908), 266. Instructions to Jehan de le Sauch, for Charles
V, June 11, 1522: "It is absolutely necessary to find money . . . for otherwise there could easily occur a conspiracy or a mutiny in the Netherlands.
Knowing their prince to be away and not about to return, seeing their
properties diminished as a result of the war, foodstuffs expensive, and the
harvest promising to be bad, they will all, if God does not provide, be
willing and ready to do this." A. Henne, *Histoire du Règne de Charles-
Quint en Belgique* (Brussels, 1858), III, 267.

[38] A. Jacopszoon, *Prothocolle van alle de Reysen . . . gedaen zedert
ick de Stede van Aemstelredamme gedient heb gehadt . . .*, MS in Amsterdam City Archives, transcript by E. van Bienna, pt. 2, fo. 232; entry
for assembly of estates of Holland, April 6–8, 1536. I would like to thank
Dr. P. A. Meilink for drawing my attention to this most important source
for the history of the estates of Holland and for sending me the transcript.

[39] Brussels, Arch Gén., *Manuscrits divers*, 237, fo. 39.

government's collection and expenditure of the taxes they should vote. The offer was rejected at that time; for the States-General insisted on peace with Guelders.[40] But in the 1520's and 1530's, the estates of Flanders, Brabant, and Holland all built up their own machinery of control.[41] In 1558, the States-General took the first step towards creating a unified financial institution under its own control for the whole of the Netherlands by appointing the Antwerp banker, Antoon van Straelen, as superintendent of taxes for all the provinces.[42]

While the monarchy was not entirely averse to such developments it was distinctly hostile to the growing habit of the estates of demanding redress of grievances and the acceptance of petitions before they would grant *aides*. In vain, provincial governors and governors-general tried to reverse this procedure:[43] the estates knew that without such insistence their power was broken, and they remained adamant.[44] Mary of

[40] Henne, *Histoire*, I, 311.

[41] J. Craeybeckx, "De Staten van Vlaanderen en de gewestelijke Financiën in de XVIe eeuw," in *Handelingen der Maatschappij voor Geschiedenis en Oudheidkunde te Gent,* nieuwe reeks, dl. 4, afl. 2, 1950, where the history of this development is described in detail.

[42] Rachfahl, *Wilhelm*, I, 566 ff.

[43] E.g., Hoochstraten, governor of Holland, and the estates of that province, May, 1537. A. Jacopszoon, *Prothocolle*, pt. 2, fo. 304.

[44] Proposals made to the emperor by Madame [Margaret of Austria], July, 1530. "In order to avoid the delays which the estates of Brabant and the other provinces usually manage, every time they are asked for a grant, and this with the excuse and under color of their diverse requests and demands, and since they do not want to make the grant unless these demands have been agreed to; it is fitting and very necessary, either by edict or by special maneuvers and agreements in each separate province, to make sure that in future the estates of the said provinces, after the demands have been presented to them, should not make requests or demands to the emperor in any matter whatever until they have first consented to the *aide*. The said lady further advises His Majesty that this were better done in his presence than in his absence." Charles did not answer this. Brussels, Bibliothèque Royale, MS, 16068-16072, fos. 135 f.

It should be noted that petitions accepted by the prince were a form of legislation initiated by the estates.

Hungary even said that the estates preferred the emperor to be poor so that they should be more powerful, "for, through their privileges, they wanted to be masters and not servants." [45]

Even when the patrician deputies themselves were willing to meet the government's financial demands, fear of their constituents at home often prevented them from doing so. In Brabant and, before 1540, in Flanders, the petty bourgeoisie of gilds and craftsmen were represented in the town councils and had to approve all financial decisions. They were perfectly capable of holding up agreements of the whole States-General, as did the guilds of Brussels and Louvain in the early years of the reign of Philip II.[46] Charles V pursued a consistent policy of excluding the more democratic elements from the government of the Netherland towns; [47] but even where the lower classes were thus excluded there was the constant fear of riots and open revolts. The great towns of Flanders, in particular, were the centers of popular revolutionary movements. Since these movements often started as revolts against heavy taxation, and since those aldermen and burgomasters who were held to be too accommodating to the government's demands were liable to lose their heads, these popular movements tended to strengthen the estates in their resistance to the crown and were generally responsible for the more extreme parliamentary claims. This happened in 1477 when popular movements broke out all over the Netherlands.[48] It happened again in Flanders during the rebellions against Maximilian, in 1485 and 1488.

Nevertheless, the patrician oligarchies usually remained in

[45] Mary to Charles V, Jan. 4, 1536. Brussels, Arch. Gén., *Pap. d'Etat,* 49, fos. 2 f.

[46] Rachfahl, *Wilhelm,* I, 562 ff. Verhofstad, *De Regering,* p. 93 ff.

[47] In Tournai in 1522; L.P. Gachard, *Extraits des Registres des consaux de Tournai, 1472–1490, 1559–1572* etc. (Brussels, 1846), p. 10 ff. Brussels in 1528; K. Lans, *Correspondenz des Kaisers Karl V.* (Leipzig, 1844), I, 279. Ghent in 1540; J. Craeybeckx, "Maria van Hongarije," in *Algemene Geschiedenis,* 4, 107.

[48] P. van Ussel, *De Regeering van Maria van Bourgondië over de Nederlanden* (Louvain, 1943), p. 67 ff.

firm control of the towns and, in consequence, also of the States-General. Their interests were local and sectional; the privileges they defended against encroachments by the crown were equally local and sectional—often diametrically opposed to the interests of other towns and provinces. Such was the case, for instance, when Holland claimed to export grain freely while there was famine in the rest of the Netherlands.[49] In the absence of a general cause for opposition, it was therefore most unlikely that the government would ever be faced by a general revolt of the States-General, and, in fact, no such movement occurred during the whole long reign of Charles V. The States-General remained a conservative force, capable of blocking important government policies disliked by the majority of provinces, such as the proposed union and standing army of 1534–1535,[50] but unable and unwilling to challenge the crown's control of government. Yet the political situation remained unstable and tended to deteriorate, especially after about 1530. The Brussels riots of 1532; the revolt of Ghent of 1537–1540; the confederation of the abbots of the great Brabantine monastic houses, formed to resist the financial demands of the crown; the increasing friction between the estates of Holland and the governor, the count of Hoochstraten [51]—all these were signs that Charles V's imperial policy was overstraining the resources of the Netherlands and the goodwill of his subjects.[52]

During the first years of Philip II's reign, the States-General became the mouthpiece for grievances which had now become

[49] Debates in the estates of Holland, 1527. A. Jacopszoon, *Prothocolle,* 1, fos. 200 ff.

[50] L. van der Essen, "Les Etats Généraux de 1534–1535 et le projet de confédération défensive des provinces des Pays-Bas," in *Mélanges d'Histoire offerts à Ch. Moeller* (Louvain and Paris, 1914), Vol. II.

[51] A. Jacopszoon, *Prothocolle, passim.*

[52] Mary of Hungary was well aware of the position. Early in 1536, when war with France was about to break out again, she asked Charles whether the Netherlands could not remain neutral. The emperor's reply was sympathetic but negative. Charles to Mary, March 2, 1536, Brussels, Arch. Gén., *Pap. d'Etat,* 49, fos. 24 f.

general: excessive taxation and the presence of Spanish troops in the Low Countries. During the governor-generalship of Margaret of Parma, the king became convinced that, if summoned again, the States-General would become the mouthpiece of the movement to moderate the placards against the heretics and the activities of the Netherlands inquisitors. Philip was undoubtedly correct in his estimate of the situation; yet it was not the States-General which initiated or organized the revolt. The economic changes of the sixteenth century had upset the social equilibrium of important areas of the Netherlands and had thus created a revolutionary situation: among the artisans and wage earners of the industrial belt of Walloon-Flanders, Calvinist preachers found a fertile field for their propaganda, and they were similarly successful among the middle and lower classes, alike in the thriving port of Antwerp [53] and in decaying old textile towns like Ghent and Leiden. The country-nobility saw their incomes dwindle with rising prices and their local influence curtailed by the extension of the activities of the central government: [54] many hundreds joined Louis of Nassau's and Brederode's Compromise. Calvinism, working on social and economic discontent, created forces and organizations which transcended provincial boundaries. These forces saw in the States-General a convenient weapon and called aloud for its summons—and this at the very moment when the king's policy had antagonized some of the most powerful members of the high nobility. Thus the stage was set for the series of revolts which began in 1566. The subsequent collapse of the crown's authority left the States-General in the center of the political stage as the only legitimate political authority. But internal

---

[53] Antwerp was traditionally the most loyal supporter of the monarchy from whose favor its merchants had received great benefits. It is a measure of the discontent created by the policies of Charles the Bold and Philip II that it was only in 1477 and in 1566 that the town had any experience of revolutionary movements.

[54] H. A. Enno van Gelder, "Bailleul, Bronkhorst, Brederode," in *De Gids*, C (1936), 217.

divergencies of interest and aim, and insufficient control over those external forces which had created the revolutionary movements, prevented the States-General from keeping the Netherlands united.

| *Rulers of Netherlands* | | *Regents and Governors-General of Netherlands* | |
|---|---|---|---|
| Philip the Good | 1419–1467 | Maximilian | 1482–1494 |
| Charles the Bold | 1467–1477 | Margaret of Austria, | 1507–1515 |
| Mary of Burgundy | | dowager duchess | and |
| (married Max. of Austria) | | of Savoy | 1518–1530 |
| | 1477–1482 | Mary of Hungary | 1531–1555 |
| Philip the Fair | 1482–1506 | Emmanuel Philibert | |
| Charles V | 1506–1555 | of Savoy | 1555–1559 |
| Philip II | 1555–1598 | Margaret of Parma | 1559–1567 |
| | | Duke of Alva | 1567–1573 |

CHAPTER 5

# Property and the Price Revolution
## (*Hainault, 1474–1573*)

DURING RECENT years, economic historians have tended to confirm the old-fashioned view that, around the year 1500, a real change took place in the development of European society; but the nature of this change is now considered to have been rather different from that postulated by nineteenth-century historians. A long period of declining population, falling grain prices, and stagnating trade (at least in many of the older centers of economic activity) was followed by more than a century of rising population, growing towns, and expanding trade. But the most distinctive economic phenomenon of the sixteenth century, and the most discussed by contemporaries, was the phenomenon of rapidly rising prices, especially rising agricultural prices. Modern economic historians have been so delighted with rediscovering this important event that, with some exaggeration, they have sometimes called it a price revolution. So much is generally accepted; but there is still disagreement about the effects of rising prices on the economic and social history of different classes, disagreements which have recently given rise to a spirited controversy about the fortunes of the English nobility and gentry during this period. These disagreements seem to arise largely from the nature of the sources and from the difficulties involved in using them as a basis for statistical analysis and in interpreting the results. Fortunately, for some parts of the Continent there exist sources which lend themselves more readily to statistical treatment. While the difficulties of interpretation are still formidable, the use of these sources may throw light not only on the economic history of the areas concerned, but may deepen our understanding of economic and social phenomena in general for this period; for rising prices were an all-European phenomenon.

In the *Archives Générales du Royaume,* of Brussels, there exist eighteenth-century copies of registers of feudal property in the county of Hainault.[1] The originals are deposited in the Archives du Département du Nord, at Lille. Sample checks with microfilm copies of these originals revealed that the Brussels copies are generally accurate—at any rate sufficiently so, as to make the margin of error due to mistakes by the copyist statistically negligible. These registers are the main source used in this article.[2]

In 1470, Charles the Bold wrote to the *bailli* of the *châtellenie* of Ypres (the district outside that town), commanding him to arrange that "all those who have and hold fees and mesne fees should make a good and true declaration of them," stating their name, situation, size, value, and rent charges. This information was to be handed to the ducal commissioners and receivers of taxes within a month of the publication of the order on pain of forfeiture of the fiefs.[3] It may be doubted whether this census was ready within a month; for it was not until January 15, 1475, that Charles wrote again to the *bailli* to fix the rate of military contributions; for, up to that time, said the duke, there had been no system of military service

---

[1] Arch. Gén. du Royaume, Chambre des Comptes, no. 1116, *Registre des Fiefs et arriers fiefs du Hainnau, 1474;* nos. 1118–20, *Fiefs et Arriers fiefs en Hainnaut, 1502;* no. 1121, *Recueil et denombrement des biens appartenans et dependans de plusieurs abbayes et des particuliers en Haynnaut et Cambresis, 1502;* no. 1122, *Fiefs et arriers fiefs du Hainnaut des années 1564 et 1573.*

[2] I would like to thank the University of Manchester for a travel grant which enabled me to study these documents during a visit to Brussels, in the summer of 1954.

[3] Letter of March 29, 1470. L. P. Gachard, *Collection de Documents Inédits concernant l'Histoire de la Belgique* (Brussels, 1823), I, 214 *et seq.*

exacted from holders of fiefs: some had been burdened too heavily and others, "by the dissimulation of our officials, or otherwise," had escaped too lightly. Fiefs of an annual rental value of about 200 *écus,* of 48 *gros* Flemish, were to furnish one knight (*homme d'armes*) with three horses; those of about 40 *écus,* one horseman; those of about 16 *écus,* one foot soldier; and those of up to 10 *livres* of 40 *gros,* were to remain exempt.[4]

The registers of the fees and mesne fees of Hainault were compiled in 1474. No ducal order about them has come to light, so far; but there is little doubt that their compilation was part of the same policy. Compared with the registers for Flanders, those for Hainault have the great advantage for the economic historian of presenting their information much more clearly and of stating the annual value of the fiefs. More important still, there are two further sets of registers of the same type for the years 1502 and 1564–1573. If these registers can be treated as statistical samples, we shall have evidence of the distribution of real property in this province, outside the towns, and of income derived from it, for a period of very nearly a hundred years. It is the purpose of this article to show how this can, in fact, be done and what conclusions may be derived from such an analysis.

A general census compiled in Hainault by the receiver of taxes, Jehan du Terne, in 1469, gives the number of hearths (i.e., households) outside the towns as 28,778.[5] The number of entries of fiefs for 1474 is 2,146, i.e., about 7.5 per cent—a very adequate sample. The position is even better for 1502 where 2,469 entries compare with 22,632 households counted by the receiver of taxes in 1501 [6]—a sample of rather more than 10

4 *Ibid.,* pp. 237 *et seq.*

5 Lille, Archives du Département du Nord, B. 196, fols. 29 *et seq.*

6 M.-A. Arnould, *Acquits ou documents justificatifs rendus par le receveur des aides de Hainaut (1496–1540).* Commission Royale d'Histoire (Brussels, 1941), pp. 44 *et seq.* The higher number of entries is due to the existence of a special book of mesne fees held from ecclesiastical institutions (Chambre des Comptes, no. 1121). Since they were held almost exclusively by laymen—sometimes the same persons who figure in the

per cent. In the register of 1564–1573 there are only 778 persons, while the number of households in the province was almost certainly higher than it was in 1502. As a sample, this is not as good as the entries for the other two dates; but it is still adequate.

In the later fifteenth and sixteenth centuries, the holders of fiefs owed certain obligations of military service to the crown. In the sixteenth century, these were mostly compounded for in money. There is no evidence that, apart from these obligations, fiefs differed either legally or economically from any other type of property. In the course of the sixteenth century even this remaining distinction tended to disappear—most probably because the owners of feudal property simply neglected to register it as such. Since the register of 1564–1573 shows a rather higher percentage of nobles than the two previous ones—13.8 per cent, as against 6.5 per cent in 1474 and 8.6 per cent in 1502—it looks as if nobles found it more difficult than other people to commit such purposeful neglect. The statistical consequences of this development will be discussed later. Any other bias in this process of disappearance of feudal property has had to be ignored; it is unlikely to have been significant.

While the registers may therefore be accepted with a considerable degree of confidence as adequate statistical samples, there remains the problem of how far the entries themselves are reliable. The owners of fees and mesne fees declared their value to the ducal commissioners under oath. When, in the 1540's and 1550's, the government of the Netherlands proposed taxes on commercial capital and other mobile property which was also to be declared under oath, the estates objected that this was an invitation to perjury.[7] No such objection was ever raised against declarations under oath about *immobilia,* undoubtedly

---

other registers—and show no differences in kind from all the other entries, I have simply added them to the register of that year. Ecclesiastical property, properly speaking, is almost entirely absent from these registers.

[7] K. J. W. Verhofstad, *De regering der Nederlanden in de jaren 1555–1559* (Nijmegen, 1937), pp. 61 *et seq.*

because the chances of cheating successfully were not rated very high: the whole village knew what houses and fields every one owned. If there was public sympathy for understating the value of one's property, that would apply to all alike. As this inquiry is concerned less with absolute values than with the proportions of the distribution of property, the factor of undervaluation may well be ignored, if indeed it exists at all.

The types of property registered include houses, gardens, cultivated land, forest, rents, labor services (where these still existed), and rights of jurisdiction. Thus, the chevalier Mahieu de Lannaix held from the seigneur de Ligne, in 1474, the fief of Dameries. It consisted of a house with two *bonniers* of garden, 52 *bonniers* of arable, 6½ *bonniers* of meadow and pasture, and 40 *bonniers* of forest; together with the rents he received, both in money and in kind, and with the profits from his exercise of high, medium, and low justice over his fief, Lannaix had an annual income of 450 *livres tournois*.[8] This was a comparatively large income and, as in all entries, it was estimated as the average of the previous five years. Since Lannaix held his fief from the seigneur de Ligne, he was not a tenant-in-chief. Others, in their turn, held fiefs from him; subinfeudation was highly advanced in Hainault and often reached five or six degrees, with the count himself sometimes appearing as vassal of the third or fourth degree. Subinfeudation had long since ceased to have any but a purely formal significance. Such obligations as still attached to fiefs were owed only to the count.[9]

By the latter half of the fifteenth century, serfdom had all but ceased to exist in Hainault; but many feudal obligations survived, especially on larger estates. In 1564, Jehan de Namur, as lord of the fief of Riauwelz, received a *taille* of six *deniers tournois* from every citizen. It was worth a man's while to pay

[8] Chambre des Comptes, no. 1116, fol. 3.
[9] I.e., the duke of Burgundy. How far sub-infeudation played a part in the exercise of noble patronage and influence has never been investigated: it may well have been important.

3 *sous* 4 *denier* for his citizenship of Riauwelz. He could buy
or sell heritable property if he paid a simple tax of 5 *sous:* but
if a noncitizen was involved, either as buyer or as seller, the
lord would claim two *sous* in the *livre* of the value of the sale.
Citizens were further absolved from the payment of a property
tax of three *sous* per *bonnier* of land, and of the *droite de
mortesmains du meilleur cattel,* a tax of two *sous* in the livre
on inheritance. Other taxes were levied on citizens and foreigners alike: a tax of 10*d.* on each *bonnier,* rents in money
or kind payable at the feast of St. John, St. Rémy, or at Christmas,
and a tax of 6*s.* 3*d.* on each plough horse, together with some
further, minor exactions.[10] Riauwelz was not exceptional.
There were other large estates on which the lords had similar
or even more extensive rights, including entry fines, marriage
fees, and even occasional labor services.[11] But the tenants were
personally free and, on most estates, simply paid their rents to
the lord in money or in kind.

Apart from rents, the most important source of seigneurial income—and power—was the exercise of the rights of
jurisdiction, high, medium or low. In contrast to their practice
in most of their other dominions, the Habsburg rulers of the
Netherlands made no attempt to prevent landowners from ac-
quiring these rights; they figured prominently in the great domain sales of the sixteenth century.[12] But, as the ducal courts
extended their competence and called up more and more cases
from the manorial to the provincial courts, rights of jurisdiction gradually lost their value, and the financial profits attached to them diminished. It is not possible to evaluate this
process in terms of loss of income; but of its existence there
can be no doubt.[13]

[10] Chambre des Comptes, no. 1122, fols. 159–161.

[11] Labor services—never very heavy—may indicate the practice of
demesne farming; but as there is no other evidence for this in the registers, it is, at best, a doubtful pointer.

[12] Cf. Bibliothèque Royale, Brussels, MSS, 13352–69.

[13] H. A. Enno van Gelder, "Bailleul, Bronkhorst, Brederode," *De Gids,*
C (1936), p. 217.

For most fiefs, the ducal commissioners added up, or aver-
aged out, the various items of income. The investigator has
only to take care that a person holding different fiefs and appearing several times in the register is not counted more than
once, and that the incomes from his several fiefs are added together. Where, however, the commissioners failed to enter the
total income from a fief, it has been necessary to make the calculation for them. Where only the number of *bonniers* or *jour-
naux* of land was set down, this has proved impossible; land
values varied far too much to allow a safe estimate for any one
fief. Nor has it proved possible to evaluate rights of jurisdiction. The only person who knew about that was the owner;
where he failed to give the required information the historian
is helpless. On the other hand, it was possible to calculate the
value of rents in kind for the registers of 1502 and 1564–1573.

The commissioners themselves used conventional and not
market prices. The same procedure has had to be followed.
For wheat and for several other commodities, these conventional values are sometimes mentioned in the registers. For
commodities where this was not the case, values have been
calculated from market prices either in Hainault itself, or,
where Hainault prices were not available, from market prices
in Brabant and Flanders. The method used was to reduce such
prices to the conventional level by keeping constant their proportion to wheat prices of which both the market and the conventional levels are known. Where it was possible to check
this method by values mentioned in the registers, it was found
to give good results. The margin of error due to these calculations is therefore likely to be very small. Conventional prices
for 1502 and 1564–1573 are set out in Table 1.

Table 1. *Conventional prices, 1502 and 1564–73*

Prices per *muid* in £ *s. d. tournois*

| Year | Wheat | | | Rye | | | Barley | | | Oats | | | Spelt | | | Capons (each) | | | Chickens (each) | | |
|------|----|---|---|----|----|---|----|---|---|----|---|---|----|---|---|---|---|---|---|---|---|
| 1502 | 3 | 0 | 0 | 1 | 15 | 0 | 1 | 7 | 6 | 1 | 11 | 0 | 1 | 7 | 6 | 0 | 2 | 6 | 0 | 1 | 2 |
| 1564–73 | 10 | 0 | 0 | 6 | 0 | 0 | 5 | 0 | 0 | 5 | 0 | 0 | 5 | 0 | 0 | 0 | 6 | 3 | 0 | 3 | 1 |

Between 1502 and 1564–1573 the gap between conventional and market prices tended to increase (cf. Table 4). This meant that where holders of land received rents in wheat or oats or capons, the real income was a good deal higher than the value given in the register or calculated here. The significance of this fact will be discussed below.

The figures in the register may, therefore, be taken as adequate statistical samples of income from real property. They do not, however, say anything about income from other sources. Some of the largest landowners, such as the Croy and the Lannoy, had estates in other provinces as well as in Hainault. Many members of the nobility derived large incomes from offices held under the crown or from the ownership of ecclesiastical benefices. Middle-class owners were sometimes salaried government officials, such as Philippe Wieland, judge of the Great Court of Malines and author of the *Antiquités de Flandre;* or, more frequently, they were merchants from Mons, Valenciennes, Ath, or towns outside Hainault. For these latter, land was only a subsidiary source of income. Many small holders can hardly have lived on the income from their holdings at all unless they, or some members of their families, supplemented it by working as craftsmen or as spinners and weavers in the growing rural textile industries. All such earnings cannot be evaluated, except in a comparatively few cases.[14] These shortcomings in the sources are most serious in the case of the small holders for whom income from land was often not even the most important source of income. At any rate, it would be hazardous to draw any but very tentative conclusions about their economic fortunes from the evidence of these registers. But with the

[14] Dr H. A. Enno van Gelder has collected a large quantity of material on personal incomes and property in the sixteenth century. Inevitably, most of this relates to the nobility and only a few instances come from Hainault. I would like to take this opportunity of thanking Dr Enno van Gelder for allowing me access to his notes and for his generous advice on problems connected with the economic and social structure of the Netherlands during the sixteenth century.

larger landowners, and especially with the nobility, we are on safer ground: the great majority of them derived by far the greater part of their income from land. Thus, while the registers do not give a complete picture of agrarian society during this period, they do give a very adequate account of the economic fortunes of its upper layer.[15]

The results of the statistical analysis of the figures derived from the registers are set out in Table 2 and in Figure 1.[16]

From the income figures it is clear that landed property was divided very unevenly in Hainault, and this disparity between the incomes of rich and poor became even greater in the course of the 28 years between the compilation of the first two registers.[17] It was a period of declining agricultural prices, punctuated by violent short-term fluctuations. Unfortunately, we have no price lists for Hainault before the year 1500. But the economic relations between Hainault and Flanders were sufficiently close to make their price movements very similar. Table 3 (*a* and *b*) shows agricultural prices in Flanders during this period.[18]

The last quarter of the fifteenth century was a disastrous period for the southern provinces of the Netherlands. Charles the Bold's and Maximilian of Austria's wars with France im-

[15] The censuses compiled in 1570 for the levying of the duke of Alva's "100th penny" attempt to give figures for total income. Unfortunately the Hainault accounts do not distinguish between *mobilia* and *immobilia*. But in Brabant, which was more urbanized than Hainault, the value of *mobilia,* including government annuities (*rentes*), amounted to only 20%. M.-A. Arnould, "L'Impot sur le Capital en Belgique au XVI⁰ Siècle." *Le Hainaut Economique,* I (Mons, 1946), 44 and *passim.*

[16] I would like to acknowledge my great debt to Mr J. Johnston, of the Department of Economics of the University of Manchester, and to Mr E. Nixon, of the Shirley Institute, for their help and advice on the statistical work in this paper.

[17] This disparity was much greater than it was in some parts of Italy at the same time. See Chapter 1.

[18] Calculated from H. van Houtte, *Documents pour servir à l'Histoire des Prix de 1381 à 1794* (Brussels, 1902).

Table 2. Income from feudal property in Hainault

| % | 1474 | | | | 1502 | | | | 1564/73 | | | |
|---|---|---|---|---|---|---|---|---|---|---|---|---|
| | No. | Aggregate income of group (£) | Average income (£) | Percentage of total | No. | Aggregate income of group (£) | Average income (£) | Percentage of total | No. | Aggregate income of group (£) | Average income (£) | Percentage of total |
| 100 | 2,147 | 67,502 | 31·45 | 100 | 2,469 | 91,624 | 37·11 | 100 | 778 | 72,419 | 93·07 | 100 |
| Top 75 | — | — | — | 99·1 | — | — | — | 99·5 | — | — | — | 99·1 |
| 50 | — | — | — | 96·4 | — | — | — | 97·1 | — | — | — | 96·3 |
| 25 | — | — | — | 89·4 | — | — | — | 91·2 | — | — | — | 88·4 |
| 10 | 215 | 52,431 | 244 | 77·7 | 248 | 74,348 | 300 | 81·1 | 78 | 53,564 | 687 | 73·9 |
| 5 | 107 | 45,427 | 424 | 67·4 | 124 | 65,499 | 528 | 71·3 | 39 | 44,316 | 1136 | 61·1 |
| Nobility | 139 | 42,231 | 304 | 62·1 | 212 | 63,423 | 299 | 69·3 | 107 | 44,180 | 413 | 57·1 |
| Non-noble | 2,008 | 25,271 | 12·59 | 37·9 | 2,257 | 28,201 | 12·49 | 30·7 | 671 | 28,239 | 42·08 | 42·9 |

| | 1474 | 1502 | 1564/73 |
|---|---|---|---|
| Q1 | £2. 2s. 10d. | £1. 19s. 3d. | £6. 4s. 5d. |
| Median | £5. 0s. 6d. | £5. 0s. 5d. | £15. 8s. 1d. |
| Q3 | £12. 17s. 3d. | £13. 3s. 1d. | £50. 17s. 8d. |
| Skewness | 0·4623 | 0·4535 | 0·5887 |
| Entries without ascertainable value | 90 | 158 | 77 |

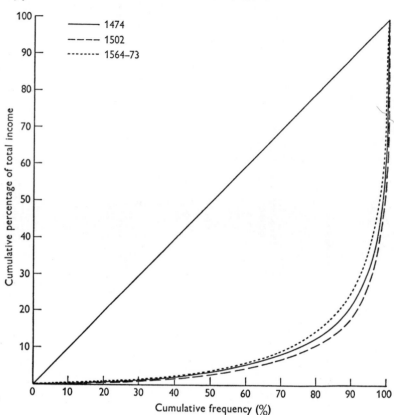

Figure 1. *Distribution of Income in Hainault, 1474, 1502, and 1564–1573.* The diagonal line is the line of equal distribution of income and the areas enclosed by this diagonal and the actual curves is a measure of the inequality of distribution. The graph starts with the poorest section of the community, while the figures in Table 2 indicate the richest sections; i.e., the richest 10 per cent of the population are those between 90 and 100 per cent in the graph.

posed a crushing burden of taxation on the provinces. Destructive border warfare was followed by civil war in 1485 and, even more ruinously, from 1488 to 1490. The loss over 6,100 houses revealed by the census of 1501—a loss of over 21 per cent—is a sinister pointer to the fate of the country population

Table 3a.  *Agricultural prices in Flanders*

| Date | Wheat | Oats (hard) | Oats (soft) | Butter 100% | Cheese | Barley | Rye |
|---|---|---|---|---|---|---|---|
| 1500 | 29s. 4½d. | 12s. 11½d. | 8s. 7¾d. | £5. 18s. | 29s. 4½d. | 27s. 2d. | 37s. 6d. |
| 1470 | 130·46 | 110·95 | 103·7 | 179·66 | 119·84 | 171·77 | 161·78 |
| 1471 | 132·54 | 104·16 | 100·34 | 207·79 | 129·68 | 147·22 | 156·45 |
| 1472 | 120·69 | 149·15 | 149·4 | 198·30 | 68·07 | 176·66 | 136·45 |
| 1473 | 134·03 | 127·93 | 123·49 | 162·71 | 86·59 | 184·03 | 131·54 |
| 1474 | 154·29 | 170·06 | 158·21 | 220·33 | 124·50 | 176·66 | 146·66 |
| 1475 | 179·82 | 125·07 | 131·13 | 169·49 | 94·04 | 154·58 | 181·33 |
| 1476 | 136·01 | 122·99 | 122·22 | 162·71 | 92·88 | 165·62 | 93·33 |
| 1477 | 147·85 | 161·34 | 158·44 | 213·55 | 124·81 | — | — |
| 1478 | 227·56 | 159·87 | 168·75 | 217·28 | 108·78 | — | — |
| 1479 | 222·83 | 190·35 | 189·69 | 299·32 | 202·14 | — | — |
| 1480 | 207·3 | 146·84 | 137·84 | 207·28 | 93·77 | — | — |
| 1481 | 233·08 | 188·19 | 175·92 | 241·69 | 136·86 | — | — |
| 1482 | 442·3 | 213·81 | 216·08 | 301·69 | 220·52 | — | — |
| 1483 | 462·04 | 288·73 | 271·06 | 299·49 | 214·43 | — | — |
| 1484 | 171·3 | 157·56 | 155·9 | 272·03 | 132·74 | 193·85 | 163·54 |
| 1485 | 172·94 | 124·45 | 124·78 | 196·62 | 85·67 | 150·9 | 137·78 |
| 1486 | 139·92 | 209·18 | 209·02 | 131·35 | 111·36 | 276·03 | 200·88 |
| 1487 | 290·04 | 198·22 | 197·68 | 160·5 | 184·85 | 272·35 | 320 |
| 1488 | 287·13 | 199·92 | 199·3 | 157·62 | 192·95 | 283·4 | 291·64 |
| 1489 | — | — | — | — | — | 345·96 | 346·66 |
| 1490 | 494·75 | 395·67 | 378·13 | 410·16 | 385·69 | 198·74 | 186·66 |
| 1491 | 292·40 | 141·43 | 140·5 | 101·69 | 147·07 | 219·61 | 237·33 |
| 1492 | 338·46 | 214·35 | 213·42 | 101·69 | 98·05 | 295·65 | 285·33 |
| 1493 | 310·72 | 200·77 | 198·95 | 169·49 | 220·52 | 345·96 | 394·66 |
| 1494 | 175·83 | 132·87 | 129·51 | 108·47 | 110·78 | 154·58 | 144 |
| 1495 | 126·99 | 109·72 | 109·95 | 101·69 | 86·79 | 118·99 | 96·88 |
| 1496 | 113·75 | 128·62 | 126·62 | 94·91 | 81·68 | 119·61 | 89·79 |
| 1497 | 137·64 | 170·06 | 158·68 | 96·61 | 85·80 | 182·55 | 157·77 |
| 1498 | 194·75 | 116·35 | 116·20 | 195·7 | 96·01 | 169·30 | 181·33 |
| 1499 | 167·36 | 122·76 | 120·83 | 106·77 | 112·32 | 184·02 | 155·54 |
| 1501 | 150·03 | 139·35 | 138·42 | 111·86 | 102·11 | 159·47 | 130·66 |
| 1502 | 209·9 | 158·64 | 156·83 | 123·72 | 124·30 | 225·72 | 193·33 |
| 1503 | 255·27 | 138·58 | 137·38 | 147·45 | 124·5 | 228·19 | 292·12 |
| 1504 | 162·62 | 193·51 | 181·36 | 188·13 | 181·68 | 198·74 | 160·0 |
| 1505 | 161·94 | 200·61 | 200·57 | 122·03 | 208·74 | 196·90 | 152 |

during those years.[19] The census of neighboring Brabant tell
the same dismal story. In the Walloon part of the quarter of

[19] Cf. above.

Table 3b.   *Mean of indices in five-yearly periods*

| Date | Wheat (%) | Oats (hard) (%) | Oats (soft) (%) | Butter (%) | Cheese (%) | Barley (%) | Rye (%) |
|------|-----------|-----------------|-----------------|------------|------------|------------|---------|
| 1470–4 | 130·4 | 132·45 | 127·02 | 193·75 | 105·73 | 171·26 | 146·57 |
| 1475–9 | 182·81 | 151·92 | 154·04 | 212·47 | 124·53 | 160·01 | 137·33 |
| 1480–4 | 303·20 | 199·02 | 191·36 | 264·43 | 159·66 | 193·85 | 163·54 |
| 1485–9 | 225·5 | 182·94 | 182·69 | 136·52 | 143·7 | 265·72 | 259·37 |
| 1490–4 | 322·43 | 217·01 | 212·1 | 178·30 | 192·42 | 242·91 | 249·59 |
| 1495–9 | 148·09 | 129·5 | 126·45 | 119·13 | 89·25 | 154·89 | 136·26 |
| 1500–4 | 175·56 | 146·01 | 142·79 | 134·23 | 126·51 | 182·42 | 175·82 |

Brussels [20] the number of inhabited houses declined from 6,175 in 1472, to 5,011 in 1496—a loss of 19 per cent.[21] In the Walloon part of the quarter of Louvain the losses were much worse: 2,485 houses in 1472, to 1,257 in 1496—a decline of very nearly 50 per cent.[22] In both quarters the losses in the open country were even more severe than in the towns; 46.6 per cent of all the households outside the towns were so poor in 1496, that no taxes could be levied on them at all.[23] In Hainault conditions may not have been quite as bad as in the quarter of Louvain; but the deputies of the estates of Hainault complained bitterly about the soldiery who had "eaten up the poor country people." [24]

In such conditions, it is not surprising to find that the nobility and other great landowners with considerable reserves of capital were able to ride out the storms better than the peasants. Often, the peasants' loss was the nobles' gain and many added to their estates and their incomes.[25] No wonder then that, unlike Flanders, Hainault remained loyal to Maximilian

[20] The province of Brabant was divided into four quarters: Brussels, Louvain, Antwerp, and Bois-le-Duc.

[21] J. Cuvelier, *Dénombrements de Foyers en Brabant (XIVe–XVIe siècles)* (Brussels, 1912), pp. clxii and ccxxxiv.

[22] *Ibid.*, pp. clxi and ccxxxiii.        [23] *Ibid.*, p. ccxlii.

[24] *Relation de Jeannet de la Ruyelle, 1482,* L. P. Gachard, ed., Bulletin de la Commission Royal d'Histoire, ser. 3, I (Brussels, 1860), 338 *et seq. Relation des états généraux tenus à Malines . . . 1492, ibid.*, 4, 332 *et seq.*

[25] This did not, of course, apply to all nobles. Cf. *Relation de Jeannet de la Ruyelle*, p. 338.

during the civil wars. The province was dominated by the nobility, and the nobility was doing well.

Between 1502 and 1564–1573 there was a clear reversal of the trends dominant in the previous generation. The Lorenz curve for 1564–1573 (Fig. 1), lying well inside the other two, shows that the extreme inequality in the distribution of income has now been somewhat reduced. The values for the lower quartile (Q1) and for the median (Mi) about trebled; i.e., the incomes from the smaller properties roughly kept pace with rising agricultural prices (cf. Table 4). But the average income of the upper 10 and 5 per cent did little more than double, and the percentage of total income received by this upper group declined quite sharply. The greatest gains were made by the medium-sized properties: the value of the upper quartile (Q3) nearly quadrupled. This comparatively large shift in Q3 is the reason for the greater skewness in the frequency distribution of the incomes in the 1564–1573 register.[26]

For the sixteenth century we have price lists for Hainault itself.[27] Table 4 shows that wheat prices rose by about 400 per cent in the period between the last two registers; but the prices of other foodstuffs did not rise nearly as rapidly. It was a period of relative agricultural prosperity for those who could take advantage of the good market for cereals. Unfortunately, we have no census of hearths for Hainault in the sixteenth century; but if we accept again the evidence from the neighboring districts from Brabant, we can see a very distinct improvement. In the open country of the Walloon part of the quarter of Brabant, the number of inhabited houses had increased by 45 per cent by the year 1526, and in the Walloon part of the quarter of Louvain by nearly 110 per cent.[28] Developments in Hainault are likely to have been, at least, in the same direction. There

---

[26] The coefficient of skewness is taken as

$$\frac{Q1 + Q3 - 2Mi}{Q3 - Q1}.$$

[27] I. Delatte, "Prix et salaires en Hainaut au 16e siècle," *Annales de la Société Scientifique de Bruxelles,* ser. 3 (1937).

[28] Cuvelier, *op. cit.,* pp. cclxxiv and cclxx.

Table 4. *Wheat prices in Hainault*

| Years | Wheat prices (per *muid* of wheat) Average yearly price in 5 years £ s. d. | | | Index 1500– 1505 = 100 |
|---|---|---|---|---|
| 1500–5 | 5 | 18 | 6 | 100·0 |
| 1505–10 | 5 | 13 | 6 | 95·8 |
| 1510–15 | 6 | 1 | 9 | 102·7 |
| 1515–20 | 5 | 19 | 10 | 101·1 |
| 1520–5 | 11 | 2 | 6 | 187·8 |
| 1525–30 | 8 | 8 | 5 | 142·1 |
| 1530–5 | 9 | 5 | 11 | 156·9 |
| 1535–40 | 12 | 14 | 3 | 214·6 |
| 1540–5 | 11 | 0 | 5 | 186·0 |
| 1545–50 | 10 | 15 | 0 | 181·4 |
| 1550–5 | 14 | 14 | 7 | 248·6 |
| 1555–60 | 19 | 8 | 1 | 327·5 |
| 1560–5 | 16 | 6 | 5 | 275·5 |
| 1565–70 | 19 | 11 | 0 | 330·0 |
| 1570–5 | 25 | 2 | 5 | 424·0 |

|  | Wheat Index 1500– 10 = 100 | Butter Index 1500– 10 = 100 | Eggs Index 1500– 10 = 100 |
|---|---|---|---|
| 1500–10 | 100·0 | 100·0 | 100·0 |
| 1511–20 | 110·2 | 106·3 | 104·4 |
| 1521–30 | 123·7 | 134·4 | 117·4 |
| 1531–*1538* | 165·3 | 137·5 | 130·4 |
| *1539*–50 | 173·7 | 162·5 | 165·2 |
| 1551–60 | 288·1 | 216·9 | 234·8 |

|  | Salt herrings Index 1500– 10 = 100 | Salt Index 1500– 10 = 100 | Olive oil Index 1500– 10 = 100 |
|---|---|---|---|
| 1500–10 | 100·0 | 100·0 | — |
| 1511–20 | 108·3 | 128·8 | 100·0 |
| 1521–30 | 137·5 | 200·0 | 124·1 |
| 1531–*1538* | 116·7 | 162·5 | 110·4 |
| *1539*–50 | 129·2 | — | — |
| 1551–60 | 183·3 | — | 165·5 |

were no major catastrophes, such as civil war, until the time when the third of our registers was already being compiled; but there were the usual intermittent border warfare with France and the inevitable depredations of the garrison troops.

While the general economic background of the sixteenth century is fairly clear, the fortunes of the different classes are rather more problematical. For the holders of very small properties the evidence is somewhat contradictory.[29] In the country-side of the Walloon quarter of Brussels the number of "poor" houses declined from 46 to 38 per cent, up to 1526; [30] but in the quarter of Louvain it rose from 62 to nearly 70 per cent, and this despite the remarkable increase in the number of inhabited houses.[31] If we follow Professor Postan's method of using the price of butter to see whether the mass of the population had sufficient money left over, after paying for bare necessities, to indulge in such a "semiluxury," [32] then the fact that butter prices lagged far behind those of cereals would suggest that there was no increasing demand for it and that the standard of living of the mass of the population did not materially improve during this period. This conclusion is born out by what is known about wage rates in Hainault.[33] Nevertheless, the sharp decline of the late fifteenth century seems to have been halted and it is fair to suggest that those with land, even small holdings, did relatively better than wage earners.

The most striking feature of the 1564–1573 register is, however, the relative decline in the income of the upper 10 per cent as against the advance of the middle income groups. There is no very obvious reason why these latter should have done so much better than large owners in a period of rising agricultural prices. It is very likely that Professor Tawney's arguments for the decline of the English aristocracy and the rise of the gentry hold good for Hainault. As in England, the Hainault aristocracy were largely absentee landlords, deriving their income from rents which it was difficult to raise. They were unable to take advantage of favorable market conditions to the extent that cultivators of medium-sized properties did. But this argument must remain an hypothesis until it can be checked by

[29] Apart from the difficulties of drawing conclusions from the registers about them which were discussed above.

[30] Cuvelier, *op. cit.,* pp. cclxxxii *et seq.*

[31] *Ibid.,* p. cclxxxii.

[32] M. Postan, "The Trade of Medieval Europe: The North," *Cambridge Economic History of Europe* (Cambridge, 1952), II, 209.

[33] Delatte, *op. cit.,* p. 23.

the study of the accounts of a number of individual estates.[34]

While we know very little about the movement of rents, the registers provide some evidence of their composition. Where a landowner received rents in kind, the value of these rents moved parallel with market prices, and he suffered no loss from their rise. Table 5 shows the proportions of total income received in this form.

At no time did anyone in the upper 5 per cent receive rents in kind alone; but fifty-one out of the 124 members of this group in 1502 received composite rents, and for these fifty-one rents in kind amounted, on the average, to almost one-third of their income. By 1564–1573, only five out of the thirty-nine in the similar group still received composite rents, and even for them the proportion of their total income which this represented had become negligible. By contrast, the middle group had maintained its rents in kind much more successfully. Whether this was a deliberate policy, or simply conservatism, it is impossible to say; but it undoubtedly helps to account for their economic advance at the expense of the large owners. For the lowest income group, the figures of this table probably mean not so much the receipt of rents in kind as a traditional valuation of the yield of their holdings, and it is therefore best not to attempt to draw conclusions from Table 5 for this class.

Since all rents in kind are calculated according to the conventional values of the registers (Table 1), their real values, in terms of market prices, were much higher than is indicated by Table 5—an added advantage for those who had managed to keep them. On the other hand, rents in kind sometimes formed part of total income figures given in the registers, so that real income in such cases was rather higher. Against this, rents nominally in kind were sometimes in fact paid in money. At other times, a lord coming to visit his estate might demand

[34] This is not the type of research which can be done in short visits to Belgium. No such work has yet been attempted by local historians, and it may well be difficult to find estate accounts. But at least one set, that for the *seigneurie* of Gaesbeke, in Brabant, is deposited in the Bibliothèque Royale of Brussels, MSS, 19,240, 19,242, and 19,247.

Table 5. *Proportions of income received in rents*

**Rents in kind only**

| | | 1502 | | | | | | 1564–73 | | | |
|---|---|---|---|---|---|---|---|---|---|---|---|
| Intervals | Items | (1) £ | Average (£) | (2) cumulative total income (£) | (1) as percentage of (2) | Intervals | Items | (1) £ | Average (£) | (2) cumulative total income (£) | (1) as percentage of (2) |
| Under £5 | 471 | 942·22 | 2 | 2,619 | 36·0 | Under £15 | 113 | 801·35 | 7·09 | 2,586 | 31·0 |
| £5 and under £112 | 362 | 5,376·56 | 14·85 | 21,665 | 24·8 | £15 and under £382 | 111 | 6,257·08 | 56·37 | 26,272 | 23·8 |
| £112 and over | 0 | 0 | 0 | 67,340 | 0 | £382 and over | 0 | 0 | 0 | 43,561 | 0 |
| Totals | | 6,318·78 | | 91,624 | 26 | Totals | | 7,058·43 | | 72,419 | 24·45 |

**Rents in kind and money**

| | | 1502 | | | | | | 1564–73 | | | |
|---|---|---|---|---|---|---|---|---|---|---|---|
| Intervals | Items | (1) £ | Average (£) | (2) cumulative total income (£) | (1) as percentage of (2) | Intervals | Items | (1) £ | Average (£) | (2) cumulative total income (£) | (1) as percentage of (2) |
| Under £5 | 31 | 37·85 | 1·22 | 2,619 | 1·4 | Under £15 | 7 | 43·93 | 6·27 | 2,586 | 1·7 |
| £5 and under £112 | 139 | 2,103·7 | 15·13 | 21,665 | 9·7 | £15 and under £382 | 26 | 1824 | 70·2 | 26,272 | 6·9 |
| £112 and over | 51 | 21,453 | 420·647 | 67,340 | 31·9 | £382 and over | 5 | 1,363·33 | 272·67 | 43,561 | 3·1 |
| Totals | | 23,594·55 | | 91,624 | 25·8 | Totals | | 3,231·26 | | 72,419 | 4·5 |

The right-hand section, 'Rents in kind and money', represents those properties in which income was received in both forms. Col. (1) shows the aggregate value of rents in kind received in this composite income. Col. (2) is the cumulative income of all properties in each of the three groups. The intervals represent the three groups, i.e. incomes below the median, incomes between the median and the top 5 %, and the incomes of the top 5 %.

grain and capons from his tenants until he left, when rents would again be paid in money.[35] These uncertainties may, to some extent, cancel out; but while it is wise not to press the evidence of rents in kind too far, it is still very suggestive, even if not entirely conclusive.

It now becomes possible to draw some conclusions about the social and political history of Hainault in the light of the economic evidence of the registers. During the first three-quarters of the sixteenth century, the peasantry—the mass of the lower income group who held land as owners or tenants—managed to hold their own in the face of rising prices far better than they had done in the period of falling prices in the latter part of the fifteenth century. This may well be one important reason why they did not join the German peasants in their great revolt of 1525 or why only very few of them embraced Anabaptism, the craftsman's religion of social protest. Calvinist preachers, appearing in the late 1550's, had their greatest successes among the craftsmen of the towns and the full-time (and often unemployed) rural textile workers of the Walloon industrial belt, from Hondschoote in the north-west to Valenciennes and Mons in the south-east. In 1563, Tournai and Valenciennes became centers of Calvinist revolts. At the time of the Union of Arras, the magistrates of Mons were very frightened of popular anti-Spanish and anti-Catholic riots. But the mass of the peasantry took no part in any of these movements.

At the other end of the social scale, the position of the nobility was more complex. Hainault was the home of many of the greatest noble families of the Netherlands. The vast clan of the Croy, with their many famous titles, such as Chièvres, Roeulx, and Aerschot; their relatives, the Lannoy, made famous by the Viceroy of Naples, captor of Francis I at Pavia; the Ligne; the Lalaing, counts of Hoochstraten; the Boussu and the Rolins, whose fortunes were made by a chancellor of

[35] There is no mention of this in the registers; but Dr Enno van Gelder's documents show at least one case where this happened.

Philip the Good—all these had vast estates in the province, even while they rarely lived there. Below them were the hundreds of lesser nobles.[36] These nobles, and especially the high nobility, all but monopolized the upper 2.5 per cent of the entries in the registers. Their share of total income dropped from 59 to 47 per cent between 1502 and 1564–1573. Nevertheless, it is unlikely that their economic position seriously deteriorated in the sixteenth century. Their influence at court, their monopoly of provincial governorships, of high military and court offices, and their claim to the disposal of the fattest ecclesiastical benefices gave them opportunities for making up losses of income from their estates which were denied to the lower nobility. They remained loyal to the crown until Philip II's methods of government drove a few of them into half-hearted but disastrous opposition.

Below these top 2.5 per cent, there were successful merchants from Mons and Valenciennes, or lawyers holding high offices in the provincial courts or the central administration; they owned estates as large as those of any knight and sometimes enjoyed the *haute justice* as well as any *écuyer*. The 107 members of the nobility in the register of 1564–1573 represent a much higher percentage of total entries than did the nobility in the earlier registers. That, in spite of this fact, the nobility as a whole had lost ground heavily (Table 2) shows that the incomes of many of them had fallen, and had fallen below those of many *bourgeois*. Yet, it is a debatable point how far the sixteenth century may be regarded as a period of long-term crisis for the Hainault nobility. Philip II's minister, Cardinal Granvelle, thought that the opposition of the *grands seigneurs* was motivated by their desire to extricate themselves from heavy debts. This may have been more true of the lower than of the high nobility whom the cardinal had primarily in

---

[36] I have included among the nobility anyone described as *chevalier, écuyer,* or *seigneur de . . . ,* unless the registers state specifically that he was a *bourgeois*. Ladies are classified in the same way: *dame de . . .* or, more usually, as the widow of *seigneur. . . .*

mind. But sixteenth-century noblemen were not unduly worried about debts.[37] What mattered more was that the income from their estates declined [38] and that it declined at a time when alternative income, from offices under the crown, was reserved to the high nobility or the comparatively few who could hope for more modest local offices. The central government and the hated lawyers were, moreover, steadily encroaching on their remaining seigneurial rights. In 1520, a proclamation prohibited the levying of new tithes and sought to abolish feudal rights existing for less than 40 years. In 1531, the crown forbade lords to exact gifts or new services from their tenants.[39] The decline of income from the exercise of the rights of jurisdiction has already been mentioned. If the decline in the real income of the lower nobility was, in fact, due to rising prices, then it was probably not spread evenly throughout the first three quarters of the sixteenth century but concentrated in the 15 or 20 years before the outbreak of the great revolt, the years after 1550, when prices rose much more rapidly than before. Thus, if there was a crisis, it was a comparatively sharp and sudden one, aggravated by demobilization from the *bandes d'ordonnances,* the aristocratic Netherland cavalry, after the Treaty of Cateau-Cambrésis, in 1559.

These developments would certainly account for the growing discontent among the nobility in the 1560's. Calvinist propaganda had its successes among them, though few were given to religious fanaticism on either side. Many joined the Compromise, the opposition movement led by Brederode and Louis

[37] Permanent obligations on estates, such as annuities to sisters or mothers-in-law, are usually mentioned in the registers. These have not been taken into account in this analysis unless they formed part of the income of another entry. Every owner of an estate had obligations of one form or another, and nearly all noblemen lived to the limit of, or beyond, their income. Moreover, most annuities were paid and received within the same class.

[38] Cf. Table 2 and above.

[39] H. Pirenne, *Histoire de Belgique* (Brussels, 1907), III, 256 *et seq.*

of Nassau, and some signed the petition of 1565, at the presentation of which the famous name *gueux,* beggars, was first applied to them. One incomplete contemporary list names nineteen Hainault nobles among them, as against twenty-one from Flanders, forty-six from Brabant, fifty-nine from Holland, and eighty-seven from Friesland.[40] A few Hainaulters, such as Marnix de St. Aldegonde, took a leading part in the Orangeist revolt. But the great majority, with the Duke of Aerschot and the Count of Boussu at their head, remained loyal to the king. Despite the decline of their incomes, the nobles maintained their dominant position in the social and political life of Hainault. The economic advance of the middle income group, shown in the registers, was not nearly sufficient to upset the essentially aristocratic nature of Hainault society. Together with the nobility of Artois, the nobles of Hainault took the lead in forming the Union of Arras and disrupting the united front against Philip II which the Prince of Orange had built up with so much patience after Spain's military power had collapsed in 1576. Whenever there was a serious threat of social revolution—from the breaking of the images in 1566, to the aggressive democratic dictatorship of the Ghent Calvinists, in the late 1570's—the Hainault nobility closed their ranks and united for the preservation of the social *status quo,* even if this meant submission to the rule of Spain.

[40] F. Rachfahl, *Wilhelm von Oranien* (Halle, 1908), II, 567, n. 1.

# CHAPTER 6

# Patronage and Bribery
# during the Reign of Charles V

PATRONAGE WAS the fuel which kept the wheels of six-teenth century political society turning. It was the civilian form of an earlier, feudal-military relationship. Governments were building up professional civil services; but they could not yet do without the help of those who possessed power and influ-ence of their own, especially in local government: great nobles or princes of the church and lay or ecclesiastical corporations. It was not necessary, nor even always desirable, that the gov-ernor of a province, for instance, should have the bulk of his property in that province. But he must be a great lord. He must have the habit of command, the firm expectation of be-ing obeyed, more especially, if he held a military, as well as a civil, appointment. The nobility were still regarded as the lead-ers of society, and rich and successful commoners aspired to join their ranks. Philip II's much criticized appointment of the duke of Medina Sidonia as commander of the Armada, in 1588, was motivated by a clear, if misguided logic. A man of lower degree, a simple Galician gentleman like Martínez de Recalde, for instance, would simply not have commanded suf-ficient authority to make himself obeyed, for all that he was one of the most experienced and efficient naval commanders in Spanish service.[1]

[1] I owe this point to Professor G. Mattingly, of Columbia University. For a recent discussion of the problem of the appointment of Medina Sidonia, cf. I. A. A. Thompson, "The Appointment of the Duke of Me-dina Sidonia to the Command of the Spanish Armada," *The Historical Journal,* Vol. 12, No. 2 (1969).

There were those, like Francesco Taverna, Charles V's chancellor of Milan, who had attained to a modern view of office. When asked by the governor general of Milan to contribute from his salary to a government loan, Taverna refused and maintained that his salary was not a matter of the sovereign's grace which he might be expected to pledge to him in the hope of a future *grazie;* if he fulfilled his duties to the governor general's satisfaction, so he said, he would expect to receive and keep his salary; if he did not fulfill his duties satisfactorily, he would expect to be dismissed.[2]

If such views were still far from universal among the class of professional administrators, they were even less so among the nobility. A great nobleman would expect to be paid the salary attached to the office he held; but, equally, he might be willing to advance money to his prince or guarantee a government loan with his private property. He would expect recognition of his services later, and this might take the form not only of money payment but of some public honor or privilege. All rulers, even the most impecunious, like Maximilian I, or the most stingy, like Elizabeth I, had many of these in their gift. It was a slight on a man's honor and self-esteem to be expected to serve his prince without such rewards. It undermined his standing with and usefulness to his own friends and clients who had attached themselves to him in the hope of their own advancement and profit. For the rewards granted by the prince also took the form of benefits to third parties, at the request of their patrons. The official papers of Charles V and Philip II are full of requests for such *mercedes* as they were called in Spain. Thus, when Charles V failed to reward the marquis of Pescara for his victory of Pavia, another Milanese chancellor, Girolamo Morone, was led to believe, quite logically, but as it happened erroneously, that Pescara might be induced to change sides.

The Habsburg rulers of the Netherlands always kept close personal control over patronage, for they knew that on this de-

[2] F. Chabod, *Lo Stato di Milano nell'Impero di Carlo V* (Rome, 1934), pp. 172 ff.

pended the loyalty and cooperation of their subjects. Both Margaret of Austria and Mary of Hungary vainly protested that they could not govern without controlling patronage. After a lifetime's experience as governor general of the Netherlands, Margaret wrote a memorandum to her nephew which epitomized her difficulties.

"In the matter of the *aides* of the Netherlands," so the memorandum ran, "and especially in Brabant and Flanders, we used to provide some benefices to the children and other relatives of the governors of the foremost towns. But before His Majesty left, he had given Madame a list for [filling] the benefices under his patronage. She therefore had no means of giving any benefice in the way it had been done formerly, not even to the children and relatives of those of His Majesty's officials who conduct his affairs, nor to her own chaplains and servants. Only twelve benefices were reserved for her own people, and that is a small number. Moreover, none has fallen vacant, nor is likely to, for a long time. . . . Madame therefore begs His Majesty that it would please him to allow her the disposal of every third benefice in his gift, and she insists on this in all humility." [3]

The emperor denied this modest, almost pathetic, request. But he knew what was happening and tried to counteract the difficulties which faced his governments by constantly journeying from one of his states to another, dispensing patronage in person. Philip II who thought he knew better than his father, but did not, made the fundamental mistake of staying in Spain while still denying the governors of his other dominions the control over patronage. This policy had not a little to do with the revolt of the Netherlands.

If service to a prince kept many of its feudal characteristics in the sixteenth century, the contemporary view of offices themselves also maintained many of its medieval ambiguities. Sixteenth-century political morality, as set out in the royal instructions to governors of provinces, for instance, certainly viewed

[3] "Articles proposez a l'Empereur . . . de par Madame," July, 1530. Brussels, Bibliothèque Royale, MS, 16068–16072, fo. 140.

the holding of a political office as a public service. At the same time, the holder of an office frequently regarded it as a piece of private property, even when he had not actually bought it. A man who was given an office, not because of his ability to fill it but as a reward for previous services in other fields, or as the price for his political support, would naturally make the most of the opportunities, financial or social, which the possession of this office offered him. The morality of such action was generally accepted, for, in the social and financial system of the time, it was inevitable. But for those who required the services of the officeholder, the situation was both simpler and more sinister: it required bribery.

Two little-known incidents in the history of the estates of Holland, during the reign of Charles V, admirably illustrate how the conduct of politics depended on these relationships. The first was concerned with gratuities, the second with fees. A gratuity was the counterpart to patronage, a gift, in money or in kind, for a service rendered to a client in the advancement of the client's interests. A fee was more strictly related to the exercise of an office, and its payment would be expected even when there was no relationship of patron and client. Neither the payment of gratuities, nor that of fees, was regarded as corrupt in itself; but both could easily lead to corruption. Whether, in practice, they did or did not, depended not only on the circumstances of the particular case but also on the different points of view of those who paid and those who were paid.

The first incident concerned the privilege of Holland freely to export grain. This was a matter of great importance to the province and more especially to Amsterdam which was establishing itself as the main *entrepôt* for the export trade of grain from the Baltic. The government in Brussels had, at different times, disputed this privilege both because, like all sixteenth-century governments, it feared that free exports of grain might raise prices to famine level in case of scarcity, and because it cast money-hungry eyes on this export as a convenient object for taxation. In 1531, the emperor had decided in favor of Holland's privilege but, in the autumn of 1535, the Brussels government returned to the attack. It published a *placard* prohibiting the export of all grain from the emperor's lands. Soon it became clear that its intention was to re-introduce the *congie,* or *verlofgeld,* the export tax on corn, from which the province claimed to be free by the emperor's decision.[4]

Holland sent its deputies to Brussels and, on December 9, 1535, they presented their case before the full council, with the governor general, Mary, dowager queen of Hungary, herself present. The lawyers of the council argued the case on theoretical grounds. Did they want to maintain, asked Carondelet, the chancellor, that the emperor did not have the power to do what he liked? It was the Roman law principle of "what has pleased the prince has the force of law" which the lawyers in government service were consistently upholding during the sixteenth century. The delegation did not allow themselves to be led onto such treacherous ground. They did not want to dispute "about the powers of princes," they said; but they knew very well that the emperor did not want to do anything which would harm the country and the proposed export tax would do just that.[5] The case was referred to a committee of the queen's council of state and the Holland delegates waited for the arrival of their governor, the count of Hoochstraten, from whom they hoped for support. On December 16, they argued with the committee, all lawyers who, as Andries Jacopszoon, the secretary of the city of Amsterdam said scornfully, produced much scholastic talk.[6] The deputies preferred to state their case in terms of practical economics, viz., that the proposed tax would ruin their trade and drive foreign merchants away.[7] Over

---

[4] A. Jacopszoon, *Prothocolle van alle de Reysen . . . gedaen zedert ick de Stede van Aemstelredamme gedient heb gehadt . . . ,* MS in Amsterdam City Archives, transcript by E. Van Bienna, pt. 2, fos. 218–219. Andries Jacopszoon was secretary of Amsterdam and represented the city in the meetings of the provincial estates and in the States-General.

[5] *Ibid.,* fos. 220–221.        [6] *Ibid.,* fo. 221, "scholastique redenen."

[7] *Ibid.,* fos. 221–222.

Christmas there was talk of a compromise and, characteristically, the delegates thought that a touch of judiciously applied bribery might now help their case. The seigneur de Molembaix, a member of the council, pressed them to accept a small impost which would not be burdensome to them but help the emperor. "It smacks like this," wrote Jacopszoon, "that he is to have a portion (of the receipts of the tax) and the *advocat* (of Holland) has secretly promised him a gratuity of 200 pieces of wainscotting, payable by the province." [8]

On January 7, 1536, the government shifted their ground. It was the other provinces who complained about the free export of grain, they now said, both because it raised prices in the Low Countries and because of the unfair advantages it gave the Hollanders in competition with the merchants from Zealand.[9] These complaints were, no doubt, genuinely voiced; but the dispute and the eventual decision had very little to do with them. Early in February, a confidential letter from Hoochstraten to the *advocat* made it clear to the estates of Holland, assembled at The Hague, how much the whole matter depended on the attitude and private interests of certain members of the council of state. The counts of Nassau and Bueren were shortly expected at Nassau. It would be a good idea, wrote the governor of Holland, to send deputies to meet them and to win them over from the party in the council who favored the tax. The estates decided to send another deputation to Brussels and resolved "that the great lords and others should be rewarded by bribes and corruption if they supported us." [10] They knew now that their most determined opponent was Ruffault, the treasurer general, who had been promised the receivership of the tax.[11]

---

[8] *Ibid.*, fo. 221. Wainscotting or paneling, was apparently a regular form of high class tip (cf. J. Wagenaar, *Vaderlandsche Historie* [Amsterdam, 1751], V, 104), perhaps because paneling of rooms was just becoming fashionable, and the Dutch merchants would be able to provide the high quality Baltic timber.

[9] A. Jacopszoon, *Prothocolle*, pt. 2, fos. 224–225.

[10] *Ibid.*, fo. 226.     [11] J. Wagenaar, *Vaderlandsche Historie*, V, 104.

These tactics worked. On February 24, 1536, the government dropped the proposed tax and the estates of Holland paid their part of the bargain: 400 pieces of wainscotting each to Nassau and Hoochstraten, 200 each to Berghes and Molembaix, 200 Carolus guilders to Bueren, 100 to Carondelet, and smaller amounts to others.[12] Ruffault did not receive anything. The secretaries, Philip Nigri and Louis Schoere, had voted against the abolition of the tax. Unlike Lord Chancellor Bacon, on a later occasion, they did not feel themselves entitled to a payment for services they had not rendered and declined the proffered gratuity.[13] As a sign of courtesy, the estates of Holland gave them a present of Rhenish wine instead.[14] The system, clearly, had its own standards of morality. But neither did Bacon consider that he had acted corruptly—precisely because he had not let the gifts he had accepted from litigants influence his decisions. He, as most of his contemporaries in official positions, distinguished between gifts and bribes. Since most officials were badly underpaid, they considered the acceptance of gifts morally justifiable; for they were performing a public service, and it seemed just that those whom they served should pay for it. Not unnaturally, these latter found it harder to see the distinction between such a gift and a plain bribe—as, for their own, more questionable reasons, did Bacon's accusers.[15]

If the bourgeois mentality of the estates of Holland looked upon such matters as simple bribery, not everyone agreed with them. The aristocratic and official society of court and government viewed it rather as the natural corollary to the practice of patronage. The two views were, at bottom, irreconcilable, and their divergence is at least one of the reasons for the strained relations between the estates of Holland and their

[12] A. Jacopszoon, *Prothocolle,* pt. 2, fo. 229.

[13] J. Wagenaar, *Vaderlandsche Historie,* V, 106.

[14] A. Jacopszoon, *Prothocolle,* pt. 2, fo. 229.

[15] Cf. J. Hurstfield, *The Queen's Wards* (London, 1958), pp. 182–184, and the whole chapter on "Corruption" which contains an excellent discussion of this problem in Elizabethan England.

governor, the count of Hoochstraten. A year after the dispute
over the export tax these came again into the open, this time
over a question which touched Holland just as nearly as the
corn trade, the freedom of her fishing fleet.

The war with France had broken out again and the French
had invaded Artois. The government, desperate for money to
pay the troops, proposed a general tax on chimneys to the
States-General, in March, 1537.[16] The usual bickering followed
and the estates of Holland demanded the redress of their grievances before voting any tax. The most important of these grievances concerned the fisheries. The admiral, the seigneur de
Beveren, had made an agreement with the French admiral for
the mutual issue of safe-conducts for fishing vessels. He sold
the safe-conducts at the rate of 15 *stuivers* per cod fisherman
and 25 *stuivers* per herring fisherman. This, he proudly
claimed, was his right as admiral which he and his forbears had
enjoyed since 1487.[17] It was the typical view of a public office
and its profits as a private possession to be exploited by the
holder. His claims seemed justified to a court which thought
highly of hereditary aristocratic rights, but they did not equally
impress the Dutch fishermen. The deputies of the estates of
Holland clamored loudly that Beveren had made a private
agreement with the admiral of France to ruin the poor mariners for the sake of these gentlemen's private profit.[18] Relations between ministers and deputies deteriorated rapidly. The
cardinal of Liège swore at the deputies.[19] The queen with
whom they had an audience said: "You are being very difficult," and then, "you are opinionated." [20]

But the deputies stood firm. They would not be commanded
by Beveren or any other admiral, they declared, but only by
their own *stadtholder,* in the name of the emperor. On May

[16] A. Jacopszoon, *Prothocolle,* pt. 2, fos. 293–297.

[17] A. vander Goes, *Register van alle die Dachvaerden by deselve Staten gehouden . . . ,* vol. I (1772), p. 279.

[18] A. Jacopszoon, *Prothocolle,* pt. 2, fos. 303–304.

[19] *Ibid.,* fo. 303.    [20] *Ibid.,* fo. 305.

28, in another audience before the council, they demanded that the queen herself should take over these safe-conducts from France and distribute them freely through a third person. They did not mention their own governor, Hoochstraten, this time, and this omission turned out to be a mistake. On June 1, the *advocat* of Holland again stated his case, so violently that Secretary Nigri said his words came close to rebellion. But the government was now very anxious to have its money and Nigri declared that Beveren would from now on issue safe-conducts without payment. The deputies thereupon agreed to the ordinary grant and, unofficially, to the extraordinary grant.[21]

On June 3, the deputies saw Hoochstraten who promised that Beveren would grant 600 free safe-conducts. The deputies then attempted to excuse the *advocat* for his ill-considered speech two days before. At this, Hoochstraten exploded. They were constantly asking him to plead their interests, he said, but they did not consult him and said things without asking his advice and pleasure. They had given Bueren and his wife a fat gratuity,[22] whereas he, Hoochstraten, had been given nothing, although he had kept the soldiery out of Holland. "I am not as stupid as you take me for," Jacopszoon quotes him as saying. "If some one gives me so much pleasure (pointing to his hand) I will give him that much pleasure (pointing to his forearm). But equally, if some one gives me so much displeasure, I will do the same to him or I will set him back as much (pointing as before). And do you think I keep pigs while others keep lambs?"[23] One of the deputies asked the governor whether he wanted a gratuity; Jacopszoon does not tell us whether ingenuously or ironically. Perhaps Hoochstraten was not certain, either, for all he answered was: "You know what you have to do."[24]

[21] *Ibid.*, fos. 306–307.

[22] Wagenaar mentions 6,000 and 200 Philips guilders, respectively. *Vaderlandsche Historie*, V, 135.

[23] A. Jacopszoon, *Prothocolle*, pt. 2, fos. 309–310.

[24] There is no indication in either Jacopszoon or Aert vander Goes that they did give him anything on that occasion.

Hoochstraten's outburst, for all its naivety, is one of the best contemporary comments both on the working of, and on the state of mind underlying, the whole system of patronage.

In the event, Beveren was most unwilling to relinquish what he regarded as his rights. Towards the end of June, Holland was complaining again that Beveren had said he had received from the admiral of France only 100 safe-conducts, instead of the promised 600, and that he was giving them to the Zealanders.[25] The Hollanders threatened to use the monies they had granted the emperor to equip warships and send them against the French fishing boats, even though these had, in their turn, received safe-conducts from Beveren.[26] The quarrel dragged on and, in 1540, the emperor finally gave the Solomonic judgment that each side should retain its rights.[27]

Relations between the estates of Holland and Hoochstraten continued strained until the latter's death and did not improve with subsequent provincial governors, least of all with the Prince of Orange, in the 1550's. Then, disputes over the prince's claims for tax-exemption for his estates in Holland were added to the perennial quarrels over patronage and the rights and obligations of his office. Only Philip II's political mistakes and the common hatred of the Spanish government brought the two sides, governor and estates, together into an alliance which meant the end of Habsburg rule in the northern Netherlands.

[25] *Ibid.*, fos. 311–312.
[26] A. vander Goes, *Register*, vol. I, pp. 379–382.
[27] *Ibid.*, p. 379, marginal note.

# CHAPTER 7

# The Powers of Deputies
## in Sixteenth-Century Assemblies[1]

HISTORIANS HAVE, for a long time, recognized and discussed the importance of the problem of the powers of the deputies in medieval representative assemblies.[2] Much less, however, is known about this problem in the sixteenth century. Neither in England nor in France did the question become controversial in the sixteenth century, and this may well be the reason for its comparative neglect. The English members of Parliament had, for a long time, enjoyed the exercise of *plena potestas*, the right to take decisions without referring back to their constituents. England had become a political unit earlier than most other European countries. English towns, with the single exception of London, were smaller and politically weaker than the great cities of Italy, Germany, the Netherlands, and Spain. From the fifteenth century onwards, perhaps even earlier, the gentry had increasingly taken over the representation of the towns in Parliament,[3] and in the sixteenth century country gentlemen made up the great majority of the members.[4] While their interests were often local or regional, they represented not so much the borough corporations as the landowning classes.

[1] A shortened version of this paper was read as the author's Inaugural Lecture, at the University of Nottingham, on March 10, 1961.

[2] E.g., G. Post, "Plena Potestas and Consent in Medieval Assemblies," in *Traditio*, Vol. I (New York, 1943), and bibliographical references there.

[3] J. S. Roskell, *The Commons in the Parliament of 1422* (Manchester, 1954), chap. 7.

[4] J. E. Neale, *The Elizabethan House of Commons* (London, 1949), p. 147.

The influence of the great landed families over county and borough elections, and the absence of a clear dividing line between the gentry and the nobility, made for a remarkable homogeneity in the composition and the interests of the House of Commons at least, when compared with Continental assemblies. Where the greatest men of the county were themselves either members of the House of Lords or of the House of Commons or where, through influence and patronage, they could get their relatives, friends, and clients elected, there was clearly every advantage in having full powers. To whom, indeed, could members of Parliament have wanted to refer back when they, or their patrons in the Lords, were themselves their most powerful constituents?

Many of the boroughs, it is true, did not elect residents or even local men, and this tendency to elect outsiders increased in the fifteenth and sixteenth centuries. But this happened mainly in the smaller boroughs which came to prefer members who could serve for reduced wages or for none at all.[5] Since the end of the thirteenth century it had been generally accepted that the members of Parliament represented the community of the shire or the borough, and beyond that the community of the whole realm of England, and that, in consequence, their decisions were binding upon every one.[6] As Sir Thomas Smith put it, in his *De Republica Anglorum,* published in 1583: Parliament "representeth and hath the power of the whole realm both the head and the bodie. For everie Englishman is entended to bee there present, either in person or by procuration and attornies, of what preheminence, state, dignitie, or qualitie soever he be, from the Prince (be he King or Queene) to the lowest person of Englande. And the consent of the Parliament is taken to be everie mans consent."[7] If, by the fifteenth and sixteenth cen-

---

[5] Roskell, *The Commons,* pp. 141 ff.

[6] J. G. Edwards, "The 'Plena Potestas' of English Parliamentary Representatives," in *Oxford Essays in Medieval History Presented to H. E. Salter* (Oxford, 1934), p. 151.

[7] Quoted in *ibid.,* p. 153.

tury, many borough members no longer had much direct connection with the borough they represented, or if, as sometimes happened, the sheriffs returned members without any election at all, then such phenomena were regarded as minor blemishes of an otherwise excellent and well-tried system. The leading families in the counties profited by having more parliamentary seats available. The great boroughs like London or Norwich were not affected. The smaller boroughs which were not prepared to pay the costs of their own representation in Parliament were not likely to put up a fight to restrict the powers of their representatives.

At the same time, it suited the crown to deal with an assembly which could take rapid and binding decisions. Whatever the origins of *plena potestas,* by the sixteenth century only legal pedants were likely to worry whether this principle implied "political and sovereign consent" or "judicial conciliar consent to the decisions of the prince and his high court and council." [8] The question had become one of political and administrative convenience and its constitutional implications were hardly considered. This attitude is very plain in Elizabeth's instructions to the earl of Leicester when she sent him to the Netherlands, in December, 1585. The queen and her advisers knew, of course, that the deputies to the States-General of the United Provinces did not enjoy full powers and had to refer all important matters to their constituents. Obviously, the system was not designed for taking speedy decisions, so necessary in wartime. Leicester was therefore instructed "to deale with the states that, for avoidinge the confusion which soe manie councelles doe breed, they wold make choice of a lesse nomber of wise, discreete and well affected persons, to whom the direction of matters of policie maie be committed and for cutting of the tediousness and delaies in matters of councell, to move them, that the deputies of the severall provinces maie have authoritie to consult and conclude

[8] For this important medieval distinction cf. Post, "Plena Potestas and Consent," pp. 407 ff.

and cutt of the often references to the particular (i.e., provincial) states." [9] The advice was admirable but, as we shall see, remarkably naïve.

It is more difficult to see why in France the question of the powers of deputies to the States-General should not have become a problem in the sixteenth century. The French deputies were not as homogeneous a group as the English members of Parliament. They were sent to the States-General by a bewildering variety of local and provincial authorities and assemblies and by an even more bewildering variety of electoral procedures. Owing to the size of France and to the surviving provincial autonomies the interests of the deputies of the third estate were much more purely and self-consciously local and provincial than those of the members of the House of Commons. Yet, no one seems to have thought, as a matter of principle, that the deputies should not have full powers to discuss and decide the issues which the government wanted to put before them. The deputies received instructions or *cahiers* from the bailiwicks they represented. If the deputies failed to obey these instructions they might find that their salaries were cut or that the bailiwicks disavowed them altogether.

Yet, this did not happen very often. In general, the bailiwicks expected their deputies to present their *cahiers* but otherwise left them wide powers, to discuss and decide the issues which the king put before them, to negotiate with other deputies, and to accept the rule of the majority. One naturally expected one's deputies not to be overenthusiastic about increased taxation. Taxes voted in the States-General would still have to be approved in the provincial assemblies and by the privileged towns. There was thus no need to be unduly concerned about the action of the deputies. Moreover, these deputies, like the English

[9] J. Bruce, *Correspondence of Robert Dudley, Earl of Leycester* (London, 1844), p. 13; quoted also in J. Huges, *Het Leven en Bedrijf van Mr. Franchois Vranck* (The Hague, 1909), p. 45.

members of Parliament, were themselves often enough the leaders of the local and provincial communities.[10] Perhaps even more important was the infrequency of the meetings of the French States-General in the sixteenth century. There was too little chance for the relations between crown and deputies to crystallize around certain recurring problems. Each of the relatively rare assemblies of the States-General was concerned only with the immediate crisis which had led to its summons. The crown made little attempt to build the States-General into its governmental system. Owing to the large number of deputies involved it could not think of wholesale bribery, as the Castilian government could when faced with only 36 deputies of 18 towns. Since the French crown did not seriously threaten the independence of the deputies, their constituents had no need to limit their powers.

The full powers of the French deputies to the States-General were therefore different from those enjoyed by English members of Parliament. They were, in fact, largely a sham. The French deputies could take decisions without referring to their constituents, but they could not legally bind their constituents by their decisions. Not surprisingly, the French crown showed little enthusiasm for regular meetings of the States-General. They were expensive and difficult to manage and, at best, they gave little more than a moral backing to a tax proposal by the government. The particular form of full powers enjoyed by the deputies therefore, did nothing to strengthen the political position of the States-General of France.

The situation was very different in the Habsburg states of Spain and the Netherlands. In both countries the third estate was represented, in Spain in the Cortes and in the Netherlands in the provincial and general estates, by a limited number of towns anxious to defend their autonomy against the encroach-

[10] For this and the preceding points cf. J. Russell Major, *The Deputies to the Estates General in Renaissance France* (Madison, 1960), pp. 5 ff.

ments of the centralized royal administration.[11] In both countries the crown was consistently using the assemblies to obtain financial aid; in both, the third estate which had to foot the bill as consistently tried to whittle down the crown's demands. In consequence, the struggle over taxation between government and assemblies became a permanent feature of the political life of Spain and, even more, of the Netherlands. The Habsburg governments, in their relations with their representative assemblies, were therefore bound to have two tactical objects in view. The first was to ensure that the members of these assemblies should have full powers to discuss and grant the crown's financial demands; the other, arising out of the first, was to have assemblies whose members were open to persuasion. These objects could not always be pursued openly and consistently; but government policy always tended in this direction. Conversely, the towns were bound to pursue diametrically opposed objectives. While they were often willing to grant the government's demands, especially for defense, they usually thought these demands too high and they were most anxious not to grant them too hastily, nor without a *quid pro quo* in the form of the redress of their grievances. For this purpose it was essential that their deputies should be able and willing to say no. Just as in England, the question of the powers of the deputies was therefore eminently one of practical politics; only it had not yet been solved to the satisfaction of all parties, as had happened in England during the Middle Ages.

It was in Castile, the largest of the kingdoms under the Spanish crown, that the problem of the powers of deputies led to the most dramatic developments. Throughout the fifteenth century, the kings of Castile had sought to extend their influence over the Cortes. As early as 1422, they paid the salaries and expenses

[11] Some towns in the States-General, e.g., Malines and Lille-Douai-Orchies, were representing not so much the third estate as whole provinces or sovereign titles of the prince.

of the deputies of the towns. In 1480 four *cuentos* (i.e., million) maravedís were allocated for this purpose.[12] The distribution of this sum was in the hands of some of the deputies; but the government could, and did, interfere by cutting the salaries of those deputies who opposed its policy. The Cortes of 1480 passed an Act of Resumption which enabled the crown to repossess itself of alienated crown domain to an estimated value of 30 million maravedís a year.[13] It meant that 13.5 per cent of this sum had to be cast on the parliamentary waters. But, since the crown obtained for it not a once-for-all tax but a permanent revenue of 30 million, the court felt, no doubt, that this was a good investment. In 1499, and again in 1506, the crown insisted that deputies be granted full powers by their constituents.[14] But the struggles for the Castilian succession, after the death of Isabella the Catholic, in 1504, seriously weakened the position of the crown. The royal position deteriorated further during the eighteen months between the death of Ferdinand of Aragon (January, 1516) and the arrival in Spain of his heir, Charles of Burgundy (the later Charles V). Despite the efforts of the regent, Cardinal Ximénez de Cisnéros, to uphold the power of the government and protect the rights of the crown, Spain became almost unmanageable. All the old feuds between the different Spanish kingdoms, between the towns and the nobles, and between different noble families broke out again and there was growing resentment at the prospect of a foreign succession. Castilian temper did not improve at the sight of their new king, an ungainly and inexperienced youth who did not speak Spanish and seemed to be surrounded by Burgundian advisers. Sober Castilian *caballeros* resented Charles's Burgundian court and the much-exaggerated plunder of his Flemish favorites and Spanish hangers-on. The Cortes of Valladolid, in February,

[12] There were 375 *maravedís* to the ducat.

[13] R. B. Merriman, *The Rise of the Spanish Empire* (New York, 1918), II, 106.

[14] J. Bernays, "Zur inneren Entwicklung Castiliens unter Karl V," in *Deutsche Zeitschrift für Geschichtswissenschaft* (Freiburg, 1899), I, 382 ff.

1518, paid him homage and gave him a *servicio* of 600,000 ducats, payable over three years. But they also presented far-reaching demands and were outspoken in their counsel and criticism.[15]

Charles spent the next two years in Aragon and Catalonia, and his renewed absence added to the distrust and resentment felt in Castile. In the late summer of 1519 news reached Spain that he had been elected emperor. He would have to go to Germany, as soon as possible, and he would need money. There was no question of getting it from Aragon and Catalonia. In their Cortes, the principle of redress of grivances before supply was firmly established. Hence, as the shocked Venetian ambassador, Contarini, reported, "every cobbler, blacksmith, or similar person had the right to hold up everything until he was satisfied." [16] It had already taken much longer than in Castile to get even the coronation grants from Aragon and Catalonia. In any case, these kingdoms were small and poor. The money would have to come from Castile.

It was obvious to the court that, with the country in such a hostile temper, this was not going to be easy. The 1518 grant had not yet expired, and the king had promised not to ask for another one until it did. He could plead necessity, but there had been no time to prepare public opinion about the imperial election. Many traditionalists in Castile—and most Castilians were traditionalists—resented their king's chasing after foreign titles and feared that it would lead to long absences and neglect of their country. More than ever it was necessary to have a friendly Cortes, able to take quick decisions.

Charles's chief advisers, the Netherlander Guillaume de Croy, lord of Chièvres, and the Piedmontese Mercurino di Gattinara, were experienced and astute politicians. The tactics they now adopted were brilliant. Their only mistake was to misjudge the

---

[15] Cf. my chapter "The Empire of Charles V in Europe," in *New Cambridge Modern History* (Cambridge, 1958), II, 304 f.

[16] E. Albèri, *Relazioni degli Ambasciatori Veneti al Senato durante il secolo decimosesto* (Florence, 1840), ser. 1, II, 30.

length to which the opposition would be willing to go. This mistake nearly cost Charles his throne.

On February 12, 1520, Charles V summoned each of the 18 cities who were traditionally represented in the Cortes, to send their customary two deputies to the Galician town of Santiago. The town councils were to elect these deputies according to custom and give them full powers to decide matters for the service of God and the king.[17] To make certain that all the towns observed this command, a model formula of the powers to be granted was enclosed. The town councils were to oblige themselves "to keep, maintain, fulfill *and pay*, and to hold firm, acceptable, stable, and valid, for now and for ever afterwards, as if we ourselves (i.e., the town councils) had done and granted it supposing we ourselves had been present," everything their *procuradores* might decide.[18]

Neither in the summons nor in the model of powers to be granted to the *procuradores*, i.e., the deputies, was there any mention of precedents for this royal requirement of a *plena potestas* for the deputies. Perhaps there were too many recent precedents the other way. On March 11, the royal judge in Burgos (*juez de residencia*) wrote to Charles that the town council would have granted all his financial demands, but that they had not willingly given free powers to grant what His Majesty might demand, for they knew that the deputies obtained favors (*mercedes*), a percentage from the grant given by the kingdom. At the time of the Catholic Queen, he continued, full powers for deputies had been introduced; but they had caused disputes in the Cortes which had to be remedied by instructions limiting these powers. If full powers were now reintroduced, they would be perpetual, they would take away the power of the kingdom, and they would be much resented. "If Your Majesty wants this," he concluded, "there would, in the end, be no one who would

[17] *Cortes de los Antiguos Reinos de Leon y Castilla* (Madrid, 1882), IV, 285 ff.

[18] *Ibid.*, p. 289; my italics.

ever dare to contradict you, for Your Majesty is such a great and so feared a prince." [19]

If this was the attitude of Burgos with its rich wool merchants, who were the class who most immediately benefited by the Flemish connection of their royal house, the attitude of Toledo and most other towns, with no such special interests, was likely to be openly hostile. Peter Martyr, the shrewd Italian humanist who knew Spain well, warned Gattinara, on March 1, 1520; "Everywhere there is nothing but maledictions; people protest that to call the Cortes in Santiago, empowered only to obey the king's command, is to filch their freedom and to order what one orders from a chattel slave." Even in Burgos, he pointed out, the *regidors* of the council had been bribed by the Burgalese bishop Mota, of Badajoz, "in order to flatter the emperor and the goat (i.e., Chièvres)." [20] Martyr at least had no doubt that full powers for the deputies implied the previous consent of their constituents to everything the king might demand.

In the towns, the feuds and faction fights were becoming increasingly bitter. Their origins had often been private and local. Now they merged with the quarrels between the royalist and antiroyalist parties. When the Cortes assembled in Santiago, on March 31, Castile was already on the edge of revolt. Only the towns dominated by the royalists, Burgos, Seville, and Granada, had given their *procuradores* what the government had demanded: *carte blanche*.[21] The Salamanca deputies were rejected because their credentials were considered defective. Toledo was not represented because the lot had fallen on royalist councillors to represent the city, and they had refused to accept the restrictions which the majority of the town council had insisted on imposing on their powers.[22] Toledo, moreover, had previously sent

[19] D. Danvila, *Historia crítica y documentada de las comunidades de Castilla* (Madrid, 1897), I, 310. Also quoted in H. L. Seaver, *The Great Revolt in Castile* (London, 1929), pp. 70 f.

[20] Seaver, *The Great Revolt*, pp. 64 f.    [21] *Ibid.*, p. 71.

[22] *Ibid.*, p. 74.

a deputation to court, to present to Charles the grievances of the kingdom caused by his proposed departure to Germany. This deputation, together with the rejected Salamancans, now registered a formal protest against the validity of any acts in the Cortes in which their cities were not represented. Chièvres countered this threat by promptly exiling the Toledans to their fiefs in remote parts of Spain.[23]

On April 1 it became clear how little support the government had in the Cortes. Only Burgos, Granada, and Seville accepted Gattinaras' tax proposals. Avila asked for further discussion. Valladolid, Jaén, Murcia, Toro, Segovia, Zamora, Guadalajara, Soria, Cuenca, and Madrid, all, more or less emphatically, supported the proposals of León and Córdova, that the towns' petitions must be considered before the government proposals.[24] It was the classic gambit of insisting on redress of grievances before supply. But it was precisely such a situation that Chièvres and Gattinara had envisaged when they had insisted on full powers for the deputies. Before the session had opened, they had sought to isolate the *procuradores* even further by requiring them to take an oath of secrecy about all proceedings in the Cortes. Already on the afternoon of April 1 some of the opposition deputies began to waver. Over Easter, Gattinara adjourned the Cortes to Coruña where the court was already embarking. By April 22 he had induced Avila, Cuenca, Guadalajara, Segovia, and Soria to join with the original three, Burgos, Granada, and Seville, in supporting the proposed taxes. The deputies of Jaén, Murcia, and Madrid were divided and did not vote.[25]

Gattinara had achieved this success simply enough. Granada and Seville were granted considerable sums in tax relief, and at least ten of the deputies obtained sums varying from 100 to 600 ducats each, as well as offices and honors. The money for these bribes was to come from the new *servicio* which they had voted.[26] For those *procuradores* who still felt scruples about the undertakings they had given to their home towns, there was a

[23] *Ibid.*, p. 69.    [24] *Ibid.*, p. 75.    [25] *Ibid.*, pp. 76 ff.
[26] *Ibid.*, pp. 80 ff.

royal writ which, on the basis of "the absolute royal power," annulled all such undertakings and pledges.[27]

It was a most dramatic and sinister demonstration of the way in which the crown could exploit the *plena potestas* of both unscrupulous and weak deputies. But, in the peculiar circumstances of 1520, it was not successful. Gattinara had blatantly overplayed his hand and had still failed to take enough tricks to win the game. The deputies of León, Córdova, Zamora, Toro, and Valladolid had maintained their opposition, even if somewhat ambiguously in the case of Valladolid whose deputies were among those bribed by the court. Jaén, Madrid, and Murcia remained divided.[28] It had to be assumed that Toledo and Salamanca would remain hostile. As Charles's fleet weighed anchor, on May 20, 1520, the revolution in Castile had already begun.

No one in Spain, not even Charles's own council, thought that the new taxes were legal or that they could be collected. Riots broke out in Toledo, Madrid, Zamora, Segovia, Cuenca, and even in Burgos, and popular juntas took over the government of the cities. Mobs burned the houses of the deputies who had voted for the new taxes. If they did not yet know the details of the bribes, no doubt they guessed at them, as indeed everyone did. One of the Segovia deputies was rash enough to face the crowd. They dragged him out of the city and hanged him by his feet.

The royal attack on the independence of the Cortes had sparked off the revolt; but the leaders of the *comunero* movement did not try to set up parliamentary government in Castile. In the *capitulos* they sent to Charles V, on October 20, 1520, they demanded that the new *servicio* should not be collected; that in any future Cortes the king should not send the cities orders about the powers of their deputies, and that the cities themselves should pay their own deputies; that the deputies should not receive any grant or favor (*merced*) for themselves or their relatives, on pain of death and confiscation of their property—if the king granted this, it would be something of a moral

[27] *Ibid.*, p. 76.     [28] *Ibid.*, pp. 76 ff.

justification for the mob violence against the Coruña deputies—and that, finally, the cities should have the right, on their own initiative, to assemble the Cortes every three years, freely to discuss all matters relating to the benefit of the crown and the kingdom.[29]

Some of these demands, especially the right of free assembly, went beyond anything that the towns had previously enjoyed or that the crown had ever acknowledged. But they were essentially conservative and defensive at least in intention.* The *comuneros* did not even propose an extension of the representation in Cortes beyond that of the privileged 18 towns. The question of popular sovereignty, or even of the sovereignty of the communes, did not arise and was not discussed. On the contrary. They demanded that the king, "from his absolute royal power and having no earthly superior," should consent to their *capitulos* as perpetual laws of the kingdom, nor should he ask the pope to release him from his oath. The subjects, in good Spanish tradition, reserved for themselves the right of resistance if the king should revoke these laws.[30]

The demands and arguments thus remained on a traditional and on a severely practical plane. The actions of the movement, however, were openly revolutionary. They had to be, if even the most conservative part of the *comunero* program was to be achieved. The rebellious towns, led by Toledo, formed a league and set up a *junta* that was in effect a revolutionary government. The royal forces were quite inadequate to resist the movement. Most of the Castilian nobility had not forgiven the king his Flemish councilors and their alleged plunder. They felt affronted by the appointment of a foreigner, Adrian of Utrecht, as regent. Even the appointment, as co-regents, of the admiral

[29] The *capitulos* are printed in A. de Santa Cruz, *Crónica del Emperador Carlos V* (Madrid, 1920), I, 297–328.

* Since this was written, J. A. Maravall, *Las Comunidades de Castilla* (Madrid, 1963), has convincingly shown that the *comuneros* were much more revolutionary than I had thought.

[30] A. de Santa Cruz, *Crónica,* pp. 327 f.

and the constable of Castile, did not immediately persuade them to help the king. But in the winter of 1520–21 radical and popular elements in the towns were more and more gaining the upper hand. They spread the revolt to the estates of the nobility and, for the first time, the nobles felt alarmed. Their old antagonism against the towns flared up again. In the towns one after another of the moderate leaders of the *comunero* movement deserted to the royalists. A respectable movement in defence of the liberties of the towns and the Cortes was turning into a social revolution, and the urban nobility would have nothing more to do with it. In the spring of 1521, the nobles raised an army of their own and routed the *comunero* forces at Villalar (April 23, 1521). Valladolid and the other towns of northern Castile immediately submitted to the king; only Toledo, the prime mover of the revolt, held out until October, 1521.

The defeat of the *comunero* movement in 1521 was, inevitably, also a defeat for the Cortes. The crown did not have to enunciate any new principles. The towns had lost the ability and the will to resist. Their deputies now had to present their full powers, and deputies' salaries were to be paid from the taxes they voted. In the Cortes of Toledo, in 1525, Alonso de Céspedes, *procurador* of Seville, protested; but his was a protest only about the division of the four *cuentos* of maravedís voted for the salaries. The deputies had no power to divide this sum, he argued, for no one could grant anything to himself. But his colleague from Seville dissociated himself from this view. He had no instructions to the contrary, he said, and he saw no reason to refuse a *merced* granted by the king. The deputies of the other towns rounded on Céspedes. The grant of the four *cuentos* was an old practice, they said, and many of the *procuradores* were either not paid at all by their cities or not paid sufficiently to meet the heavy expenses of their journey. Céspedes himself received four ducats a day from Seville, more than they would get from the division of the four million maravedís.[31] And so

[31] British Museum, MS, Add. 9930, *Colección de Cortes*, XVI, fos. 245–247, 18th century copy. At 375 *maravedís* to the ducat, the 4 *cuentos*, or

the matter went through. But even in this debate it was not taken for granted that the deputies necessarily had full powers. The immediate argument was clinched less by an appeal to principle than by a smear on the man who had raised the matter.

Full powers did not prevent the deputies from receiving instructions from their constituents: the grievances, protests, and proposals on all matters, financial, economic, political, and religious, which they presented at every meeting of the Cortes. But the crown usually refused attempts to revive the principle of redress of grievances before supply, and it granted or refused petitions as it saw fit. Even if the government did accept the petitions first, as it did in 1525 in order to get a quick vote on the taxes, it no longer made any difference. The government simply did not act on the petitions it had allowed. The next Cortes, in 1528, then started with a demand for the execution of accepted petitions. The government simply ignored this demand, like the petitions themselves.[32] The steep rate of increase in parliamentary taxation in Castile during the sixteenth century is a measure of the crown's success in its efforts to make the Cortes into a pliable instrument of its own will.[33]

It may be that Chièvres was one of those conservatives—the duke of Alva was certainly another—who approved of a degree of autocracy for the government of a foreign country which he would not have tolerated in his own. At any rate, he never tried the gambit of demanding full powers for delegates in the Netherlands assemblies. If in the Netherlands the problem never took as dramatic a turn as it did in Castile in 1520, it played just

---

4,000,000 came to 10,666⅔ ducats. Hence, if the division had been an equal one, which was not necessarily the case, each of the 36 deputies would have got 296.3 ducats. If the deputies claimed that this was less than 4 ducats a day, the Cortes and the journeys to and from its meeting place would have had to last more than 74 days.

[32] Bernays, "Zur inneren Entwicklung Castiliens," p. 387.

[33] Koenigsberger, "The Empire of Charles V," in *New Cambridge Modern History*, II, 320 ff.

as important a role in the parliamentary politics of that country.[34]

In the Netherlands it was firmly established that the representatives of the towns (who were the ones most immediately touched by proposed taxes) would generally have powers only to listen to government proposals and then report back to their constituents, usually their town councils. They then returned to the assembly with further instructions. But this was rarely the end of the matter. The instructions, even of the deputies of any one province, were not always similar. In almost every assembly some would grant less than the government had asked for. Then those who had already agreed to the full demand withdrew their assent because they had been instructed to agree only if all other members agreed. There followed then a period of negotiations and haggling, and, frequently, the deputies were sent home a second or even third time to obtain further instructions.

For the government the system was a great waste of time and of nervous energy. From the fifteenth century onwards, exasperated ministers therefore tried to induce towns and provincial assemblies to grant their representatives full power, at least for decisions on specific government proposals.[35] Sometimes, the initiative came from the provinces themselves. Thus, in the States-General of Brussels, in March, 1537, Tournai demanded that all deputies should come with full powers.[36] Tournai was at that time threatened by a French invasion and was therefore anxious for the government to obtain rapid help from the other provinces. But, until the beginning of Philip II's reign, Netherlands governments never seriously attacked the problem as one of principle. The case of Mons is a good example.

At Brussels, in December, 1514, the emperor Maximilian I, guardian of the young archduke Charles (later Charles V), asked

[34] For the origin and structure of the States-General cf. Chapter 4.
[35] *Ibid.*

[36] A. Jacopszoon, *Prothocolle van alle de Reysen . . . gedaen zedert ick de Stede van Aemstelredamme gedient heb gehadt . . . ,* MS. in Amsterdam City Archives, transcript by E. van Bienna, pt. 2, fo. 295.

the States-General for an *aide* of 500,000 florins, besides another
100,000 for the dowry of the archduchess Isabella, and also the
expenses for a guard of 500 men-at-arms for Charles. Maximilian had never been known for the modesty of his financial demands, but the Netherlanders had, from long experience,
learned how to handle him. The high nobility, led by Chièvres,
were anxious to obtain Maximilian's consent for declaring
Charles of age and thus bring to an end the regency of Charles's
aunt, Margaret of Austria. They were powerful in the estates of
Brabant, and it seems not unlikely that it was their influence
which induced the deputies of Brabant to propose that, since
the emperor would have to be paid something, the States-General
should agree immediately to grant him 100,000 florins. From
previous experience they knew that Maximilian would be content to take what he could get. The Brabant proposal was accepted by the deputies of the other provinces, apparently without reference back to their constituents.[37] But the town council
of Mons in Hainault decided that there was no precedent for
such a decision and refused to be bound by it.[38] The governor
of Hainault then tried to arrange the matter amicably, promising remission of certain duties to Mons; but he also threatened
that Charles, the nobles, and the ducal council would not suffer
the town council's arrogance if they persisted in their refusal.[39]
On January 13, 1515 the town council of Mons was still discussing the matter when a government bailiff appeared and demanded immediate payment of Mons's share of the 100,000
florins. The councilors protested and tried to stall him, but the
next day he ordered ten of them to remain in the town hall
until the city's share of 2,000 fl. had been paid.[40] The Mons
deputies in Brussels then talked to Chièvres who promised to

[37] Report by the deputies of Mons, Dec. 11, 1514. Brussels Archives
Générales du Royaume, transcript from Archives Communales de Mons,
Reg. 5, fo. 141.

[38] Decision of the council, Dec. 30, 1514. *Ibid.,* fo. 144.

[39] The deputies to the council of Mons, Jan. 1, 1515. *Ibid.,* fo. 145.

[40] *Ibid.,* fo. 148.

smooth the matter over if Mons paid 1,000 fl. immediately and the rest as part of the *aide* they would grant to Charles on his first state visit to Hainault. After some hesitation Mons agreed to this proposal, specifying, however, that the 1,000 fl. were to be regarded as a pure gift.[41]

At no time during this dispute did the government insist on the a priori binding force of the vote of the deputies in the States-General. They only argued that Mons should accept the vote as a loyal city, since none of the other towns, whether in Hainault or in the other provinces, had made difficulties. They put pressure on Mons over the actual payment, but not over the question of principle: the right to contract out of a grant which they had not empowered their deputies to vote for.

Successive Netherlands governments were not at all certain, in fact, that they wanted the deputies to have full powers. The advantages were obvious, but there were also disadvantages. If one of the important delegations, Flanders or Brabant, for instance, opposed a grant, it might well persuade others to do the same.[42] Mary of Hungary, Charles V's sister and governor general from 1531 to 1555, was particularly anxious to avoid joint discussions, for, as she wrote to Charles, "there are always those who will put it into other people's heads that promises made to them in the past have not been kept."[43] The revolt of Ghent in 1539—essentially a taxpaying strike—showed the danger of such influence. In 1540, Charles V therefore ordered that henceforth three of the four "members" of Flanders (Ghent, Bruges, Ypres, and the group of small West Flemish towns called the *Franc* of Bruges) could overrule the fourth. This ordinance, however, left out of account the other small towns and *châtellenies* in Flanders who traditionally had a right to be consulted about taxation even though, in practice, they generally voted with the big towns. Just because of this, it might well work to the detriment of the government if they were not consulted; it was never

---

[41] *Ibid.*, fos. 148–152.     [42] For examples cf. Chapter 4.

[43] Mary to Charles, Jan. 4, 1536. Brussels Arch. Gén. du Roy., *Papiers d'Etat*, 49, fo. 4.

with them that resistance to government proposals originated. In 1542, Mary therefore ordered that the representatives of the small towns and *châtellenies* were not to consult with those of Ghent, but only to listen to the government proposals, report home, and then bring their answers. As the eighteenth-century writer Zaman pointed out, this made a joint agreement on a government proposal virtually impossible and, in practice, left the four "members" of Flanders with even greater powers than before, since they had to draw up the agreement on the government proposals.[44] If one imagined the English House of Commons no longer allowed to debate, Zaman argued, and the rank and file members, after once stating their opinion, leaving the act to be drafted by the M.P.'s for London, Bristol, Cambridge, and Wales, then the representatives of these four would soon have complete control over the House. In just such a way, he claimed, the four "members" of Flanders were able to impose themselves on the small towns.[45] Zaman was wrong in thinking that the preponderance of the four "members" of Flanders in matters of taxation dated from the ordinance of 1542. It had effectively existed much earlier. But the ordinance clinched it, and Zaman was correct in his appreciation of the dilemma in which the Netherlands government found itself in the question of the powers of deputies.

In practice, the deputies had to be allowed a certain degree of initiative, for otherwise no agreement could ever have been reached at all. The deputies of the smaller provinces were often specifically instructed to vote with the majority or to discuss a common policy with the deputies of Flanders and Brabant.[46] As long as money was not involved, the patricians who dominated the town councils were generous over the powers they granted their deputies.[47]

[44] P. de Zaman, *Exposition des Trois Etats du Pais et Comté de Flandre* (Ghent, 1711), pp. 217 ff.

[45] *Ibid.*, p. 224.     [46] Cf. Chapter 4.

[47] L. Wils, "De Werking van de Staten van Brabant, omstreeks 1550–1650," in *Anciens Pays et Assemblées d'Etats* (Louvain, 1953), V, 11 ff.

Underlying the problem of the powers of the deputies was the subjects' fundamental distrust of their government's intentions. After a particularly bitter debate on defense expenditure in the assembly of the estates of Holland, in November, 1523, the deputies of Leiden said bluntly that those who brought reports of government promises were liars. "This was as much as to say that princes are liars, promising much and doing nothing," the secretary of Amsterdam, Andries Jacopszoon, noted in his diary. Jacopszoon does not sound as if he was shocked by such a sentiment.[48] There were obvious objections to being represented by some one who held a government office. Albert de Loo, the advocate of Holland, was also an imperial councilor and the estates tried to have him dismissed "since he has to keep his oath both to the emperor and to the estates, and often he has to speak against the emperor and does so with fear." [49] Sir Roger Owen, M.P. in 1614, made the same point when he said: "King's livery hindereth their sight" (*Journal of the House of Commons,* I, p. 456).

Even where no divided loyalties were involved, it took a great deal of courage for a deputy to stand up to the government. For what was a burgomaster or secretary of a Dutch town, compared with the great lords and councilors at the court in Brussels? He was not even a gentleman, as most of the members of the English House of Commons were, after the gentry had taken over the majority of the borough seats. In 1530, the representatives of Amsterdam, the burgomasters Boelenszoon and Banninck, had to tell the governor of Holland, the count of Hoochstraten, that there was little chance of meeting his tax proposals unless the government upheld Amsterdam's privilege of free grain export. The governor flew into a rage and threatened to flatten Boelenszoon and Banninck like dogs.[50] This outburst was neither his first nor his last. A choleric old gentleman, he had little understanding of economic matters—a serious handicap,

[48] Jacopszoon, *Prothocolle,* pt. 1, fo. 59.
[49] Jan. 22, 1523. *Ibid.,* fo. 4.
[50] Feb. 11, 1530. *Ibid.,* fos. 127 f.

this, for a governor of a commercial province. His relations with Banninck were particularly bad. "I shall be governor when you are no longer Banninck," Jacopszoon reports him as sputtering, when what he meant to say was "when you are no longer burgomaster." The matter was serious, however, for there was a good deal of aristocratic solidarity against the pretensions of commoners. The counts of Nassau and Bueren, and the lord of Brederode were heard to remark that they would not have suffered a man like Banninck in one of their own towns. Master Vincent, one of the councilors, had to intervene for the burgomaster and make his peace with the lords.[51]

Banninck and the other bourgeois deputies would have been in an intolerable position if they had had to speak only for themselves. In the circumstances, they could plead their instructions and stand firm in the knowledge that the government would not lightly offend a powerful city, however much individual ministers might personally detest its representatives. The aldermen and burgomasters in the town councils found it easier, for their part, to be brave among friends and within the familiar walls of their own town halls than in the daunting presence of the governor general and her court. Although the same deputies were often sent to the provincial and general assemblies, there was too much jealousy between town and town, and between province and province, for a strong enough feeling of solidarity to grow among the deputies which would give them the sense of protection which the growth of such a feeling gave to the members of the English Parliament.

The restrictions which the estates imposed on the powers of their deputies were a very useful weapon in the defense of local and provincial privileges and in the struggle to keep down the rate of taxation. But would these restrictions still be useful when the estates themselves became responsible for the government of the country? When in the summer of 1576, after the collapse of Spanish authority in the Netherlands, the States-Gen-

[51] June 5–7, 1535. *Ibid.*, fos. 209 f.

eral found itself in this position, nobody had as yet thought about this question. Holland and Zealand had been in a state of rebellion since 1572, and the Spaniards had failed to subdue them. When Philip II's governor general died, in March, 1576, the unpaid Spanish regiments mutinied. Effective government ceased almost completely. The estates of Brabant began to raise troops of their own and on September 4, 1576, these troops arrested the Spaniards and their sympathizers in the Council of State. The estates of Brabant then summoned the States-General to meet in Brussels.

The States-General was confronted with the urgent task of concluding peace with the rebellious provinces of Holland and Zealand and with protecting the country from the mutinous Spanish soldiers and getting them out of the country. It was necessary to raise troops and therefore to impose taxes and collect money.

In Brussels, the purged Council of State and many of the deputies quickly appreciated the constitutional implications of these problems. Brabant and Hainault were the first provinces to grant their deputies full powers. On September 30, 1576 they sent the seigneur de Courteville to the estates of Flanders with the request that the Flemish deputies be given sufficient powers.[52] Flanders, like Brabant, was threatened by the Spanish soldiery and seems to have quickly complied with the request. In the other provinces, the old suspicions and habits of thought were not so easily discarded. When the deputies of Namur, Artois, Lille-Douai-Orchies, Malines, Utrecht, Tournai, and Valenciennes presented their powers, they were found insufficient.[53] Throughout October, 1576, the Council of State and the States-General as a whole both negotiated with these provinces to persuade them to give their deputies sufficient powers at least for the conclusion of the Pacification of Ghent, i.e., the peace with Holland and Zealand. In the end, most of them agreed,

---

[52] N. Japikse, *Resolutiën der Staten-Generaal van 1576 tot 1609* (The Hague, 1915), I, 9, n. 1.
[53] *Ibid.*, pp. 9 ff.

often after heated discussion. But many, like Artois, would grant full powers only for the political questions of the Pacification and the expulsion of the Spaniards. On financial matters they would not budge: their deputies would have to refer back all tax proposals.[54]

It was not long before the Council of State and the States-General found themselves haggling with the separate provinces almost as the governor generals had done before the revolt.[55] Don John of Austria, the new governor general, did his best to discredit the States-General by assuring the provinces that he had nothing to do with the new taxes which were the work of the ambitious politicians in Brussels. He, the king's legitimate representative, only wanted to restore the old privileges.[56] When, in March, 1577, the States-General made regulations for its own procedure, with the avowed purpose of speeding up its business, the question of the powers of the deputies was not even mentioned.[57] The provinces had rebelled against Spain to preserve their liberties. Yet, to carry on the war against Spain they needed a representative assembly able to take effective decisions and this meant giving up some of the very liberties for which they were fighting. The southern provinces never fully resolved this dilemma. As the prince of Orange said, in 1579, the deputies at the States-General were not councilors gathered together to discuss the common weal, but advocates of their own provinces and towns, whose interests they tried to further even if that meant the ruin of the other provinces.[58] In this respect, the Union of Arras (the union of the southern, Catholic provinces which returned to their old allegiance to Philip II) was a reaction against the attempt to introduce full powers for the

[54] C. Hirschauer, *Les Etats d'Artois de leurs origines à l'occupation française* (Paris-Brussels, 1923), I, 257.

[55] Japikse, *Resolutiën*, I, pp. 120 ff.

[56] Hirschauer, *Les Etats d'Artois*, I, pp. 259 ff.

[57] L. P. Gachard, *Actes des Etats Généraux des Pays-Bas, 1575–1585* (Brussels, 1861), I, 440.

[58] R. Fruin, *Geschiedenis der Staatsinstellingen in Nederland*, H. T. Colenbrander, ed. (The Hague, 1922), p. 183.

deputies of the States-General at the expense of the powers of
the towns and provinces. In this respect, too, Don John of Austria and his successor, the duke of Parma, were right when they
claimed that they wanted to restore the old privileges. When
Secretary de Moy, of Antwerp, wrote a treatise on the States-
General and the estates of Brabant, about 1595, he described
the powers of the deputies exactly as they had been before the
revolt.[59] But, by that time, these privileges had become almost
irrelevant. The States-General of the southern provinces could
do little more than fight ineffective rearguard actions against
the financial demands of a now all-powerful government.

In Holland and Zealand the problem of the powers of deputies and of effective government by an assembly of estates had
arisen already in 1572 when the cities of these provinces had
opened their gates to the Sea Beggars. In September, 1573, the
representatives of the nobles and towns of Holland began to
discuss the problem formally and, on February 1, 1574, they
passed a resolution on their own constitution. The deputies
were to take an oath that, in all matters concerning the welfare
of the country, they were to "advise and decide in such a way as,
according to their reason and right conscience, they should find
for the general weal, without affection, favor or disfavor, to particular towns or persons." Decisions were to be taken by majority vote, except that no one was to be forced to consent to taxes
or contributions against his will. In case of disagreement, the
prince of Orange, as governor of the province, and members of
the Council of Holland whom he deputed for the purpose were
to arbitrate.[60]

Clearly, this ordinance was open to conflicting interpreta-

---

[59] H. de Moy, *Tractaet van Beden by den hertogen van Brabant gedaen
aen Staten General oft van Brabant* . . . , Antwerp, City Archives, MS,
fo. 5, 18th century copy.

[60] P. Bor, *Oorspronck, begin ende vervolgh der Nederlantsche Oorlogen*
(Amsterdam, 1621), Vol. I, Bk 7, fo. 7. Partly quoted in S. van Slingelandt,
*Staatkundige Geschriften* (Amsterdam, 1784), I, 108 f.

tions. It did not attempt to define the powers of deputies, except in financial matters. But, if it did not specifically endow deputies with powers beyond those given them by their constituents, it could be, and was in fact, interpreted as doing this. Orange managed to make the system work, because of his position as governor of the provinces and, more importantly, because he was generally trusted. In the Articles of Union which Holland, Zealand, and West-Friesland concluded in 1575, at least one difficult point was cleared up when the provinces agreed that resolutions taken by the estates in common should have binding force, and that if any one of the allies refused to be bound by them, he should be compelled to do so by the others.[61] Even so, the insistence of the towns on withholding from their deputies full powers in financial matters still led to much friction with the prince. In practice, it was the prince's skill in handling the estates which overcame the inherent difficulties of the system. Thomas Wilkes, Leicester's representative in The Hague in 1587, has left us an account of William's methods: "He always entertained some five or six of the most credit; the needy ones with pensions, the rest with presents, and all with calling them to his table and society. Through these he wrought upon the rest, and there was nothing handled in their assemblies but he knew of it beforehand." When he had anything to propose, he always consulted with these persons "whether the matter would pass or be impugned." He knew the arguments that would be brought against his propositions and came "armed with the answers and counter-reasons to the wonderful admiration of all, and so prevailed." [62]

Perhaps those who told Wilkes about Orange's methods deliberately exaggerated his political virtuosity and its effective-

[61] "Articulen van Verbondt tusschen de Landen ende Steden, onder gehoorsaemheydt des Princen van Orange, als Stadthouder ende Capiteyn Generael over Hollandt, Zeelandt end West-Vrieslant . . . ," para. 9. *Holland Staten Resolutien 1575*, p. 246.

[62] Wilkes to Elizabeth I, July 12, 1587. *Calendar of State Papers, Foreign* (London, 1929), XXI, pt. 3, April–Dec., 1587, p. 164.

ness, calculating, quite correctly, that when Wilkes wrote to the queen, he would point the contrast with Leicester's political ineptitude and advise her to emulate the prince. The Dutch certainly did not fail to give Leicester his chance, though it was not entirely Leicester's fault that he failed to take it.

The assassination of Orange, in Delft on July 10, 1584, had shocked the States-General and, more especially, the estates of Holland, into an immediate reappraisal of the constitutional problem. The States-General was in session in Delft on that very day and immediately wrote to the members of the Union of Utrecht, requesting them to despatch deputies with full powers to take decisions on the government of the country.[63] The estates of Holland and Zealand wrote in the same sense to Utrecht inviting its deputies to a separate meeting of representatives of the three provinces. In Utrecht, however, anti-Holland feeling was strong. On July 15 the estates of Utrecht instructed their deputies at The Hague that they should object to absolute powers for deputies in the negotiations about the confirmation of the Union of Utrecht. The estates of Utrecht did not think it suitable, in the prevailing circumstances and in such an important matter, to give anyone absolute power to decide on the government of the country, so ran the instructions. "Not only was this not suitable for the estates, but in the aforesaid country (of Utrecht) nobody could be found of sufficient intelligence to be allowed to exercise such absolute powers." The deputies should only consult with those of Holland and Zealand and with those of the neighboring provinces, and then refer their proposals back to their own estates.[64]

Nevertheless, there was general agreement to continue the Union of Utrecht, i.e., the union of all provinces which had ab-

[63] J. Huizinga, "De Vergadering der Staten-Generaal op 10 Juli 1584 na den noen," in *Bijdragen voor Vaderlandsche Geschiedenis en Oudheidkunde* (The Hague, 1907), ser. 4, VI, 368.

[64] July 15, 1584 (o.s.), "Instructie voor den edelen . . . Meester Floris Heermade. . . . M. L. van Deventer, *Gedenkstukken van Johan van Oldenbarnevelt*, (The Hague, 1860), I, 50 ff.

jured their allegiance to Philip II. Holland, Zealand, and
Utrecht still had their separate assembly and a common council,
and the States-General as a whole appears to have been willing
to accept the leadership of this group of provinces. After heated
debates, the States-General on August 18, 1584, accepted the
*acte van vereeninge,* the act of union by which the Union of
Utrecht was formally confirmed and a new council of state was
created as the highest executive organ of the Union. Orange's
son, the young Maurice of Nassau, was invited to become the
first councilor.[65]

The central government of the Union of Utrecht was now at
least formally stronger than it had ever been before. During the
debates of the provincial estates and of the States-General, in
July and August of 1584, most of the deputies had enjoyed full
powers. Otherwise they would not have been able to resolve so
quickly the political and constitutional crisis caused by the
death of the prince of Orange. But no one had suggested that
the deputies should enjoy such powers permanently. Very soon
the estates of Holland even showed themselves unwilling to
abide by their own resolutions of 1574 and 1575: that majority
votes were to be binding in all matters except taxation.

They debated the problem in February and March of 1585. It
was agreed that deputies should always present their instructions and powers. They were to swear to uphold all privileges,
laws, and customs of the country, "in so far as these should not
be prejudicial to the privileges and laws of individual towns."
They were "to help to further all matters concerning the whole
country . . . and decide as they were instructed by their principals (i.e., their constituents) and, moreover, to serve in all matters according to their reason and conscience for the common
welfare." They were also to keep all discussions secret—except
from their principals.[66]

This masterpiece of constitutional obscurity proved emi-

[65] L. Delfos, "Die Anfänge der Utrechter Union 1577–1587," in *His-
torische Studien* (Berlin, 1941), Heft 375, pp. 260 ff.

[66] *Holland Staten Resolutien 1585,* pp. 110 ff.

nently acceptable to all parties. It tilted back the balance of power in favor of the town councils; but it still left a good deal of elbow-room for skillful politicians, like Oldenbarnevelt, whose influence was strong both in their own town council and in the assembly. It proved, however, much more difficult to come to an agreement on the question of majority votes. Up to this time, no member of the estates could be forced to accept majority decisions in financial matters. This immunity was now extended to cover religious and constitutional matters and questions of war and peace, "and similar important matters concerning the state of the country." But if in such cases there was a two-thirds majority for a proposal, the matter was to go to arbitration before a neutral commission nominated by the estates.[67] Gouda immediately protested that they would not be bound by a two-thirds majority, nor by arbitration, in the proposal to offer the sovereignty over the provinces to the king of France.[68] Amsterdam went further and threatened to withdraw altogether if the two-thirds majority rule was applied to financial matters.[69] Faced with this ultimatum by the greatest town of the province the assembly committed several members of the Council of Holland to go to Amsterdam and try to win over the city fathers.[70] There is no evidence that the commission was successful, and the matter was left undecided.

In the meantime, further and even more important decisions had to be taken. The duke of Parma was closing in on Antwerp, and the military position of the Union was rapidly deteriorating. On May 11, 1585 the States-General of the provinces constituting the Union of Utrecht resolved to offer the sovereignty to Elizabeth I.[71] Gouda had given its deputies to the estates of Holland powers to discuss requests for help from England. But when the question of sovereignty came up for discussion the magistrates of the city ordered the deputies to return home. Again the estates of Holland sent a commission but Gouda remained unmoved. In the formal offer of sovereignty to Eliza-

[67] *Ibid.*, pp. 113 f.    [68] *Ibid.*, p. 110.    [69] *Ibid.*, pp. 165 ff.
[70] *Ibid.*, p. 165.    [71] *Ibid.*, pp. 268 f.

beth by the estates of Holland, Gouda was not mentioned with the other cities.[72]

We now know that Gouda's attitude was due to the Catholic and Spanish sympathies of its magistrates.[73] Contemporaries knew it, too, no doubt, although this explanation is not even hinted at in the official resolutions of the estates of Holland. At least one of Gouda's representatives in the estates of Holland, the pensionary Franchois Vranck, certainly did not share the Spanish sympathies of his town council. Once more it is clear that there were very good practical reasons, and in this case rather sinister ones, why a town should want to restrict the powers of its deputies to commit it to resolutions of the assembly of estates. If the estates were doubtful as to the powers they would allow their deputies, they were still convinced that only a strong central government could retrieve the desperate military situation. When Leicester arrived in the Netherlands, in December, 1585, the States-General made him governor general and, in February, 1586, gave him greater powers than they had been willing to allow any of his predecessors, including even the great prince of Orange.[74]

The constitutional position of the States-General and its deputies, however, as well as that of the provincial estates, was obscure in the extreme. Leicester certainly did not understand it, any more than he understood all the other confused political problems of the Netherlands. Soon he was quarreling violently with the estates of Holland which thereupon tried their best to limit his powers.[75] In March, 1587, while Leicester was back in England, Thomas Wilkes, the English representative at The Hague, tried to clarify the position in a memorandum ad-

[72] J. Huges, *Mr. Franchois Vranck*, pp. 42 f.

[73] A. M. van der Woude, "De Goudse Magistraat en de Strijd tegen de Koning," in *Bijdragen voor Geschiedenis der Nederlanden*, 13, No. 2 (1958), 101–107.

[74] P. Geyl, *The Revolt of the Netherlands (1555–1609)*, 2d ed. (London, 1958), p. 203.

[75] Cf. my "Western Europe and the Power of Spain," in *New Cambridge Modern History*, III, chap. 9, 297 ff.

dressed, in French, to the States-General and the estates of Holland. "Sovereignty, in the absence of a legitimate prince, belongs to the people," Wilkes wrote, "and not to you, gentlemen, who are only servants, ministers, and deputies of the said people, and all your instructions and commissions are limited not only in time but also in subject matter. . . ." Sovereignty, he continued, was limited neither in power nor in time,[76] and the deputies of the States-General did not represent this sovereignty, for the people had given the general and absolute government to His Excellency (i.e., Leicester) to exercise it as sovereign power. He was the guardian of this sovereignty until the prince or the people chose to revoke it. In the state of the United Provinces there was, in fact, only the people who could do this. According to the principle of common law, that only he who has given power can take it back, only the people, the masters of the deputies in the provincial estates and in the State-General, and not these deputies themselves, could take any power away from the governor general. The deputies had not received any such commission. They had either not understood this position, Wilkes concluded triumphantly, or they were guilty of the crime of disobedience.[77]

For the first time in the long history of the problem of the powers of the deputies in the Netherlands, some one had tried to argue it on the basis of political and legal principles and to link it systematically with a theory of sovereignty. There is some irony in the fact that it should have been a foreigner, and an Englishman at that, even if his theory of sovereignty was no more than a pastiche of Bodin's. Previous arguments with Wilkes had already led some deputies of the estates of Holland to claim sovereignty for the estates.[78] Now Wilkes had forced them to

[76] Cf. J. Bodin, *Les Six Livres de la République*, I, VIII (Paris, 1583), pp. 122 ff.

[77] Quoted in Huges, *Mr. Franchois Vranck*, pp. 69 f.

[78] Wilkes to Leicester, March 22, 1587. H. Brugmans, "Correspondentie van Robert Rudley, Graaf van Leyster, 1585–88," pt. 1, in *Werken . . . Historisch Genootschap . . . Utrecht*, ser. 3, No. 57 (Utrecht, 1931), pp. 145 ff. Also quoted in Huges, *Mr. Franchois Vranck*, p. 72.

define their position. They entrusted Franchois Vranck, the pensionary to Gouda, with drawing up a reply. Vranck's long justification was to become the basis of Netherlands political thought for a long time.[79]

Vranck argued that sovereignty in Holland and Zealand did not reside in the common people, as Wilkes had maintained, nor in the 30 or 40 persons assembled at the meetings of the estates. Holland and Zealand had been ruled for 800 years by counts and countesses to whom the nobles and towns, i.e., the estates, had entrusted the sovereignty. In cases of minority or other incapacity of the ruler, the estates had exercised this sovereignty by appointing guardians. The origins of the present wars (i.e., against Spain), whatever people had said about them, were due to Philip II's attempt to introduce Spanish and other foreign soldiery into the country and force it to do what the estates had not approved. The towns were governed by councils constituted of the most notable persons of the whole community, anything from 24 to 40. These bodies (*vroedschappen*) were as old as the towns themselves and their members took their oaths to the cities and not to the prince. They served for life and filled vacancies by cooption. They elected the burgomasters and other magistrates. These councils and the nobles, therefore represented the whole state. They sent their deputies to the meetings of the estates of Holland with such powers and resolutions as they judged to be for the service of the country. Besides, for the duration of the war, the deputies were empowered "to discuss and resolve on all matters concerning the welfare and the preservation of the state." Their authority derived from the commissions granted them by their principals with whom they must keep in constant touch during the assemblies and by whom they could be called to account if they did not carry out their instructions. "For what is the power of a prince, unless indeed he were a tyrant," Vranck concluded his argu-

[79] It is printed in Bor, *Oorspronck*, Vol. III, Bk. 22, fos. 49–54; and partly in Huges, *Mr. Franchois Vranck*, pp. 75 ff. It is also summarized by Grotius, *Verantwoordingh van de Wettelijke Regieringh van Hollandt* (Paris, 1622), p. 8.

ment, "without a good understanding with his subjects? What understanding can he have, what support can he draw from them, if he lets himself be persuaded to become a partisan against the estates who represent the community or, to speak more clearly, against his own people? And secondly, how can the state continue to exist if it could happen that the community should be persuaded to become a partisan against the estates, that is, against the nobles, the magistrates, and the councils of the towns?" [80]

Vranck's knowledge and use of history was certainly highly dubious. His argument that the *vroedschappen*, the urban oligarchies in their town councils, represented the whole community was quite arbitrary, and his peroration was mere rhetoric. But he had produced a masterly description of the facts of the political situation in Holland and of the true seat of authority and, consequently, of sovereignty. There was a respectable medieval tradition for the grounding of rights in custom and in actual practice, and this empirical and conservative tradition remained alive and important in Europe. Burke might well have approved of Vranck.

Wilkes certainly seems to have been impressed. At any rate, by July, 1587, he had retreated far from his unaccustomed role of a Bodinian political theorist. He wrote to the queen that, if she refused the proffered sovereignty for herself, she would think that it should "remain with such as now, by the laws of those countries, do retain the same, which is not the common people, as some are persuaded, but in the *Vroetschap,* who are the chiefest burgers in the cities and out of whom are drawn the magistrates and out of them the persons called the Estates. This *Vroedschap* are most jealous of their liberties and privileges for defence whereof they now make war against their lawful sovereign and charge themselves with impositions which no prince could force them to." [81] Considering Wilkes's former arguments, both to Leicester and the Estates of Holland, this

[80] Bor, *Oorspronck,* Vol. III, Bk. 22, fo. 50.

[81] Wilkes to Elizabeth, July 12, 1587. *C.S.P., Foreign,* XXI, pt. 3, April–Dec., 1857, p. 163. Same letter as cited in n. 62.

was certainly cool, and it may have been just as well that the Dutch did not see the remark about their making war against their lawful sovereign. But Wilkes was a realist and he appreciated that Vranck had given him an accurate picture of the actual political situation.

Vranck had been very precise about the problem of sovereignty. He had been much less so about the powers of the deputies in the estates of Holland. He was clear, just as Wilkes had been, that they derived their powers from their constituents and that they were bound by their instructions; but nobody had ever doubted that. The question was rather, how much discretionary power the deputies were to be allowed and how far their decisions were to be accepted as binding in those "matters concerning the welfare and preservation of the state," of which Vranck had spoken but which he did not define. But, once the theory of the sovereignty of the estates of Holland and of the other provinces in the Union was accepted—and the States-General itself reiterated it, in 1621 [82]—a theory such as the English theory of the sovereignty of the "king in Parliament" could not develop. The question of the powers of the deputies and of the binding force of decisions remained what it had been all along: a matter of practical politics, to be decided in accordance with the willingness of the members of the estates to trust one another and the central government of the Union at any particular time.

The problem of the powers of the deputies in sixteenth century assemblies was not an abstruse and theoretical question. It was a practical problem, at the very heart of the conflict between monarchy and estates. In France it did not become a live issue because this conflict was fought in terms of a struggle, not

---

[82] Grotius (H. de Groot), *Verantwoordingh*, p. 8. On Vranck, cf. now also P. Geyl, "The Interpretation of Vrancken's *Deduction* of 1587 on the Nature of the Power of the State of Holland," in *From Renaissance to Counter-Reformation: Essays in Honor of Garrett Mattingly*, C. H. Carter, ed. (New York, 1965).

between the crown and the States-General, but between the crown and highly organized political-religious parties. In England, owing to its different social structure and the unusually great power of the crown in the Middle Ages, the question of the powers of members of Parliament had been settled already at the end of the thirteenth century. In the sixteenth century it was therefore not a subject for conflict. Nevertheless, it colored the whole history of the relations between crown and Parliament. For the crown it meant that Parliament, with its highly developed *esprit de corps* and its sophisticated committee procedure, was a much more useful instrument of taxation and legislation than the continental assemblies with their cumbrous procedure of referring back all government proposals to the individual provinces and towns. But it also meant that Parliament could become a much more formidable instrument of opposition to the crown; for the crown, unlike the governments of the Netherlands, could never by-pass Parliament by negotiating directly with shires and boroughs. The Habsburg governments of the Netherlands were fully alive to the possible dangers of such a pattern—more so, perhaps, than the Tudor governments of England, which never looked beyond the advantages of the full powers of members of Parliament.

In the Netherlands and in Spain the problem of full powers had not been settled by the beginning of the sixteeth century, and, in both countries, it remained a fruitful source of conflict. Neither crown nor estates bothered about the theoretical implications of sovereignty which the question involved; but both were highly conscious of its practical importance. In Castile the conflict over the powers of deputies was one of the immediate causes of the revolt of the *comuneros,* in 1520. But the *comuneros* did not think of the Cortes as an alternative government to the crown, nor even as its partner. They were therefore content with the purely defensive demand for the strict limitation of the powers of deputies. When the rebellion was defeated and the will to resist the crown had been broken, the monarchy, on its side, did not have to abolish the Cortes. To get what it wanted, it only had to insist on full powers for deputies who could be bribed or bullied into acquiescence in its demands.

In the Netherlands the state had only recently been formed by the union of independent duchies and counties under the House of Burgundy. The towns had kept their autonomy and a tradition of resistance to the demands of their princes. As in Spain, the limitation of the powers of their deputies was a defensive weapon. During the rebellion against Philip II, the estates became directly responsible for the government of the country. Immediately it became clear that the deputies would have to have far greater powers of decision than they had been allowed hitherto. This was regarded as an unfortunate necessity. One might argue about it in detail, but it did not alter the accepted principles of representation. It was realized only gradually that these principles themselves were involved. The debates about the form of government which followed the death of William the Silent showed the beginnings of this realization. But it was the English intervention in the Netherlands, the ambiguous position of the earl of Leicester, and the political theories propounded by Thomas Wilkes which finally forced the estates of Holland to produce a comprehensive analysis of the principles on which they based their actions and authority. Even then, there remained the old reluctance to argue the question dogmatically. Franchois Vranck said nothing about natural law or natural rights. He developed a purely historical theory of sovereignty and he firmly put the deputies of the estates of Holland in their place, as mere delegates of the regent class, the nobles and patricians who ran the towns. From them alone the deputies received their powers and authority. But the extent of these powers he left vague. That was still only a practical problem. Vranck and the rest of the regent class of the Netherlands thought it best to leave it to their own common sense and practical experience.

# CHAPTER 8

# The Reformation and
# Social Revolution

FROM THE TIME of the great peasants' revolts of the four-teenth century social revolution became a part of European life. From England to Bohemia, and from Italy to Denmark, peas-ants rose against their lords in the country, and artisans went on strike and rioted against their patrician employers in the towns. It did not, of course, happen all the time, or everywhere at once. Many provinces and towns remained peaceful for gen-erations or, like Venice, never suffered any social upheavals at all. But a bad harvest in the country, a new tax, a sudden rise in the piece of bread, or a winter of unemployment in the towns—such an event was always liable to cause an outburst of popular fury. Such outbursts, directed against the lords' *chateaux* or the patricians' town halls, were usually purely local. Their aims, where they were formulated at all, were limited and prac-tical: the abolition of a tax or a *corvée*, that is, a labor service on the lord's estate; the raising of wage rates or the participation of the craft guilds in the government of the town.

There were times, however, when such movements spread over wider areas and when they aimed at much more funda-mental changes in social relationships and political structure. Examples are the English peasants' revolt of 1381 and the Hus-site wars of Bohemia and central Europe in the first half of the fifteenth century. In both cases a certain type of religious teach-ing and propaganda transformed local rebellions into national, or even international, revolutionary movements. Popular preachers interpreted the theological speculations of university dons from Oxford and Prague in fiery sermons or crude slogans. The crudest and most effective of these was the famous couplet:

> When Adam delved and Eve span
> Who was then the gentleman?

It translated easily into other Germanic languages and spread over much of central Europe.

Respectable contemporaries, that is, those who believed in the social *status quo,* were appalled by the effectiveness of this fusion of social and religious aims; but they were not surprised by it. Indeed, even in the sixteenth century, few men, outside Italy, thought of social and political matters in purely secular terms. The social order was held to be divinely ordained and political authority was derived from God. Rebellion was not only a treasonable but an impious act. Conversely, social movements were likely to acquire a religious tinge. This was not so much a matter of finding a moral justification for rebellion—though such a motive often played its part—as a way of thinking about relations between man and man. At the same time movements which started with a purely religious appeal tended very rapidly to acquire social or political overtones. This was also generally recognized in the sixteenth century. A Venetian ambassador to France, one of the coolest of contemporary political observers, wrote that experience had always shown that changes in religion led to changes in the State, that is, to political revolutions. This was certainly true of the Reformation in Germany, as Dr. Elton has shown; [1] but in Germany the Reformation also coincided with a number of previously quite independent social movements. The result was a series of particularly violent social and political explosions. These are the events I shall be discussing in this chapter.

By sixteenth-century standards Germany was a prosperous country. In the countryside the ravages of the Black Death of the fourteenth century had been made good. German towns

---

[1] *The Reformation Crisis,* J. Hurstfield, ed. (New York, 1966), pp. 76–77.

grew rich from the transit trade between Italy and the Netherlands. German craftsmen led the rest of Europe in metal- and woodwork and were beginning to catch up on the Italian and western European lead in textiles. German silver mines, in Saxony and the Tyrol, were flooding Europe with silver coin. German engineers were mining and German capitalists were financing and exploiting Hungarian copper. German merchant bankers and mineowners were the richest in Europe, and were already beginning to tap the wealth of Spain and its rapidly expanding overseas empire. But, politically and socially, Germany was the most unstable country in Europe.

Dr. Elton has written of the division of Germany into hundreds of large and small political units over whom the central government of the emperor held little more than nominal sway.[2] But the authority of all these princes, bishops, and imperial cities was itself often ill-defined. Territorially, their states presented a jigsaw puzzle of disconnected units and enclaves. Politically, they had for centuries acquired, or usurped, their rights and prerogatives as occasion arose. By the early sixteenth century the princes were busy trying to round off their territories and to extend their authority. They began to build up their own civil service. They introduced Roman law in place of local custom and common law. They arrogated to their courts village and seigneurial jurisdiction. They strove to incorporate the smaller autonomous towns into their territory. Above all, they attempted to impose new taxes.

For a generation before the Reformation this policy had produced chronic unrest, especially in the German-speaking Alpine countries. Local peasant communities rose against their local princes, especially against ecclesiastical princes—the prince-bishops and prince-abbots who had been foremost in pursuing the new policy of reducing their peasant vassals to subjects. The peasants' aims varied locally and from time to time. But, in general, they demanded a return to the old law, their village self-government and the abolition of new taxes. Opposition to more

[2] *Ibid.*, pp. 75–77.

purely seigneurial rights, the imposition of additional labor services or the burdens of serfdom, were rarer though not unknown. All these demands were limited and practical. Quite frequently the lords and princes had to grant them, or an arbitrator arranged a compromise. Just as frequently, however, the princes returned to the attack. In consequence, the revolts continued.

There was, however, another tradition of peasant movements, one which the authorities, from the very beginning, viewed with much greater alarm. These were the religious movements based on an old chiliastic tradition, that is, the attempt to set up the thousand-year reign of Christ on earth which was to precede the Day of Judgment. From Professor Norman Cohn's book, *The Pursuit of the Millennium,* we now know a great deal about this chiliastic tradition in central Europe and its extraordinary tenacity. It had never died out in Germany and it mingled with the egalitarian religious traditions which the Hussites had taken from Wycliff and the English peasants' revolt and which they introduced into Germany in the fifteenth century. Such ideas found a particularly fertile soil in southwest Germany, where political fragmentation had gone farthest and where quite small lords were setting themselves up as princes and adding taxes to ever-increasing manorial burdens. On the upper Rhine there appeared a movement called the Bundschuh, or the peasant's laced boot. Unlike the other peasants' risings in southern Germany, which had been local, secular, and conservative in aim, the Bundschuh was a highly organized movement, covering a large area. It appealed not to traditional but to divine law, with the aim of overthrowing the existing social order and setting up a popular religious peasant society directly under the emperor.

The leader of the Bundschuh, Joss Fritz, could never manage to keep his organization and plans secret, for his supporters gave themselves away in the confessional. The authorities always had sufficient time to take effective countermeasures. But Fritz himself always escaped and, all over southern Germany, the authorities remained nervous of the continued appearance of the Bundschuh emblem and the Bundschuh slogans. From about the year 1515, or a little earlier, the two types of peasant movements, the secular and the religious, began to coalesce. Growing population pressure was causing an ever-increasing division of peasant land and a good deal of rural unemployment. Here was the chief recruiting ground for the *Landsknechts,* the famous German mercenary troops of the time. Their employment was notoriously irregular and the large number of paid-off soldiers in the villages added a further explosive element to an already unstable situation.

From the beginning of the century food prices had been gradually rising, owing to increasing population and to the inflationary effects of silver mining in Germany. In 1516–1517 bad harvests caused them to soar to hitherto unheard-of heights. Joss Fritz's revolutionary propaganda found more support than ever before, and the Bundschuh conspiracy of 1517 was the most widespread and dangerous so far. What was particularly alarming was the spread of the unrest to many of the towns. High bread prices were a traditional, almost respectable, cause for rioting in the towns. Moreover, like the peasants, the artisans and small traders of the towns suffered from the imposition of new taxes and the encroachments of princely authority on their traditional rights.

Thus Germany was already in a state of incipient social revolution at the moment when Luther, to satisfy the demands of his own conscience, broke with the established Church. Only someone of Luther's own naïve singleness of mind could imagine that his inflammatory attacks on one of the great pillars of the established order would not be interpreted as an attack on the whole social order, or on that part of it which it suited different interests, from princes to peasants, to attack. Indeed, if this had not been so, Luther's Reformation could not possibly have been as successful as it actually was.

The first to interpret Luther's writings as a signal for revolution were, however, not the peasants but the imperial knights.

The knights were a very varied social group of noble land-owners who had thrived during the centuries of imperial impotence and political chaos in southern Germany. But from the beginning of the sixteenth century they had come under increasing pressure from the princes who taxed their peasants and encroached on their rights of jurisdiction and the profits they derived from their seigneurial courts. Rising prices ate into the value of their income from rents, and when they tried to raise rents they added to the already dangerous peasant unrest. Many who had the opportunity took service with the princes. Others clung fiercely to their old independence. To them, Luther's pamphlet addressed to the German nobility seemed a clarion call against the hated power of the princes and the Church. In 1523 Franz von Sickingen, a former imperial general, led the knights against their archenemy, the archbishop of Trier. Among Sickingen's followers the traditional greed and bellicosity of the robber baron mingled with half-baked plans for a political and religious regeneration of the empire. The burghers of Trier failed to share this knightly enthusiasm and remained loyal to their archbishop. Sickingen had to raise the siege and soon the archbishop's professional mercenary army blew up Sickingen's castles and scattered his followers.

The peasant risings which began a year later were a very different matter. There is little evidence that their immediate cause was economic distress. Prices were high, in some areas, but do not seem to have approached the famine level of 1517. But there was a feeling of unease and impending catastrophe in the air. The astrologers were predicting great disasters for 1524 and 1525. Local unrest had never entirely ceased since 1517. In many places the peasants refused to pay the tithes to their clergy; it was their most immediate reaction to Luther's teachings. The peasant movement itself started in the Black Forest, close to the Swiss cantons with their infectious anti-princely and antinoble traditions. In Zürich and Basle, moreover, Zwingli and his friends had already overthrown the authority of the old Church.

Soon the movement spread through the whole of southern Germany, excepting only Bavaria. It spread by example and by propaganda. The example was the rising of the peasants in a neighboring area with their traditional demands for the return to the old law and the abolition of specific grievances. In detail these demands varied from locality to locality, as they had always done. Much of the propaganda, however, was of a more general and, often, religious character. Luther's little tract on *The Freedom of a Christian Man* was interpreted—misinterpreted, so Luther thought—as an attack on all serfdom. Divine law, as the peasants saw it, and the old traditional law were often sufficiently close to intermingle in their minds and in their demands. Thus, the appeal to divine law generalized local grievances and was the reason for the widespread adoption by different peasant bands of the famous Twelve Articles as the basis of their demands. The Twelve Articles were drafted by Sebastian Lotzer, a tanner from the Swabian town of Memmingen. They demanded the free election of ministers by their congregations. The ministers were to preach the gospel plainly and without additions. They were to be paid by the "great," or grain, tithe. The "small," or cattle, tithe was to be abolished. Serfdom and all duties arising from it were contrary to divine law. So was the nobles' appropriation of hunting, fishing, and forest rights. Rents and services were not to be arbitrarily increased, and justice was to be exercised equally and according to the old law. Widows and orphans were not be unjustly harried by death duties. If any of these demands could be shown to be contrary to God's word, Lotzer concluded, they would be dropped.

The Twelve Articles and other sets of peasants' demands are remarkable mainly for their moderation and conservatism. The peasants' leaders and their allies in the towns were often substantial and respectable men. Most of them did not, like Joss Fritz, want to overthrow the existing social order. They wanted their traditional rights, and Luther and Zwingli seemed to have made their demands even more respectable by apparently giving them the sanction of Scripture. The princes of the Church, it was widely believed, had kept the true word of God from the common man, and they had done this from pride. The peasants plundered and burnt monasteries and castles; but on only one occasion did they massacre the defenders of a castle, Weinsberg, after they had surrendered. The massacres of the Peasants' War were nearly all perpetrated by the other side.

In the first months of the risings the majority of lords, abbots, and princes were too terrified to resist and made agreements with the peasant leaders, accepting their demands. The imperial government, as usual, was helpless. But soon the greater princes recovered their nerve. The Swabian League, a military alliance of princes and large towns in southern Germany, raised an effective professional army. The peasants for their part were accustomed to bearing arms. They were led by unemployed professional soldiers. They captured artillery in the towns and castles they took. But the peasant bands were undisciplined. They had no cavalry. They had no military leader who could stand up to the experienced generals of the Swabian League. Worst of all, the peasant bands of the different areas did not cooperate. The largest of the peasant armies made a treaty with the enemy and dispersed. Most of the other bands tried to fight. But the peasants usually broke ranks at the first charge of the *Landsknecht* regiments and the League's cavalry then cut them down by the thousand. By the summer of 1525 all resistance had virtually ceased. Only the Tyrolese peasants threw up an effective leader, Michael Gaismair, who won a pitched battle and held out for another year.

The peasants had counted on Luther's support for their demands. They had misunderstood him. The princes, after the initial shock, certainly did not misunderstand him. Many were badly shaken by the revolt. Luther's own prince, the elector Frederick the Wise of Saxony, had wondered whether it was not God's will that now the peasants should rule. Luther would have none of this. Himself the son of peasants, he had sympathized with their grievances; but he condemned their actions.

In May, 1525, he published a pamphlet *Against the Murderous and Thieving Hordes of Peasants*. They had committed three mortal sins, Luther wrote. They had broken the obedience they had sworn to authority; they had committed rebellion, riot, and murder; and finally they had forced other Christians to commit similar sins. There was, he thundered, "nothing more poisonous, obnoxious, and devilish than a rebellious man." He had to be killed like a mad dog. The princes had been given the sword and must now use it. "So wondrous are the times now," Luther concluded, "that a prince can attain to heaven through bloodshed where others have attained it through prayer." If Luther's appreciation of divine judgment was correct, many of the princes must have earned their crowns of glory. Their *Landsknechts,* during the battles, and their hangmen, after the fighting was over, slaughtered some hundred thousand peasants.

Luther's own experience of the Peasants' War was in Thuringia. This province had a long history of millennial movements. It now produced the greatest of its chiliastic prophets and the most interesting figure of the Peasants' War, Thomas Müntzer. Müntzer had moved from a position close to Luther's to one of the bitterest hostility to the reformer. The kingdom of God, now close at hand, was for the elect only, those who had experienced the "living" or "spiritual" Christ within themselves and who had suffered his cross in their own afflictions of body and spirit. After the princes had failed him, Müntzer came to identify the elect with the poor. As a preacher, first in the new mining town of Zwickau, and then in the decaying town of Mühlhausen, he built up a tremendous personal prestige among unemployed miners and the poorer artisans. Though the peasants' demands in Thuringia showed only faint traces of Müntzer's millennial and egalitarian visions, there is no doubt of his influence among the rebels. The princes who marched their army against the Thuringian peasants, encamped at Frankenhausen, recognized this when they offered the peasants their lives if they handed over Müntzer and his disciples. Münt-

zer persuaded the peasants otherwise. God had promised him
the victory for the elect. Müntzer himself would catch the can-
non balls of the ungodly in the sleeves of his cloak. But at the
very first salvo the peasants fled. Some five thousand perished in
the rout and its aftermath of massacre and executions, Müntzer
among them.

Since Engels, writing about the Peasants' War, elevated
Müntzer into a hero of the class struggle, Müntzer's beliefs and
his political role have been hotly debated by Marxist and anti-
Marxist historians. The debate is based largely on an anachro-
nistic contrast between religious and political beliefs. Müntzer
certainly thought primarily in religious terms; but he did not
separate these from their social and political consequences. Nor,
for that matter, did his opponents.

Much more important than this modern historiographical
shadow boxing was Müntzer's influence on the development of
sixteenth-century Anabaptism. The Anabaptist movement included a variety of beliefs; but in general, Anabaptists were
agreed in holding that they alone constituted the elect of God,
and that for them all external authority whether of Church or
State was irrelevant and did not apply. These ideas spread
rapidly among the lower classes of Switzerland and Germany
after the Peasants' War, primarily in a pacific form: the Anabaptists preached nonresistance and suffered martyrdom by the
thousand. But Müntzer's appeal to violence for the setting up
of the kingdom of the elect on earth could not be forgotten;
and alongside the peaceful majority of Anabaptists there appeared also a revolutionary Anabaptist movement with its focus
in Holland and northwestern Germany. Economic distress seems
to have played a much greater part in this movement than in
the Peasants' War of 1524–1525. Wages had not kept up with
rising prices during the first decades of the sixteenth century.
In the early 1530's bad harvests caused bread prices to rise, often
twice as high as in the famine year of 1517. Warfare in the
Baltic and the closing of the passage of the Sound to Dutch ship-

ping prevented the import of Polish and Prussian grain into Holland and caused widespread unemployment in the Dutch shipping and textile towns. In these conditions the revolutionary wing of the Anabaptists, led by the Haarlem baker, Jan Matthys, made rapid converts. As so often in the sixteenth century, the social and religious protests intermingled.

Matthys's chance to set up his kingdom of God came not, however, in Holland, where public authority was too firmly established, but in the northwest German cathedral town of Münster. Here the gilds had forced the town council to hand over the churches to Lutheran preachers. In February, 1534, the Anabaptists won control of the council. Matthys himself now arrived and, together with his disciple Jan Bockelson, known as John of Leiden, he soon dominated the town.

The revolution in Münster ran the classic course of revolutions. Quite rapidly the moderates were driven out by the extremists. When the bishop of Münster gathered forces to besiege the city, Matthys set up the revolutionary dictatorship of the elect, that is, his own party, over the rest of the citizens. After his death in a sortie, his successor, John of Leiden, made the dictatorship even more effective and arbitrary. He introduced community of property and, some time later, polygamy; it would be hard to say which of these two measures caused greater scandal in respectable society, both Catholic and Protestant. Within Münster opposition was stifled by draconian laws and frequent executions. John had himself proclaimed king and, significantly, came to rely more and more on his own countrymen, the Dutch, to hold in check the German majority of the citizens.

In 1536, when John of Leiden had become the bishop's prisoner, he was interviewed by Lutheran divines. These worthies were less concerned to find out his views than to impress him with their own learning and orthodoxy. But their report makes it clear that John stuck to his view that God showed men his will through images. The Anabaptist kingdom of Münster had been such an image of the millennial kingdom foretold by the prophets. John had believed that it would last until the second coming of Christ.

In fact, Münster had held out for over a year, while both the hunger and the terror inside the city grew apace, until the bishop's troops finally captured it in June, 1535. John had sent his preachers out to obtain support. In Holland thousands answered the call, only to be intercepted on their way and massacred by the troops of the Netherlands government. An Anabaptist attempt to capture Amsterdam failed equally; but it increased still further the authorities' fear of the Anabaptists. The executions of Anabaptists in the Netherlands and in northwestern Germany more than matched John of Leiden's terror against his opponents. In Münster the bishop's power and the catholic religion were restored.

The kingdom of Münster was the last of the German revolutions of the sixteenth century. They had all failed, and the reasons for this failure are not far to seek. The social and religious beliefs animating these movements were too narrow. They appealed only to the peasants and the artisans of the towns. Only a handful of nobles and patrician burghers took an active part in the movements, and none of them became a leader of the first rank. The knights had had their fling before the peasants struck. When the peasants plundered their castles and burnt the monasteries the knights found themselves, inevitably, on the side of authority. Left to themselves, the peasants and artisans proved incapable of providing their movements with capable leaders or of creating an adequate organization. The German historian, Günther Franz, has suggested a reason for this failure. For centuries the most talented children of the peasants and artisans had tended to enter the priesthood. Both as persons and as parents they were lost to their own class. In its immediate application to the problem of leadership in the social revolutions of the sixteenth century, this theory cannot be proved; but it seems at least plausible.

Much more formidable revolutionary movements than the

German ones appeared in western Europe during the second half of the sixteenth century. These were based on a religious faith, Calvinism, which was respectable in a way that the egalitarian millennarianism of Müntzer and the Anabaptists could never be. Calvin did not preach the overthrow of established authority. Still less did he preach those Anabaptist doctrines of community of property which were abhorrent to respectable people, who thought nothing of picking up cheaply scraps of church property for themselves. But Calvin did allow resistance to established authority for the sake of true religion, provided it was led by those who themselves enjoyed some legitimate authority such as peers of the realm or an assembly of estates. At the same time the Calvinist preachers could rouse artisans and unemployed workers as effectively as the militant Anabaptists. With such a varied appeal and on the basis of the Calvinist church organization, the French Huguenots and the Netherlands Sea Beggars could build up effective revolutionary political parties. They included members of all classes, from artisans and fishermen to knights of the Order of the Golden Fleece and French princes of the blood. In financial and military resources, in organizational talent, and in political leadership the Sea Beggars and the Huguenots and, in Scotland, John Knox's "Brethren" and the Lords of the Congregation, were the equals of the governments they opposed. They could and did achieve successful political and religious revolutions. Yet, in the end, even these revolutions left the social structure of their countries essentially intact. The day for a successful democratic and egalitarian revolution had not yet come.

# CHAPTER 9

# The Organization of Revolutionary Parties in France and the Netherlands during the Sixteenth Century

IT IS a commonplace of modern historical writing that the sixteenth century was the age of "new monarchies" in western Europe. The establishment of centralized government and capitalist finance, the introduction of Roman law and of professional civil servants, have been extensively studied; the work of Habsburg, Valois, and Tudor rulers in unifying great kingdoms is well known. Not so well know is the nature of the oppositions which the governments of the sixteenth century had to face. Too often these oppositions have been represented as the survivals of the old feudal nobility fighting a rear-guard action for their medieval privileges, or as the first stirrings of the "rising middle classes," staking a claim for religious liberty and a more active citizenship against monarchial despotism. It is true that some historians have described the organization of sixteenth-century oppositions and have appreciated that their revolutionary activities were possible only through the efforts of a highly developed party organization.[1] The present chapter attempts to show that these organizations were not isolated phenomena, but rather the logical counterpart of the increased

[1] Notably Lucien Romier, for the Huguenots, and Pieter Geyl and Enno van Gelder and their school, for the Calvinists of the Netherlands. Herbert Butterfield has been fully aware of these problems and has stressed the organizational aspect both of the Huguenot movement and of the Holy League in his lectures. I would like to acknowledge my great debt to these and to discussions of these problems with Professor Butterfield.

power of the state; that they were nearly always the result of the efforts of determined minorities who tried to impose their views on the country by force; that without such organization these minorities could not hope to succeed; and that they did succeed only where the government was temporarily weak.[2] If the orgins of the organization of the modern state can be found in the monarchies of Francis I, Henry VIII, and Philip II, the origins of the organization of the Jacobins and of the totalitarian parties of the twentieth century can be found in the Huguenots and Holy League of France, the Sea Beggars and Calvinists of the Netherlands and, to a lesser degree, in Knox's "brethren" and the Lords of the Congregation of Scotland.

European governments had been faced with oppositions before the sixteenth century. These oppositions had nearly always been limited to one class, or group of classes, as in the medieval peasant revolts and in feudal movements such as the League of the Common Weal in France; or they had been revolts on a limited territorial basis.[3] In the sixteenth century, almost for the first time, opposition movements became nationwide and included classes, or elements of classes, ranging from princes of the blood to unemployed artisans. These opposition movements might act through a parliament or assembly of estates, or—and this happened to all of them at some time in their careers—they could become openly revolutionary. It is only this revolutionary aspect of sixteenth-century oppositions which will be discussed in this chapter.

The new factor which made possible these formidable parties was religion. Religious belief alone, no matter whether it was held with fanatic conviction or for political expediency, could bring together the divergent interests of nobles, burghers, and

[2] Or where, as in Scotland, it lacked some of the advantages of the "new monarchies."

[3] There were some exceptions, such as the war of the Sicilian Vespers and the Hussite wars. But the former had the nature of a national movement against a foreign army of occupation, and the latter added a religious to a nationalist element—the distinguishing feature of the sixteenth-century movements.

peasants over areas as wide as the whole of France. And it was religious organizations from which developed the organization of political parties or which provided the prototype for party organization. "It is common knowledge, confirmed by many examples," wrote the Venetian ambassador to France in 1561, "that, with a change of religion, there will of necessity follow changes of states" (i.e., revolutions).[4]

France, the classical land of revolutions, provided two of the sixteenth-century revolutionary movements, the Huguenots and the League. The transformation of the scattered Calvinist communities into the highly organized Huguenot party, capable of surviving a generation of civil wars, was the answer to the attempts of Henry II to exterminate heresy through the machinery of the state. The initiative in this response was taken not only by the French Calvinists, but by Calvin himself, in Geneva. The Huguenot movement had, therefore, from its beginnings the characteristics of an international, as well as of a national, party. Wherever a Protestant community was established it elected its elders and deacons to assure the discipline of the faithful, administer the funds of the community, and, in general, look after the physical and spiritual welfare of its members. In the larger towns the organization was more elaborate, with the election of *quarteniers, centeniers,* and *dizeniers.*[5] The pastors of the larger communities, or of groups of smaller ones, were often appointed by Theodore Beza or by Calvin himself; thus spiritual control was centralized in Geneva.[6]

As the Protestant communities grew and attracted persons from an ever wider range of classes, secret conventicles changed into open mass meetings.[7] By 1557 assemblies of two or three thousand in the Cévennes offered armed resistance to the king's

[4] Giovanni Michiel, "Relazione di Francia nel 1561," in E. Albèri, *Le Relazioni degli ambasciatori veneti al senato durante il secolo decimosesto,* ser. 1, III (Florence, 1853), 428.

[5] L. Romier, *Le Royaume de Cathérine de Médicis* (Paris, 1925), II, 188, 189.

[6] *Ibid.,* II, 189, 217.    [7] *Ibid.,* II, 192–196.

officials who sought to prevent the scandal of the public preaching of heresy.[8] From the end of 1559 such events became common over the greater part of France. The new doctrines had
appealed, at first, to the small artisans and shopkeepers and to
the unemployed workers and journeymen of the towns, all of
them hit by rising prices, heavy wartime taxation, and the growing influence and rigidity of the guilds which blocked economic
advance to all but the favored few.[9] To them the eloquence of
the Geneva-trained preachers brought a message of hope and
hate that the local curé could not hope to emulate. At the same
time, many of the richer bourgeoisie and the professional
classes, and more especially their womenfolk, were drawn towards the new doctrines. Disgust with the generally admitted
abuses of the old church, the half-understood or misinterpreted
Calvinist doctrine of the lawfulness of usury, or, simply, the
hope of gain from the vast wealth of the church—these were the
powerful inducements that made men accept protestantism.[10]
After the end of the war with Spain, large numbers of the
nobility, especially the impoverished lower nobility of the
south, began to join the new movement for a similar variety of
reasons.[11]

Two results followed immediately upon this marriage of social and religious forces. Within the short period of about two
years, from the end of 1559 to the beginning of 1562, the

[8] Henry II to the seneschal of Nîmes, July 3, 1557, C. Devic and J.
Vaissette, *Histoire générale de Languedoc* (Toulouse, 1889), XII, 559.

[9] H. Hauser, "La Réforme et les classes populaires en France au XVIe
siècle," from *Revue d'histoire moderne el contemporaine,* 1 (1899), 1–14.

[10] See the brilliant analysis of the spread of Calvinism in France in
Romier, *Le Royaume,* II, 152–300.

[11] Giovanni Correro, probably following a common Catholic opinion,
divided the Huguenots into three types: the great ones, driven by ambition; the medium ones, "made sweet [on the new religion] by the free
life and the hope of getting rich, especially from church property," i.e.,
motivated by greed; the lower orders, attracted by a false creed, i.e., by
ignorance ("Relazione di Francia, 1569," in Albèri, *Relazioni,* ser. 1, IV,
183).

majority of the Calvinist communities placed themselves under the protection of a local seigneur.[12] His influence would bring new converts, especially from the country population which had been comparatively untouched by the new religion. The price revolution of the sixteenth century had tended to benefit the French peasant and left him reasonably well contented with his lot; with the natural conservatism of the countryman he was averse to changes in religion. The best chance for the reformers to make headway among the peasantry was, therefore, to act through the local country gentlemen whose change of religion the peasant on his estate would be obliged to follow.[13] But even more important was the military element introduced by the nobility. The conventicles became military cadres; mass meetings of armed men, protected by the local nobility and their retainers, began to invade the churches to celebrate their services in open defiance of public authority and of the majority of the Catholic population.[14] Nor did this happen only in the south. In May, 1560, their assemblies in Rouen were said to be 20,000 strong. The royal commander, with 5,000 troops, could not prevent the scaffolds and gibbets he had set up from being pulled down again and he did not dare to take further action.[15]

The Huguenot military cadres were now organized on a provincial and national basis in the same way as the religious communities already had been organized in their provincial and national synods. The synod of Clairac, in November, 1560, divided the province of Guienne into seven *colloques,* each with its captain. In 1561 the synod of Sainte-Foy decided on the election of two "protectors," one for the region of Toulouse

[12] Romier, *Le Royaume*, II, 264–265.

[13] Thus the seigneur de la Feste-Fresnel declared, in 1561: "God has set me in authority over many men, and by this means one of the most superstitious parts of the kingdom may be won for Christ" (Hauser, "La Réforme," p. 13).

[14] Romier, *Le Royaume*, II, 264–267.

[15] Throrkmorton to Elizabeth I, May 13, 1560, P. Forbes, *A Full View of the Public Transactions in the Reign of Queen Elizabeth* (London, 1740), I, 459.

and one for that of Bordeaux. Under them were the colonels of the *colloques* and under these the captains of the individual communities, each strictly responsible to his immediate superior. When the first civil war broke out, in 1562, this organization was more or less fully developed in Guienne, Languedoc, Provence, and Dauphiné, and it existed at least in outline in the rest of France.[16] As the government sought to break Calvinism by increasingly severe edicts and official persecution, the Calvinist communities came to rely more and more on their noble patrons and their military organization. Inevitably, the control of the movement tended to shift from the preachers to the nobles, despite Calvin's misgivings and his efforts to prevent it.[17]

Now it only remained for the movement to find a leader among the higher nobility. When Condé took the title of protector-general of the churches of France [18] all the enormous influence of the Bourbon connection was added to the Huguenot party.[19] The combination of feudal power with the military organization of the Calvinist communities, the financial backing of wealthy bankers and merchants,[20] the voluntary contributions of the faithful,[21] the religious faith kept aflame by skillful

[16] Romier, *Le Royaume,* II, 264–265.     [17] *Ibid.,* II, 267.

[18] Romier, *Le Royaume,* II, 266.

[19] While Condé's assumption of the leadership of the Huguenots weakened the control of Geneva over the movement, it provided the constitutional loophole by which Calvin could countenance resistance to established authority, for Condé was a prince of the blood and claimed the constitutional right for himself and his brother, Anthony of Navarre, to advise the king during his minority.

[20] C. G. Kelley, *French Protestantism, 1559–62* (Baltimore, 1918), pp. 42–47.

[21] Correro, "Realizione," p. 184: "[The Protestant preachers] very frequently made collections of money in their churches, to which the common people contributed readily and generously; and of these monies the great and middling people had their share. Without this help, the princes [Condé, Coligny, etc.] could not have spent the money which they did; and there is no doubt that they regarded these sums more in the manner of kings than of princelings or private noblemen."

propaganda and organized in a strict communal discipline that held together in a common purpose social groups with basically divergent outlooks and interests—all these provided Condé with a political instrument such as no "overmighty subject" had disposed of before. The international organization of Christian communities which Calvin had built up and controlled from Geneva had become a national French revolutionary movement. It never broke with its international connection; it could still obtain material aid from Protestant England and Calvinist Palatinate; it supported William of Orange and provided the Sea Beggars with a base of operations at La Rochelle; its preachers still looked to Geneva for spiritual guidance; but all its energies, its hopes and aims, were now concentrated on France.

Nevertheless, this organization could not have been built up if it had not been for the weakness of the government after the death of Henry II. Local Catholic officials and magistrates were halfhearted in the execution of the king's edicts and, after his death, were less inclined than ever to visit the full rigor of the law on their Huguenot neighbors and countrymen.[22] Many officials, moreover, secretly sympathized with the Huguenots or had frankly joined the movement.[23] Throughout the years 1560 and 1561 the Vicomte de Joyeuse, acting governor of Languedoc, wrote to the king and to the constable, Montmorency, painting in ever darker colors his waning authority, the unreliability of his officials, and the increasing power and influence of the Huguenots who added insult to injury by claiming to act in the king's name.[24] Worst of all, the central govern-

[22] Even after a generation of civil war the knight in the *Dialogue d'entre le Maheustre et le Manant* ([Paris(?), 1594], p. 71), is made to object to the League's policy of terror: "We are all Frenchmen and we should use courtesy towards each other and not force and violence. . . ."

[23] Romier, *Le Royaume*, II, 277–278.

[24] Devic and Vaissette, *Historie générale*, XI, 339, 358–359, XII, 361–364, 567–568, 570–571, 577, 583. See also the *procureur-général* of the parlement of Toulouse to the Cardinal of Lorraine, Sept. 1, 1560, *ibid.*, XI, 333.

ment itself failed to back its provincial governors. While Guises, Bourbons, and Montmorencys were maneuvering for position and Catherine de Medici was trying to prevent any one of the factions from becoming too powerful, no consistent policy could be maintained. "I never sawe state more amased than this at somtyme, and by and by more reckless," the English ambassador reported from the court at Amboise, "they know not whome to mistruste, nor to truste. This day they licence som to departe: to morrowe they revoke theym. He hath all the trust this daye, that tomorrow is leste trusted." [25]

In sharp contrast to the vacillation of the court were the determined actions of the Huguenot party. In October, 1561, they seized Montauban and a number of smaller towns around Toulouse.[26] Once established in any town they acted with great ruthlessness to carry out their aims and maintain themselves in power. They plundered churches and committed them to their preachers; they sacked monasteries, chased away the monks, and forcibly married off the nuns.[27] Joyeuse reported that even good Catholics were so terrorized by the Huguenot mob that there was not a clerk who would write, nor a witness who would testify, against them.[28] In the course of the first two civil wars

[25] Throckmorton to Cecil, March 15, 1560, Forbes, *A Full View*, I, 375. Also quoted by L. von Ranke, *Französische Geschichte* (Stuttgart, 1852), I, 211–212.

In Scotland, the atmosphere at the court of Mary of Guise was very similar. D'Oysel, the French ambassador, wrote to his colleague in England, June 14, 1559: "In short, here you do not know your friend from your enemy, for he who is with you in the morning will be with the Protestants after dinner" (A. Teulet, *Relations politiques de la France et de l'Espagne avec l'Écosse au XVI siècle* [Paris, 1862], I, 319).

[26] Devic and Vaissette, *Histoire générale*, XI, 358–359.

[27] *Ibid.*

[28] Joyeuse to Montmorency, Sept. 17, 1561: "As to inflicting punishment through the magistrates, the greater part of these latter are participants in this evil and will do nothing against these scoundrels; and those who have behaved well and still do so are so much threatened by these scoundrels that they do not dare to do anything against them. There is no clerk who will write nor witness who will testify" (*ibid.*, XII, 583).

the movement took over the government's financial machinery in the provinces they controlled, imposed taxes on both Protestants and Catholics, prevented all payments to the Catholic church and to the government, and even struck coins with Condé's image.[29] Where they could not dominate a region completely, they infiltrated into public offices, until there was a Huguenot hierarchy of officials intermingled with the royal administration and owing allegiance not to the king but to Condé and Coligny.[30] "Thus," said the Venetian ambassador in 1569, "they could, in one day, at one definite hour, and with all secrecy start a rising in every part of the kingdom and unleash a cruel and perilous war." [31]

The organization of the Huguenot movement reached its fullest development only after the Massacre of St. Bartholomew,[32] and its survival after that terrible blow was, in itself, evidence of its strength. But in the later stages of the civil wars it gradually lost much of its revolutionary ardor. By 1588 the duke of Nevers—a very astute observer—thought that the Huguenots had had their fling and that they were now on the defensive: whole provinces and towns were no longer joining them he wrote.[33] Where they were not forced to do otherwise,

[29] J. H. Mariéjol, "La Réforme et la Ligue," in E. Lavisse, *Histoire de France* (Paris, 1904), VI, 142; Kelly, *French Protestantism,* pp. 47–50.

[30] Correro, "Relazione," p. 83. "In every province of the kingdom they had a great personage who counterbalanced the royal governor, if perchance this governor was not one of them. Under him there were many subordinates, each according to their social position and quality. These were distributed throughout the whole country, and with their authority and power (for they were all honorable gentlemen and of noble blood) they patronized and kept the small men in office."

[31] *Ibid.,* p. 184. Romier, *Catholiques et Huguenots à la cour de Charles IX,* 2d ed. (Paris, 1924), pp. 344–345, points to the efficiency of the Huguenot organization as witnessed by the speed with which Condé could concentrate 2,000 cavaliers at Orleans, in April, 1562, and the prompt local revolts that enabled the Huguenots to seize Tours, Blois, Le Mans, Angers, Rouen, Lyons, and other towns.

[32] Kelly, *French Protestantism,* p. 81; Mariéjol, "La Réforme," p. 142.

[33] Nevers to Henry III, Aug. 20, 1588; Louis de Gonzaga, Duc de Nevers, *Les Mémoires* (Paris, 1665), I, 855.

the vast majority of Frenchmen preferred to remain loyal to the old faith. Even the succession to the crown of France of the Huguenot leader Henry of Navarre could not alter this fact. But it did save France from the fate of the Netherlands: permanent division. Thanks to their military organization the Huguenots became the "state within the state," an organization beyond the control of the central government but bent no longer on its overthrow.

In the Netherlands, as in France, the organization of the opposition had its origin in the religious communities of the Protestants. The closely disciplined Calvinist congregations, with their preachers trained in Geneva and their carefully planned and directed propaganda, showed much greater powers of survival in the face of official persecution than the unorganized Lutheran and Baptist groups.[34] When the lower nobility joined the reformed religion in large numbers, the movement rapidly acquired the same military characteristics that made the Huguenots so formidable to the French government. Open mass meetings were held with the women in the center and the men, armed with every conceivable weapon and commanded by the noble members of the congregation, standing guard.[35] By 1565 the court at Brussels, undoubtedly with events in France before their eyes, began to fear open rebellion or, at least, the seizure of some important towns by the Protestants.[36]

---

[34] F. Rachfahl, *Wilhelm von Oranien und der niederländische Aufstand* (Halle, 1906), I, 409–416. Rachfahl stresses Calvin's enormous authority and his direct personal contact with many of the Netherlands reformed communities. This influence preceded their contact with the French Huguenots which became important only after the Treaty of Cateau-Cambrésis (pp. 416–417).

[35] Kervyn de Lettenhove, *Les Huguenots et les gueux* (Bruges, 1883), I, 329.

[36] Instructions to Egmont, Jan., 1565; L. P. Gachard, *Correspondance de Philippe II* (Brussels, 1848), I, 402, where there is talk of revolt in the whole north. J. de Wesenbeke, *Mémoires* (Brussels, 1859), p. 159, reporting rumors of a rebellion of the Protestants, ". . . or that, at least, they want to make themselves masters of some important cities . . .

Public officials in the Netherlands, often imbued by Erasmian ideas of church reform, and disliking the Inquisition, were as little inclined as their French colleagues to execute systematically the rigorous "placards" against the heretics.[37] The movement therefore continued to grow, albeit at a slower rate than it had done in France but finding its converts among very similar groups and classes.

Nevertheless, the Calvinists were as yet only the radical wing of the widespread opposition to religious persecution and to the government's threat to the country's privileges. If, at the assembly of St. Trond, in July, 1566, Louis of Nassau, Brederode, and the lower nobility agreed to cooperate with the Calvinist communities, the higher nobility held apart, frightened as they were by the breaking of the images and other Calvinist excesses.[38] With their help Margaret of Parma was able to reassert the government's authority against the extreme opposition.

The capture of the whole anti-Spanish movement by the Calvinists was the result of the new situation produced by the arrival of Alva: the establishment of a determined and ruthless government with an efficient army at its back.[39] Such a situation

---

among which Antwerp seemed very likely." These references also in H. A. Enno van Gelder, "De nederlandse adel en de opstand tegen Spanje, 1565–1572," *Tijdschrift voor geschiedenis,* No. 43 (1928), p. 9.

[37] Rachfahl, I, 432. P. Geyl, *The Revolt of the Netherlands (1555–1609)* (London, 1932), pp. 83–84.

[38] Geyl, *The Revolt,* p. 92.

[39] Philip II has been almost universally condemned for sending Alva to the Netherlands. But have not these judgments been based largely on the historian's hindsight? Could a strong sixteenth-century ruler have acted differently when faced with the double opposition of the high nobility (albeit a constitutional opposition) and a revolutionary religious movement with a military organization (albeit only in its infancy)? In France and in Scotland the Calvinists had built up their formidable organizations because of the weakness of the French and Scottish governments. It was a commonplace of sixteenth-century statecraft that rebellion should be crushed in its infancy. Moreover, this policy very nearly succeeded. It failed because it was, perhaps, already too late, even in 1567, and because Alva did not command the sea power to crush the Sea Beggars. Undoubt-

never existed in France after the death of Henry II. Against Alva and his *tercios* a general dislike of the foreigner and platonic protests against the illegality of the new governor's edicts could never produce a revolution. That became painfully obvious when not a single major town rose spontaneously to support the Prince of Orange's invasion of 1568.[40] The revolt did not become successful until, in 1572, a naval and military force, the Sea Beggars, had been organized *outside* the Netherlands and had concentrated their attack on Holland and Zealand where the government's military power could be counterbalanced by control of the sea. During the last twenty years Dutch historians have revealed the mechanism of this revolt; and the resulting picture is very different from the traditional one of the Dutch population rising in a mass against economic and religious tyranny.

Having seized Brill by surprise, the Beggars set out systematically to capture the towns of Holland and Zealand. In most cases, the pattern of events was remarkably similar. The patrician councils of the towns had nearly all large Catholic majorities who were loyal to the government, even though they generally detested Alva's religious persecution and heavy taxation. The great mass of the burghers were with them in preferring peace and loyalty to war and revolution, however tyrannical their government. Organized as *schutters* in the citizen guards they nevertheless proudly maintained that they were sufficient to protect their own towns and they therefore opposed the entry of the Spanish garrisons. Alva, menaced by invasion from the south and short of money and troops, had no choice but to ac-

edly, Philip misunderstood the complexity of the situation, and Alva proved to be the wrong choice for his purposes. But that also was not so obvious as it became later; for Alva had behaved with considerable tact in the war against Pope Paul IV. Yet, as will be shown below, even Alva's cruelty did not raise a spontaneous outburst of rebellion from an oppressed people: the revolt of 1572 became possible only through the action of the highly organized and ruthless Sea Beggars and their equally highly organized "fifth column" in the Holland and Zealand towns.

[40] Geyl, *The Revolt*, pp. 107–108.

cept this position. The Beggars, on their side, could rely on a small but determined minority of fanatical Calvinists in the town councils, and on the sympathy of sections of the citizen guard. Calvinist preachers and organizers worked among the townspeople, making converts especially among the poor artisans, and among sailors, shipbuilders, fishermen, and weavers in towns and ports hit by the decline of the Dutch textile and brewing industries and by the disorganization of commerce caused by the privateering of the *gueux*.[41] When the Beggar troops were near enough, the Calvinist minorities would invite them to their towns and open the gates or force the authorities to treat. Even then, the Beggars had to capture some towns by brute force, especially in Friesland and Overyssel.[42] In most towns the Beggars entered by agreement when the authorities had realized that resistance had become militarily impossible,[43] or would cause much bloodshed. On the other hand, where the strategic situation allowed, and where the authorities were sufficiently determined, they could prevent the entry of the Beggars. Thus the burgomasters of Amsterdam raised two companies, provided work for the unemployed on the building of fortifications and the manufacture of munitions, and successfully maintained the city's loyalty to the king until the collapse of Spanish authority after the death of Requesens.[44] Middel-

[41] J. C. Boogman, "De overgang van Gouda, Dordrecht, Leiden en Delft in de zomar van het jaar 1572," *Tijdschrift voor geschiedenis,* 51 (1942), 81–109. In Delft, for instance, Van der Werff, later famous as the defender of Leiden, worked as an underground agitator until expelled by the authorities (*ibid.,* p. 104). In March, 1572, Morillon wrote to Granvelle about Dordrecht: "The sailors are rough and unreasoning men, and the heretics mingle with them and have greater hopes and chances of stirring them up than ever before" (quoted in *ibid.,* p. 95, from *Correspondance de Granvelle,* IV, 149).

[42] Gelder, "De nederlandse adel," p. 140.

[43] As in Rotterdam, where the authorities invited the Beggars to occupy the town peacefully when the Spanish garrison had withdrawn (*ibid.,* p. 154).

[44] *Ibid.,* p. 157; J. Tergouw, *Geschiedenis van Amsterdam* (Amsterdam, 1891), VII, 32–33.

burg resisted a siege by the *gueux* for eighteen months (1572–
1574) and its burghers showed no less heroism in their loyalty
to Philip II than did those of Leiden in their resistance to him.[45]
In both cases, a determined minority wielding ruthless power
forced this heroism upon the mass of the citizens.

Once the Beggars were inside a town the agreements with
the authorities rapidly broke down. Public preaching of the
reformed faith was followed by image breaking, the conversion
of churches for Protestant use, and attacks on monasteries and
convents, accompanied by the expulsion [46] and, at times, by the
murder of monks and the raping or forcible marriage of nuns.[47]
Such atrocities, though generally carried out by the mobs of
the towns, were frequently organized by the Beggars—sometimes as a deliberate policy of terrorizing the population.[48]
Loyalist and moderate magistrates and officers of the *schutters*
were replaced by Beggar officers and ardent Calvinists in the
months following occupation.

It was hardly possible for the revolutionaries to act otherwise.
Despite the appeal of the movement to the mass of the poorer

[45] Gelder, "De nederlandse adel," p. 156.

[46] E.g., at Alkmaar and Leiden (H. A. Enno van Gelder, *Revolutionnaire reformatie* [Amsterdam, 1943], pp. 20, 26–27).

[47] E.g., at Gouda (Boogman, "De overgang," pp. 91–93).

[48] The Beggar leader Lumey was notorious in this respect. Sonoy, Beggar leader and Orange's governor of the Noorderkvartier, arrested a number of Catholic peasants and had them tortured to obtain confessions of
treachery—a very effective method of establishing his party in the predominantly Catholic countryside (Gelder, *Revolutionnaire reformatie*, pp.
21–22). Knox's "brethren" behaved little better in the sack of the monasteries of Perth, in 1559, when "the priests were commanded, under pain
of death, to desist from their blasphemous mass" (Knox to Mrs. Locke,
June 23, 1559, quoted in A. Lang, *John Knox and the Reformation* [Lon-
don, 1905], p. 112). In his *History of the Reformation* (ed. W. Croft Dick-
inson [London, 1949], I, 162) Knox, however, blamed the "rascal multitude" for this act and disclaimed responsibility for the gentlemen and
the "earnest confessors." It is, at any rate, a characteristic of sixteenth-
century revolutionary movements that they had learned the political value
of terror and mob violence.

classes, and its ability to mobilize the mob at strategic moments, the number of convinced Calvinists remained very small for a long time. In 1576 the Calvinist congregation in Alkmaar numbered only 160 in a population of 6,000; [49] in Dordrecht, more than a year after the occupation, the *Grote Kerk* counted only 368 Calvinist communicants against 8,000 of the old church earlier in the century. [50] These may have been extreme cases; but where no attempt was made to change the old regime after occupation by the Beggars the magistrates might attempt to negotiate with the Spaniards at the first favorable opportunity. This happened in Haarlem where the situation was only saved when the *gueux* captain, Ripperda, called upon the citizen guard to resist the magistrates, and Philippe de Marnix replaced the town councilors by safe Orangeists. [51] For the same reason of the security of the revolution the Calvinist congregations could not be allowed to elect their own ministers but had to accept their appointment by the Calvinist consistory [52]—a reversal of the original democratic program of the Calvinist communities. [53] Only very gradually, through the work of schools, propaganda, and official pressure, was the mass of the population won over to the new faith. [54]

The revolution of Holland and Zealand was the work of a highly organized minority, officered and controlled by the nobility, disciplined and united by the Calvinist faith, and sup-

---

[49] Gelder, *Revolutionnaire reformatie,* p. 20.     [50] *Ibid.,* p. 25.

[51] *Ibid.,* pp. 36–38.     [52] *Ibid.,* p. 26.

[53] It is interesting to compare this with Knox's disillusioning experience of democratic election. In 1563 Knox told the queen that he had proposed her cousin, Alexander Gordon, for election as superintendent of the kirk at Dumfries. Mary warned him that Gordon was worthless and dangerous. "And yet, Madam," Knox answered, "I am assured God will not suffer his Church to be so far deceived as that an unworthy man shall be elected, where free election is, and the spirit of God is earnestly called upon to decide betwixt the two." But the queen proved right; for Gordon corrupted "most part of the gentlemen, not only to nominate him, but to elect him." Knox stopped the election but, characteristically, allowed Mary no credit for the warning (Knox, II, 73).

[54] P. Geyl, "De protestantiseering van Noord-Nederland," *Leiding,* 1, No. 5 (1930), 123.

ported by the discontented workers and artisans, and by those members of the bourgeoisie whose hatred of the Spaniards and their exactions was greater than their loyalty to the government and their love of peace. Once the revolutionaries had seized power, the mass of the Catholic population showed no more desire to rise against the new tyranny (often highly unpopular after a very short time) than it had shown against the old.[55] While the Prince of Orange failed to check all the excesses of the *gueux* and was unable to preserve full toleration for the Catholics as he would have preferred to do, he could still use the Beggar movement for his wider political purposes.

Up to this point the position of the Protestant movement in Holland and Zealand was therefore essentially similar to that of the Huguenot movement in France; but with the temporary collapse of Spanish power, in 1576, the situation changed completely. Orange's ideal of the union of all the provinces in revolt against Spain now became a practical possibility; but it could be achieved only at the expense of the homogeneity of the revolutionary movement. The large industrial towns of Flanders and Brabant on the one hand and the Catholic high nobility of the Walloon provinces on the other were amenable neither to control by the Beggar movement nor willing to accept Orange's policy of limited revolution. The Pacification of Ghent left the towns of Brabant and Flanders in the hands of Catholic magistrates, often those appointed by Alva himself. Anti-Catholic speech and action was still punished.[56] The Calvinists could never accept this. From August, 1577, revolutions broke out in Brussels, Antwerp, s'Hertogenbosch, and Ghent. In contrast to the events in Holland and Zealand, the Calvinist minorities here acted from the inside. In Brussels they set up a

[55] Sixteenth-century observers, innocent of the Protestant and nationalistic romanticism of the nineteenth century, did not find this surprising —e.g., Scipio de Castro, "Discorso sopra l'andata dell'arciduca Matthia d'Austria in Fiandra," *Thesoro politico terza parte* (Turnoni, 1605), p. 134: "The multitude is fierce as long as it sees danger far off, but weakens and turns tail when it begins to see it close by; for no one who can live wants to die."

[56] Gelder, *Revolutionnaire reformatie*, pp. 45–50.

War Council of Eighteen. It was chosen by the popular element in the city government and soon came to dominate it. Other towns followed the example of Brussels and soon had their own Councils of Eighteen.[57] The now familiar pattern of events repeated itself: the mobs were allowed, or incited, to sack churches and monasteries; Catholic magistrates were replaced by Calvinists; the Councils of Eighteen appointed their own creatures as captains of the citizen guard; Catholic burghers were terrorized into silence. By the end of 1578 the traditionally Catholic and patrician governments of the towns had been replaced by democratic dictatorships which interpreted the toleration clauses of the Pacification of Ghent as confirming liberty of conscience only to the Calvinists.[58]

Nowhere was the revolution carried so far as in Ghent. Fired by the demagogic preaching of Peter Dathenus, and organized by the able and ambitious lord of Rijhove and Jan van Hembyze, the Ghenters carried their revolution through the length and breadth of Flanders. With the help of native sympathizers they set up revolutionary Calvinist governments in Bruges, Ypres, Oudenaarde, and other towns.[59] For the last time

[57] *Ibid.*, pp. 49–51.

[58] This interpretation of liberty of conscience was common to all Calvinist communities in the sixteenth century. Thus in Scotland the Congregation refused to accept Mary of Guise's proposal that the reformed religion should be allowed except where she herself resided. "That as we would compel her Grace to no religion, so we could not of conscience, for the pleasure of any earthly creature, put silence to God's true messengers; neither could we suffer that the right administration of Christ's true sacraments should give place to manifest idolatry; for in so doing we should declare ourselves enemies to God, to Christ Jesus his Son, to his eternal verity, and to the liberty and establishment of the Church within this realm; for your request being granted, there can no Kirk within the same be so established but at your residence and remaining there ye might overthrow the same" (Knox, I, 197–198). The last argument was fair enough, although there is no evidence that the regent intended to act in this way. From the whole of Knox's *History* it is clear that he would not accept any compromise if he could help it.

[59] Gelder, *Revolutionnaire reformatie*, pp. 58–59; V. Fris, *Histoire de Gand* (Brussels, 1913), p. 226.

in her long revolutionary history, Ghent became the leader of
an artisans' revolution, but this time with the help of a revolutionary organization that the Arteveldes would have envied.[60]
Only through rigid organization could the Ghenters now hope
for success; for the city had long since declined from its greatest
period of economic power and prosperity. But this revolution
was no longer controlled by the nobility, as it had been in Holland, nor could it be tolerated by them. The Catholic Walloon
magnates bitterly complained to Orange [61] and Orange in turn
tried to moderate a movement, the fatal results of whose actions
he clearly foresaw.[62]

In August, 1579, the breach became open. Supported by
Rijhove, the lower nobility, and the moderates, Orange entered
Ghent and disarmed the Eighteen. Hembyze and Dathenus
fled. But the harm was done: both the Walloon high nobility
and the Calvinist extremists had become Orange's irreconcil-

[60] In July, 1578, the first open synod of the reformed churches of Flanders was held in Ghent with delegates from 17 congregations. The discussions centered mainly on the appointment of preachers for the province
and other measures to increase the unity of the movement (Gelder, *Revolutionnaire reformatie,* p. 58).

[61] E.g., the Seigneur de Masnuy to Orange, Dec. 24, 1578: "In few places
in Flanders where the storm of the Ghenters has broken, has the Roman
religion been able to maintain itself: which shows that it was not so much
the zeal to advance their religion, as their greed and desire for revenge
which has driven them. It is clear at a glance that they wanted to attack
the nobility; for some of them have been so long and unjustly imprisoned
[i.e., the nobles arrested by the Ghenters in October, 1577, of whom only
the duke of Aerschot had been released] and others have been exiled,
banished and deprived of their property, estates and offices, and finally
chased from the assembly of the States-General which was summoned for
the common good of our country—truly an insupportable matter for any
man of true heart and noble condition." He added that they were only
exchanging one tyranny for another and that, in these popular movements, the name of "the people" was no more than a label (L. P. Gachard, *Correspondance de Guillaume le Taciturne* [Brussels, 1854], IV,
130–131).

[62] Letters from Orange to the burgomasters and *échevins* of Bruges and
Ghent, throughout the summer and autumn of 1578, *ibid.,* pp. 51, 52–53,
72–79.

able enemies. As military reverse followed upon military reverse, the extremists once more gained the upper hand. Four years after their flight Hembyze and Dathenus returned to Ghent. The dictatorship was re-established. But, just as it was to happen in later revolutionary movements, the struggle for power within the revolutionary movement now became more important than the fight against the common enemy. Hembyze and Dathenus opened negotiations with the duke of Parma and started replacing Calvinist officials by Catholics. This was too much even for their own supporters. In March, 1584, they arrested the old dictator, Hembyze, and on August 4 he was executed. But the revolution was lost; six weeks later Ghent surrendered to the Spaniards.[63] From then on, the issue between the rebels and the Spaniards became almost entirely one of purely military power. The period of revolutions was over.

It is not surprising that Calvinist extremism should have evoked the reaction of a similar Catholic extremism. In the Netherlands the Spanish government itself represented Catholic extremism. Independent Catholic organization, as in the Union of Arras, was therefore largely conservative and nonrevolutionary. In France, however, the Catholic government was weak and willing to compromise with the Huguenots. Local Catholic unions, or leagues, therefore began to be formed by local authorities, nobles, and prelates as early as 1560 and 1562, especially in the south where Huguenot pressure was at its strongest.[64] But it was only in 1576, after Henry III's far-reaching concessions to the Huguenots in the Peace of Monsieur, that the local leagues were organized into a nationwide league, or holy union. Where the Huguenot party had been built on

---

[63] The whole account from Fris, *Histoire de Gand,* pp. 231–236, and from Gelder, *Revolutionnaire reformatie,* pp. 128–131.

[64] Kelly, *French Protestantism,* pp. 78–79. The earliest Catholic leagues seem to have been formed in Bordeaux, in 1560. In May, 1562, the parlement of Paris directed the *échevins* and all loyal Catholics, in every quarter of the city, to organize under arms.

the union of the militarized Calvinist communities with the Bourbon family connection, the League was built on the union of the military Catholic nobility with the Guise family connection. Where the Huguenots and the Sea Beggars looked to Geneva for spiritual guidance and to England and the Protestant princes of Germany for material help, the Leaguers looked to Rome and to the Catholic rulers of Spain and Savoy. Thus, all three revolutionary movements were linked with powers and interests outside their national boundaries. This added to their strength, but it also set up tensions within the movements that greatly increased the difficulties of unified leadership.

The League of 1576 was founded as a Catholic party of the nobility [65] with essentially conservative aims: Henry III and his successors were to be preserved in their authority according to their coronation oaths and without prejudice to the estates; [66] the provinces were to have their ancient rights restored to them.[67] This program did not differ substantially from many similar feudal programs of the Middle Ages. But the remaining nine articles had a most unmedieval ring; they were the articles dealing with the organization of the League.[68] All members were to defend each other, by force of arms if need be; the governors of towns and villages were secretly to advise Catholics to join the association and to provide arms and men according to their faculties; all were to swear prompt and strict obedience to the chief of the League, without respect for any other authority; [69] all who refused to join were to be regarded as enemies and those who, having joined, wanted to withdraw were

[65] Article I of the League defined it as an association of princes, seigneurs, and gentlemen to establish the law of God and protect the service of the Catholic church (P. V. Palma Cayet, "Chronologie novenaire," in Petitot, *Collection des mémoires sur l'histoire de France,* Ser. 1, XXXVIII [Paris, 1823], p. 254).

[66] Article II, *ibid.,* p. 255.      [67] Article III, *ibid.*

[68] Articles IV–XII, *ibid.,* pp. 255–57.

[69] Article VII, *ibid.,* p. 256. Palma Cayet pointed out that this article was clearly an invitation to rebellion if the king should oppose the League (*Ibid.,* p. 259).

to be effectively outlawed and hounded down while their pur-
suers would be protected from all public and private reprisals.[70]
A powerful religious sanction was provided by the oath which
every member had to take, binding himself to observe the
articles on pain of anathema and eternal damnation.[71]

In many parts of France the League was broadened to include the clergy and the third estate [72] and, just as in the Huguenot movement, the lower orders were enrolled to provide mass
support.[73]

The power of this new party became immediately apparent
in the States-General of Blois of 1576. The agents of the League
were everywhere. They manipulated the elections and intimi-
dated voters; League *baillis* and *sénéchaux* tried to prevent the
Huguenots from attending the electoral meetings.[74] Within the
assembly they organized an adroit attack on the king's powers
in the name of the old privileges of the estates and provinces.[75]

[70] Article VI, *ibid.,* p. 256.

[71] The oath, in Article XII, is worth quoting in full: "I swear before
God the Creator, touching this bible and on pain of anathema and eternal damnation, that I have loyally and sincerely entered into this holy
Catholic association according to the form of the agreement that has been
presented to me, be it to command in it or to obey and serve; and I
promise on my life and honor to remain in it [the association] to the last
drop of my blood, not to oppose it nor to withdraw from it for any order, pretext, excuse nor occasion whatsoever" (*ibid.,* p. 257).

[72] E.g., in the Bourbonnais and in Burgundy (J. Loutchitzky, *Documents inédits pur servir à l'histoire de la Réforme et de la Ligue* [Kiev,
1875], pp. 30–34, 35–37).

[73] In Toulouse all those capable of bearing arms were eligible. Those
who could not afford to buy arms were to be assisted. The signatures of
many artisans appear under the oath, and behind the names of most of
these appeared the remark: "cannot write nor make a mark" (*ibid.,* pp.
23–25).

[74] M. Wilkinson, *A History of the League or Sainte Union, 1576–1595*
(Glasgow, 1929), pp. 9–10.

[75] A discussion of the parliamentary aims and tactics of the League falls
outside the scope of this article. In essence, it was the classical situation of
a strong group, balked from direct influence over the government, using
the representative assembly as an indirect means of attaining its aims.

For all its formidable organization, however, the League was not yet a revolutionary party. But as a threat to the king's independence it was too dangerous to be ignored, the more so, as its close links with Madrid were well known. To draw its teeth, therefore, and if possible to make it serve his own purposes by providing troops and money against the Protestants, Henry III declared himself chief of the League in January, 1577.[76] As head of such an organization he hoped to have far greater powers and authority over his subjects than he had ever had as king. But, as the duke of Nevers pointed out immediately, the nobility were not likely to exchange their vague obligations to serve the king for the very precise and far-reaching obligations they would have to the king as chief of the League.[77] The organization which had been created to coerce the king disintegrated in his hands when he tried to use it for his own purposes. If this was disappointing, it was still better than leaving such a weapon in the hands of the duke of Guise. In the Peace of Bergerac, in September, 1577, all leagues and associations were dissolved by royal edict.[78]

The League of 1576 had been dominated by the nobility and its aims had been primarily constitutional. Until the king's interference unified control by the duke of Guise had been comparatively easy. The League which appeared in 1585, after the death of the duke of Anjou had revealed to Catholics the specter of a Protestant succession, was at once more revolutionary and much less homogeneous. It started as a secret society of a small number of fanatical Catholics among the Parisian bourgeoisie, mostly priests and professional men.[79] Its discipline, dedication to the cause and puritanical insistence on the personal virtue of its members, was as severe as in any Calvinist community.

[76] Loutchitzky, pp. 42–44, and corrections of this version of the documents by Mariéjol, p. 178, n. 1.

[77] Mariéjol, p. 178.

[78] *Ibid.*, p. 191.

[79] For a full account see *Dialogue d'entre le Maheustre et le Manant*, pp. 50–53.

When they had built up a strong party among the artisans, guilds, and public officials of the municipality they entered into relations with Guise and the Catholic princes.[80] Immediately, the old League of 1576 reappeared all over France.[81] In town after town the Leaguers removed royalist commanders and governors and replaced them by their own men, on the pretext of insuring a firmer anti-Huguenot policy.[82] Not for the last time, a moderate government fighting a revolutionary party found itself outbid by an extremist and equally revolutionary party on its own side.

In Paris, the League rapidly gained in strength and confidence. Their growing tyranny over the city has been brilliantly traced in the diary of Pierre de l'Estoile, their bitter enemy. The Paris mob, which had already proved its talent for murderous pogroms in the Massacre of St. Bartholomew, was being systematically roused by the League preachers—for once the oratorical equals of their Calvinist rivals—until every misfortune and every crime was attributed to the Calvinists and Politiques.[83] The famous "Day of the Barricades," May 12, 1588, when Henry III and his Swiss mercenaries were driven out of the capital had been planned and organized as much as a year before.[84]

Once again, it was the weakness of the government which made possible the rapid progress of the League; for the League, again like other revolutionary parties, was only a small minority,[85] achieving its aims by strict organization, ruthless determi-

---

[80] Mariéjol, pp. 243–244.

[81] The signal was a declaration of the old Cardinal of Bourbon, the cat's-paw of Guise, claiming the succession against the heretic Henry of Bourbon, King of Navarre (in S. Goulart, *Mémoires de la Ligue,* new ed. [Amsterdam, 1758], I, 56–63).

[82] P. de l'Estoile, *Journal de règne de Henri III,* L. R. Lefèvre, ed. (Paris, 1943), p. 93.

[83] *Ibid.,* p. 567.     [84] *Dialogue,* p. 56.

[85] On this point both the royalist L'Estoile (p. 583) and the Leaguer author of the *Dialogue* (pp. 57–58) are agreed. Where the former blamed the fear from which the majority suffered, the latter saw in the success of

nation of aim, and the tactics of infiltration into public offices.[86]

After the murder of the duke of Guise, on December 23, 1588, the League came out in open rebellion against the king. In Provence the parlement declared for the League and the towns renounced their allegiance to "the assassin Henry III."

Elsewhere it needed the appearance of Leaguer troops to overawe the loyalist provincial parlements.[87] In almost every town the League had a strong party in the council and among the *échevins*. Members of the League now swore allegiance to Mayenne. With the help of his troops, or with the force provided by the retainers of the local Leaguer nobility, revolutionary governments were set up in almost all towns outside the Loire valley which the king managed to hold. Secret or open League committees, composed of members of the three estates, supervised the councils and imprisoned nobles and officials suspected of royalist sympathies.[88] In Toulouse, always fanatically Catholic, the *capitouls* (mayor and corporation) declared for the League, and when the parlement wanted to maintain the king's authority, the mob invaded the court and murdered the president-general.[89]

---

the League the hand of God. In a few towns the Catholic and royalist population (and, probably, the local authorities) managed to throw out the League troops (L'Estoile, *Journal*, pp. 390, 392).

[86] After the "Day of the Barricades" Henry III was no longer in a position to prevent this. In July, 1588, he made concessions to the Parisians over the control of the police and the fortifications of the Bastille but reserved for himself the right to appoint the commander of the Paris region ("Remonstrances des habitans de la ville de Paris: avec les responses du roy . . . Juillet 1588" in Gonzaga, I, 733–735). Later in the same year Guise simply replaced royalist officials by his own adherents (J. A. de Thou, *Histoire universelle*, livre 90, X [1734] quoted in L'Estoile, p. 736, n. 527).

[87] Wilkinson, pp. 77–79.

[88] *Ibid.*, pp. 78–80; Loutchitzky, pp. 229–294, *passim*.

[89] Wilkinson, pp. 80–81. If we are to believe L'Estoile (*Journal*, p. 621), the League terror, or threat of terror, was at times carried to extraordinary length. At Anger, in March, 1589, "the count de Brissac left by one gate just as the marshal [d'Aumont, the royalist commander] entered by

But it was in Paris that the revolution was carried to its furthest extremes. The League organization in each of the sixteen quarters of the city set up a committee charged with police functions and the supervision of the municipal officials.[90] These committees, in turn, formed a central committee, called the Sixteen, after the number of quarters in the capital, but with an actual membership of up to fifty. The Sixteen established the first revolutionary reign of terror that Paris was to experience. To coordinate the movement in the provinces the Sixteen sent their agents to the provinces and received those of the provincial towns.[91] The general council of the League was thus in full control of the whole network of Leaguer towns in France.

The aristocratic members of the general council, however, were becoming increasingly uneasy about the revolutionary and democratic policy of the Sixteen. L'Estoile was not alone in resenting the appointment of "small tradesmen and a bunch of Leaguer scoundrels" [92] to the captaincies of the citizen guards and to high municipal offices. Already in February, 1589, Mayenne had tried to counterbalance the democratic wing of the general council by appointing to it fourteen members of the Parisian *haute bourgeoisie* and the parlement.[93] The Sixteen answered by setting up a Committee of Public Safety with ten members. In November, 1591, they struck against their most hated enemy in Paris, the parlement. Brisson, its president, and the councilors Larcher and Tardif were arrested and executed for alleged treason.[94]

the other, leaving him the place faint-heartedly enough and without carrying out what he had loudly threatened—to drown the wives and daughters of all those who would not sign for the League."

[90] Mariéjol, p. 293; *Dialogue,* p. 42.

[91] *Dialogue,* pp. 48–49. Some of the larger towns, such as Toulouse, sent their own propaganda agents to the smaller towns (Loutchitzky, pp. 262–263).

[92] L'Estoile, p. 566.      [93] Mariéjol, p. 293.

[94] *Ibid.,* p. 345. The Sixteen later claimed that the other councilors of the parlement approved this action. Brisson was alleged to have wanted

This act made the breach between the aristocratic Politiques and the democratic Sixteen irreconcilable. In December, 1591, Mayenne arrested several of the Sixteen. Others who were implicated in the execution of the councilors fled. But Mayenne refused to act against the preachers or to destroy the Sixteen completely.[95] Yet his attempt to hold together and balance the revolutionary and aristocratic wings of the League was doomed to failure just as the similar attempts of the Prince of Orange in the parallel situation in Flanders and Brabant, ten years before. While Henry IV steadily advanced, Mercœur and others of the high nobility, maneuvered to rescue private empires from the approaching defeat. The lower nobility began to play for safety by placing a son in each of the opposing camps.[96] When Henry IV became a Catholic, the only effective bond between the different sections of the League, fear of a heretic king, disappeared. With the desertion of the Politiques and the mass of the lower nobility, the League broke up: Mayenne's ambition was left face to face with the Catholic fanaticism of the Parisian democracy. Besieged, and isolated from the provinces, their interurban contacts broken by Mayenne's intrigues and Henry's advance, their position in the capital undermined by Mayenne's "Thermidor" of 1591, the revolutionary leaders of Paris were left with only one ally—the Catholic autocrat, Philip II of Spain. It was the *reductio ad absurdum* of revolu-

to bribe the commander of the *Lanzknechts* to desert to Henry of Navarre; Larcher was said to be the leader of a party against "the cause of bread and peace" and his eldest son was found armed in the *palais* of the parlement; Tardif was alleged to be an agent of the duke of Nevers, the renegade Leaguer (*Dialogue*, p. 70). The author of the *Dialogue*—possibly Cromé, one of the Sixteen, according to Palma Cayet ("Chronologie novenaire," p. 272), and also according to a MS note in the British Museum copy of the *Dialogue*—later produced what seems to be the first theoretical justification of revolutionary terror in modern European history: "All treason against the public must receive exemplary punishment, and failing ordinary methods, extraordinary ones are allowed." He claimed that God himself acted in this way, allowing men to act in extraordinary fashion when ordinary methods failed (*ibid.*, p. 71).

[95] Mariéjol, p. 347.    [96] *Dialogue*, p. 43.

tion and it was its end. The Spanish armies failed to relieve Paris, and on March 22, 1594, Henry IV entered his capital almost unopposed.[97]

It was the paradox of the revolutionary movements of the sixteenth century that they were led by men who were not revolutionaries. Condé and Navarre, Orange, Guise and Mayenne did not create the organization of their parties. Their aim, as that of many aristocratic rebels before them, was to capture the existing machinery of state without subverting the social order or radically changing the political, or even religious, structure of the country. Yet they found themselves carried far along the path to political and social revolution by the revolutionary parties of which they were the leaders.[98] The lower nobility who formed the most active elements in all three movements as well as their military cadres, the rich burghers and impoverished artisans of the citizen guards in the towns— these were the revolutionary forces, and they were effectively revolutionary by virtue of their economic ambitions and their religious beliefs. Religion was the binding force that held together the divergent interests of the different classes and provided them with an organization and a propaganda machine capable of creating the first genuinely national and international parties in modern European history; for these parties never embraced more than a minority of each of their constitu-

[97] Mariéjol, p. 387.

[98] The same, *mutatis mutandis,* was true in Scotland. Thus Maitland of Lethington wrote to Cecil, April 17, 1560: "As I have often touched to your honour, the points necessary for our safety are (1) the removal of the French, and (2) government by our own born men" (*Calendar of Scottish Papers* [Edinburgh, 1898], I, 364). But Knox and the "brethren" who provided the ideological driving force of the movement against Mary of Guise aimed at a democratic religious revolution. The divergence of purpose was illustrated very clearly in Knox's disputation with Lethington, on the question of non-resistance to magistrates, in June, 1564. It illustrates, incidentally, Knox's outstanding grasp of the problem of power (see Knox, II, 121–122).

ent classes. Moreover it was through religion that they could appeal to the lowest classes and the mob to vent the anger of their poverty and the despair of their unemployment in barbarous massacres and fanatical looting. Social and economic discontent were fertile ground for recruitment by either side, and popular democratic tyranny appeared both in Calvinist Ghent and Catholic Paris.[99]

In the long run, not even religion was able to reconcile the nobility with democratic dictatorships,[100] and one side or the other was driven into alliance with the formerly common enemy. The result was, in every case, the breakup of the revolutionary party and the defeat of the popular movement.[101] Where the nobility and urban patriciate managed to maintain control over the revolutionary movement they also managed to achieve a great part of their revolutionary aims. Significantly,

[99] Gelder, "De nederlandse adel," p. 139, and Boogman, "De overgang," pp. 111–112, have rightly stressed the importance of the religious factor in the Netherlands revolt of 1572, as against the almost exclusive stress on the economic factors—notably Alva's tax of the tenth penny—by the older historians. As a "common denominator" religion has the advantage, for the historian, of being homogeneous and easily recognizable. But it does not follow that economic and social motivation was therefore less important, and the evidence provided by Gelder and Boogman themselves does not support such a view. The social and economic factors were, however, much more complex and less homogeneous than had been supposed. There was no a priori connection between Calvinism and social discontent. The connection was rather between social discontent and a revolutionary religion, and this the League preachers of Paris could provide as well as the Calvinists. Which particular version, Calvinist or Catholic, was successful depended on the whole complex political and social situation of a particular country or town, on the traditions of the different classes, and on the opportunities for, and effectiveness of, revolutionary organization.

[100] The clearest contemporary exposition of this problem is in the *Dialogue d'entre le Maheustre et le Manant, passim.*

[101] The Anabaptist movements in Germany were never part of a wider revolutionary party including the privileged classes. This may well account for their complete failure as against the partial success of the revolutions in France, the Netherlands, and Scotland.

however, the Huguenots and the Dutch Calvinists, once firmly in the saddle, abandoned the greater part of their revolutionary organization. Only in the field of religion did they carry their revolutions to the full conclusion. The Huguenots maintained their religious rights for another hundred years while the Dutch Calivinists succeeded in converting the majority of the population.[102] Yet, in neither case did the radical wing of the Calvinists succeed in establishing a rigorous theocracy on the Geneva model. Despite the constant insistence on religious unity, the possibilities of the political single-party state were not yet fully recognized. Henry III's tentative moves in that direction ended in complete failure. A Calvinist (or Catholic) theocracy had come to be equated with democratic tyranny, and neither nobility nor urban patriciate were willing to accept this. The traditional governments, when firmly led, were still too powerful and commanded the traditional allegiance of the subject.[103] The traditional social and political structure of Europe had still too much toughness, the traditional ruling classes still too much vitality. It was another two hundred years before they were effectively challenged and before a revolutionary party appeared that was as highly organized as those of the sixteenth century.

[102] This was substantially true in Scotland as in the United Provinces and in southern France. In none of these countries, however, were these social and religious tensions fully resolved until the seventeenth century.

[103] Cf. Argyll and Lord James Stuart to Sir James Croft, English agent in Scotland, Aug. 6, 1559: "You know, sir, how difficult it is to persuade a multitude to revolt of established authority" (*Calendar of Scottish Papers,* I, 240).

# CHAPTER 10

# The Revolt of Palermo in 1647[1]

"When Antichrist comes, he shall seem as Christ. There shall be great want, and Antichrist shall go from land to land and give bread to the poor. And he shall find many followers."

(*Old Sicilan Legend*)

THERE IS no stronger proof of the stability of the empire which Charles V and Philip II had built, and of the vitality of

[1] This account is based primarily on the following contemporary Sicilian and Spanish diaries and chronicles which, to a varying degree, are all hostile to the popular movement: V. Auria, "Diario delle cose occorse nella città di Palermo e nel Regno di Sicilia," in G. di Marzo, *Bibl[ioteca] Stor[ica] e Lett[eraria de Sicilia]* (Palermo, 1896), Vol. III; D. Aragona (?) "Continuación de los tumultos de Palermo," etc., L. Boglino, ed., in *Archivo storico siciliano*, N.S., D. Aragona, "Epitome delle seconde rivoluzione di Palermo," di Marzo, trans., in *Bibl. Stor. e Lett.*, Vol. IV; A. Collurafi, *Tumultuationi della plebe in Palermo* (Palermo, 1651); Rocco Pirri, "Annales Panormi sub annis D. Ferdinandi de Andrada," etc., in *Bibl. Stor. e Lett.*, Vol. IV; Placido Reina (Andrea Pocili), *Delle rivolutioni della città di Palermo avvenute l' anno 1647* (Verona, 1648); M. Serio, "Veridica Relazione di tumulti accorsi nell' anno . . . 1647 e 1648 nella citta di Palermo," in *Bibl. Stor. e Lett.*, Vol. IV; "Breve Relazione [del come si scoprà la congiura macchinata da alcuni per sollevare Palermo . . .]," di Marzo, trans., in *Bibl. Stor. e Lett.*, Vol. IV.

There is an excellent and detailed nineteenth-century account, mainly of Alesi, in I. La Lumia, *Storie Siciliane* (Plermo, 1883), Vol. IV; and a full and very competent article by A. Siciliano in *Archivio Storico per la Sicilia*, vols. 4 and 5 (Palermo, 1938–39), based on much unpublished material. There is, however, no attempt to place the revolt in its historical setting.

There are shorter accounts in the eighteenth- and nineteenth-century general histories of Sicily, notably in G. B. di Blasi, *Storia Cronologica de' Vicere*, (Palermo, 1791), Vol. III.

the monarchic idea in the seventeenth century, than the ability of the Spanish monarchy to survive the crisis of the years 1647 and 1648. In a dispatch to his senate the Venetian ambassador in Madrid [2] characterized Spain's history in those years as a string of disasters: Portugal and Catalonia in open revolt; Andalusia in the grip of corruption owing to the treachery of the duke of Medina Sidonia; the East Indies with Brazil (a country large enough for four kingdoms) lost with Portugal; the West Indies hard pressed by the Dutch; the royal revenues mortgaged, credit extinct; friends become enemies or vacillating neutrals, and the government abandoned to the inexperience of a new favorite. Thus the Spanish monarchy resembled that great colossus which for many years had been the wonder of the world and which during an earthquake had collapsed in a few moments while every one hurried along to enrich himself with the fragments.

The ambassador could have added the popular revolts in the Spanish dependencies of Naples and Sicily, revolts which Mazarin described as "very important" in a letter of August 16 to the French delegate at Muenster,[3] and which he hoped would lead the Spaniards to make peace. But it was not only in the Spanish Empire that revolutions broke out; between 1647 and 1660 there were revolutions in England, France, and the Netherlands, so that the middle of the seventeenth century saw revolutions more widespread than at any other time except in 1848.[4] The causes of these revolutions differed as widely as the degree of success which they achieved. The revolts in the Spanish Empire, however, have in common the fundamental factor of a reaction against a system of government which, after a series of heavy defeats in a long war, had been driven to a progressively increasing exploitation of its dependencies—putting unbearable financial burdens on the lower classes or infringing

---

[2] Pietro Bassadonna in *Relazioni degli Ambasciatori Veneti,* Barozzi and Berchet, ed., ser. I, vol. II (Venice, 1860), p. 197.

[3] *Lettres du Cardinal Mazarin,* A. Chéruel, ed. (Paris, 1879), II, p. 473.

[4] [R. B.] Merriman, *Six Contemporaneous Revolutions* (Oxford, 1938).

the political privileges of aristocracies and commercial middle classes in traditionally autonomous states, in its efforts to create a centralized Spanish state. In Naples and Sicily this reaction developed into an attack on the whole social system, while in Catalonia and Portugal the movement was socially on the defensive and was therefore content to aim at political independence. The revolt of Sicily therefore, although it exerted no permanent influence on the general course of European history, has historical significance as part of the general revolutionary movement at the end of the Wars of Religion.[5]

Sicily was the oldest Spanish dominion in Italy, and the Sicilian nobles and towns had called in the Aragonese kings as early as the thirteenth century, so that they had been able to retain most of their feudal privileges intact. As a result, Spanish rule, exercised by viceroys sent from Spain ever since 1410, was not nearly as oppressive in Sicily as in Naples and Milan, but was certainly less efficient. The viceroy had to balance between the two poles of the Sicilian parliament—representing the enormously powerful and largely hispanicized absentee landowner class of nobles and prelates who had also come to fill the most important positions in the Sicilians cities—and the government at Madrid to which all important decisions had to be referred and which was always willing to sacrifice any particular viceroy to the clamor which the general unpopularity of Spanish rule would evoke in Sicily.[6] Skillful exploitation of class antagonisms and of the rivalry of the large cities had to make up for the small size of the Spanish garrison which Spain, at the end of the Thirty Years' War, was in no position to reinforce. The mass of the people, as artisans in the towns, or working on the nobles' estates in the country, were without political rights and helpless against the proverbially corrupt Sicilian officials and the ever-increasing taxation which the government in Madrid had demanded for its wars and which the parliamen-

[5] It is not discussed by Merriman.

[6] Cf. Ranke, "Die Osmanen und die Spanische Monarchie," in *Sämtl. Werke* (Leipzig, 1877), xxxv–xxxvi, 209 ff.

tary classes had done their best to pass on to them. The interests of the merchant bourgeoisie in the towns, which was more Catalan and Genoese than Sicilian, approximated to those of the nobility to whose ranks they were always hoping to be raised.[7]

Throughout the first half of the century there had been a gradual increase of prosperity [8] and the population of Palermo had risen to 130,000.[9] The growing wealth was, however, unequally distributed and while enterprising nobles and merchants made fortunes, the mass of the population was only aware of the increasing taxation on the necessities of life. The peasants, as everywhere in southern Italy, lived only just above starvation level, and one bad harvest, like that of 1646, was enough to upset the delicate balance of the complicated food economy of the island.

Like most seventeenth-century officials, the Sicilians dreaded famine unless their granaries were full to overflowing. In consequence, harvests were immediately bought up and stored in special granaries, called *caricatori,* so that domestic needs could be satisfied and at the same time duties imposed on all exports. The necessary money had to be borrowed from the banks, which further increased prices, and it was not always possible to prevent private local monopolies and speculation, despite commissioners sent into the country to hunt for hidden foodstuffs, and minute prescriptions for quality, weight, and price of bread.[10]

Messina, situated in a non-corngrowing area, was most heavily hit by the failure of the corn crop in the autumn of 1646. When the senate decided to decrease the weight of bread there were riots which were not put down until the viceroy, the

[7] E.g., in 1637 Antonio Colonna was invested with the "Barony of Biscuits" which meant the rights of the gabelle on biscuits. D. Orlando, *Il Feudalismo in Sicilia* (Palermo, 1847), p. 73.

[8] Siciliano, *Archivio Storico,* pp. 192–193.

[9] La Lumia, *Storie Siciliane,* p. 12, with discussion of authorities for this figure.

[10] *Ibid.,* pp. 20 ff.

Marquis de los Vélez, had hurried from Palermo to Messina, frightened the crowd by summarily executing its leaders, and provided more food. Fully alive to the danger of further outbreaks of bread riots, Vélez returned to Palermo in February, 1647, to find the population of that town much increased. The senate of Palermo had been buying grain at high prices and selling bread at a loss to keep food prices within the reach of the poor. This had attracted starving peasants from miles of surrounding countryside where prices had soared and foodstuffs had disappeared into the hands of aristocratic speculators and peasant hoarders. With the peasants came the bandits, the *fuorosciti,* as common in those days and as greatly feared as they were in the twentieth-century days of the Mafia.

The situation did not improve: torrential winter rains were succeeded by drought in the spring, with plague following in its wake and no hope of a better harvest. In May the authorities ordered public penances to be performed. Day after day, processions of monks, nuns, and high dignitaries marched through the streets, with bare feet and bare heads, flagellating themselves or panting under heavy crowns of spikes and chains, crying and praying for rain and for the forgiveness of their sins; and the viceroy and his court, as well as the people, joined in the processions or thronged the churches to confess and be absolved. Palermo, in the words of the diarist Auria, was transformed into a Nineveh of sorrow.[11]

On May 8 it started to rain, the air cleared, and the epidemic showed signs of abating. The public penances became processions of thanksgiving, for there was now hope of a better harvest. But the immediate situation remained critical until a ship with 2,000 *salma* of grain from Sardinia arrived on the 18th.[12] Then it seemed that the worst was over and that God had been merciful in the end. But when the people went to buy their bread on the following morning they found to their utter consternation that the loaves were much smaller than they had been. In its efforts to keep down the price of bread the senate

[11] Auria, *Bibl, Stor. e Lett.*, pp. 40 ff.    [12] A *salma* is about 275 litres.

had been losing money at the rate of up to 500 ducats a day.[13]
When an order came from Madrid that bread was to be sold at
cost price the senate decided to reduce the weight of bread from
11¾ to 10 ounces. This seemed reasonable to the government
and was not as drastic a reduction as had been carried out at
other times.[14] Both the *pretore,* the head of the city administration, and the viceroy appear to have opposed this step,[15] but
they gave way to the pressure of the senators and the *maestri
razionali,* the judges of the Court of Royal Patrimony, who
feared the Madrid government's threat that they would personally have to make good the financial losses if they continued
their policy of cheap bread.

When the crowds and especially the women had recovered
from their first shock, the small loaves were held up with tears
and lamentations and their mood changed from despair to wild
fury against the government. After the week-long strain of hys-
terical religious emotion, after apparent delivery by a merciful
providence from the threatening horror of starvation, they had
to suffer a blow which seemed to come only from the malicious
wickedness of man. There were immediate riots in front of
the palace while men shouted: "Long live the King and down
with the taxes and the bad Government." They broke into the
prisons and freed some 600 prisoners who immediately joined
them. They burned the gates of the palace and could hardly be
prevented by the Theatine monks from burning the houses of
the most unpopular senators. The crowds which on the day
before had still thronged the churches now told the archbishop
of Palermo that they would lose their respect for him if he in-
terfered and that they wanted the sacrament which the monks
were carrying to protect persons and property only inside the
churches.[16]

[13] Collurafi, *Tumultuationi,* p. 8.

[14] C. Giardina, "Letter of de los Vélez to Philip IV on the 23 May
1647," in *Atti della Reale Accademia di Scienze, Lettere e Belle Arti di
Palermo,* ser. 3, 16 (1931), 262.

[15] di Blasi, *Storia Cronologica,* pp. 204 ff.

[16] "Letter of de los Velez," p. 262.

On the 20th the mood of the mob was growing still uglier. It now had a leader in the huge miller, Antonino La Pilosa, and its main efforts were directed against the treasury and the tax offices. But according to one eyewitness [17] the rioting crowds and their leaders were confined entirely to the lowest classes. Their slogan of "Long live the King and down with the taxes and the bad Government" was a traditional one—it was used in Naples and had been well known as the revolutionary slogan *par excellence* even in the sixteenth century; [18] its first part, "Long live the King," therefore probably did not mean very much at the beginning, although it is interesting to notice that, with the possible exception of the Dutch, all seventeenth-century revolutions were directed in the first place against unpopular ministers and not against the king himself. The constant repetition of the slogan, however, cannot have been without its effects and later helped to prevent the calling in of the French.

The immediate demand of the crowd itself was the abolition of the hated "five gabelles," the taxes on grain, wine, oil, meat, and cheese,[19] although murmurings were heard against the whole existing social order, reminiscent of the slogans of the medieval peasant revolts.[20] The viceroy's concessions, however, went considerably further: apart from restoring the loaves to their former weight (or even increasing them beyond it) and abolishing the five gabelles, he issued an amnesty to those who had broken prison,[21] deposed the senate and granted the people the right of electing two popular senators.

Siciliano, the most recent historian of the revolt, has suggested that the last two concessions were not due to the demands of the illiterate crowd but to pressure from the artisans' guilds and a number of middle-class intellectuals, notably the

[17] M. Serio, p. 24.
[18] Cf. Argisto Giuffredi, "Avvertimenti Cristiani," in *Documenti per . . . la Storia di Sicilia*, ser. 4, 4 (1896), 53 ff.
[19] Reina, p. 15.    [20] Rocco Pirri, p. 72.
[21] Printed by La Lumia, together with other documents of the revolt, in *Storie Siciliane,* p. 201.

then famous writer Francesco Baronio.[22] The guilds now co-operated with the government by taking over the fortifications and the city gates and by restoring order; the leaders of the riots were arrested, publicly tortured, and executed. The two popular senators, or *giurati*, were looked upon as Roman tribunes, and the guilds and their middle-class friends imagined that they would sufficiently safeguard the interests of the people. In actual fact Francesco Salerno and Simone Sabatini who were elected were both rich merchants whose interests were rather with the nobility than with the people, and Salerno especially always worked for the government.[23]

The contemporary chroniclers blamed Vélez for weakness and cowardice in the early stages of the revolt. But it is difficult to see how he could have behaved differently with the few Spanish troops available in Sicily and the impossibility of expecting military help from Spain. He had been fully aware of the critical nature of the situation. On April 27 he had written to Madrid [24] about the drought and on May 10 he had sent urgent appeals for grain to his colleagues in Naples and Sardinia, apart from not very successful attempts to stop speculation in grain inside Sicily. The immediate responsibility for the outbreak lay rather with the government in Madrid which, as so often, gave orders without exact knowledge of the facts. During the rioting Vélez had prevented the few Spanish guards from firing on the crowds which would only have resulted in their massacre, he had made the nobles attempt to calm the rioters, and had moved the galleys away from the piers to prevent their crews being liberated. On May 25 he unsuccessfully tried to introduce troops into the town: the guilds remained in control of the city, and for the moment the government was

[22] Siciliano, *Archivio Storico*, p. 203 ff.

[23] This is clear from a letter of recommendation by Trivulzio dated Feb. 18, 1648, from R. Arch. di Stato, quoted by Siciliano, *Archivio Storico*, p. 211.

[24] Letter of Vélez to Philip IV on May 23 1647 in *Archivio Storico*, p. 261.

too weak to take decisive counteraction. The nobles, solidly behind the government, retired to their country estates.

As no further political action could be taken, the financial position created by the abolition of the five gabelles became the most immediately pressing problem. The revenue from these taxes, about 4,000 ducats annually,[25] had been appropriated for the bimonthly payment of the interest on the city of Palermo debt which was held by noble families, hospitals, religious communities, guilds, and private persons. There was therefore an immediate and widespread demand for the reestablishment of some gabelles. In consequence, at a meeting on July 1 of the new senators and the consuls, i.e., the heads of the guilds, new gabelles were decided on which represented an attempt to create some form of direct taxation weighing more heavily on the rich than on the poor. Its main points were taxes on windows (the hovels of the poor very often had none), taxes on horse and mule carriages and on bottled wine; these were probably among the first luxury taxes in Europe. The other taxes were more orthodox; they were duties on barley, slaughtered meat, tobacco, and certain types of fish, plus a personal tax on rich merchants according to their wealth. The most revolutionary feature, for Sicily, was the absence of any exemptions for privileged classes.[26]

Throughout June and July the revolt spread outside Palermo. The immediate popular demands and slogans were similar to those in Palermo and were often summarized in posters which ranged from heavy satire in Sicilian verse to threats against local captains at arms or reasoned demands for a new census and fairer distribution of taxes.[27] The political and social alignments, however, varied. In Girgenti the bishop sup-

[25] Vélez, letter to the duke of Montalto, viceroy of Sardinia, of June 1, 1647 in *Archivio Storico,* p. 266.

[26] Cf. Auria and Reina; also di Blasi, *Storia Cronologica,* pp. 212 ff., Siciliano, *Archivio Storico,* p. 215, and L. Bianchini, *Storia economica-civile della Sicilia,* 1, 281 ff.

[27] F. Lionti, "Cartelli Sedioziosi del 1647," in *Archivio Stor. Sicil.,* N.S., vol. 19 (Palermo, 1894–1895).

ported the people against the nobles, only to be chased out of the town on the charge of hoarding grain to raise its price,[28] while in Syracuse, Cefalù, and elsewhere even monks, the lower clergy, and middle-class elements supported the people, and bread riots led to wider movements. In other towns again the guilds combined with the nobles against the *basso popolo*. Messina, almost alone among the Sicilian towns, did not follow the lead of Palermo and throughout the revolution remained the strongest supporter of the Spaniards.

The viceroy was not inclined to accept the new situation. On June 17 he wrote to the senate of Messina "that he had thought in no wise to confirm the abolition of the gabelles which had been made throughout the kingdom." [29] He did his best to support the local governors and on July 6 he summarily annulled the abolition of the gabelles which had been forced on the *giurati* of the various towns outside Palermo.[30]

In the meantime the tension inside Palermo was steadily growing. While the administration was still in the hands of the nobles, the greatest power inside the city was in the hands of the guilds who controlled the fortifications. Within the guilds, and particularly among their heads, the consuls, the political party which wanted further constitutional reconstructions seems to have been gaining ground. Auria wrote that "with truly unspeakable audacity they began to treat of the reform of the city, not knowing how to govern their own house," and that they prepared new laws (*capitoli*).[31] The government was clearly very sensitive to this dangerous shift from economic to political action and reacted with great vigor. Already on June 1 Vélez had written a postscript to a letter to the duke of Mon-

---

[28] Siciliano, *Archivio Storico*, p. 231, seems to think that it was not the bishop but the speculators trying to sell corn elsewhere who caused the rise in prices.

[29] Idoplare Copa (i.e., Placido Reina), "Raccolta d' alcune lettere del Re . . . al Senato di Messina," in *L' Idra Dicapitata . . .* (Vicenza, 1662), pp. 255 ff.

[30] Lionti, *Archivio Storico*, p. 443.

[31] Auria, *Bibl. Stor. e Lett.*, p. 87.

talto, the viceroy of Sardinia, which breaks through his usual formal and reticent style: "Señor mio, these facts demand the most urgent consideration; do your utmost to help extinguish the fire." [32] Shortly afterwards Francesco Baronio, whom the government regarded as its most dangerous opponent, was imprisoned by the Inquisition, ostensibly on grounds of heresy, and on July 14 the police chief of Palermo quietly arrested and sent to Pantellaria, Giovanni Colonna, a young doctor who had been warning the guilds not to trust the government.

Towards the end of July, 1647, news arrived of the outbreak on the 7th of the revolt in Naples, and Masaniello's name became as famous in Palermo as it had become there. It is probable that from that time onwards meetings of the consuls and other leading officers of the guilds began to take place in which an overthrow of the Spanish government and the nobles on the Neapolitan pattern was discussed.

There, where the present Piazza Moderna is, was the seventeenth-century tanners' quarter, a closely built-up slum area with subterranean connections between the houses. The tanners were important because of their prosperous export trade in dressed leather. They kept together more than other guilds and often hid criminals.[33] No government officer would lightly venture into their quarter, and it was to this place that Giuseppe d'Alesi, the former gold-beater who had escaped from prison, went after his return from Naples. He had taken part in Masaniello's revolt, or had at least been a witness of it. This fact, added to his relationship to the consul of the tanners, gave him great influence in that guild. The chroniclers have described what was probably one of many meetings in a tavern where Alesi and a number of consuls drew lots for the leadership of the popular movement to overthrow the viceroy, the ministers, and the nobles, and to do away with anybody else who might oppose them.

As in every other plot during that period, there were spies

[32] Letter of Vélez, June 1, 1647, *Archivio Storico,* p. 266.
[33] La Lumia, *Storie Siciliane,* pp. 79 ff.

who informed the viceroy. The insurrection was to take place on August 15, and on the morning of that day the viceroy ordered two of the consuls to visit him, apparently with the intention of keeping them until after the appointed hour or of reasoning with them, for up to then the guilds had not been inclined to violence and their consuls had shown considerable respect for the viceroy personally.[34] He argued with them for some time when suddenly the rumor spread among the crowd who had seen them enter the royal palace that the two consuls were being murdered. There were instant riots throughout the town. Eyewitnesses said that the mob was urged on by the clamor of the consuls' wives; but it seems likely that at least the tanners and the fishing guild (like the tanners, a powerful and well-organized community of between 700 and 1,000 members who had been incensed by the failure of the government to abolish all gabelles on fish) were prepared for the rising. The immediate release of the two consuls was not sufficient to stop the movement. After the Spanish guards had repulsed the crowds who attacked the palace with stones, Alesi put himself at their head and stormed the armories of the senate and the customs houses. In white armor and on horseback—with his own standard bearer and a trumpeter who was always out of tune [35]—Alesi rode through the streets and was proclaimed captain-general by the crowds. In face of the new armed attack, the Spanish guards could give the viceroy just enough time to escape to one of the galleys, while some of the nobles took his pregnant wife with her children to the fortress of Castellammare, just outside Palermo.

Under the moderating influence of his brother Francesco, a bank clerk, Alesi set guards in the palace to prevent all looting. Both thought that the best way of establishing the revolution was to come to terms with the government as quickly as possible. But Alesi was not prepared to take any chances. All city gates except six were to be closed and these strongly guarded.

[34] Cf. Collurafi, *Tumultuationi*, p. 75.
[35] Serio, *Bibl. Stor. e Lett.*, p. 36.

No ship was to leave the harbor so that no news of the revolt could reach Naples and help be sent to the viceroy, and, finally, everyone was to go armed. One of the consuls claimed to be the *capopopoli*, the leader of the people, in opposition to Alesi: he was promptly executed when he threatened to cause a breach in the ranks of the revolutionaries.

For the next six days Alesi attempted the impossible task of establishing a popular government on the basis of cooperation with the Spaniards. On the night of the 15th Francesco d'Alesi secretly visited the viceroy on his ship to apologize for his brother's actions.[36] Vélez was exceedingly polite to him. He could be nothing else, as the revolutionaries had arms and he had not. But secretly he did his best to undermine the movement, ably assisted by the Inquisitor Trasmiera, who prevented the release of Francesco Baronio whom Alesi wanted to appoint as his secretary. That Alesi should have been convinced by the religious arguments of the wily Trasmiera shows how little even the leader of the revolution had emancipated himself from the beliefs of his time, on which the power of the ruling classes rested.

On the 16th the senate wrote him a flattering letter asking him to cooperate in finding an answer to the financial problems which had not been solved by the imposition of the new gabelles. In consequence several meetings took place in the church of San Giuseppe attended by the consuls and many artisans, by the popular senators and other officials, together with Trasmiera and a number of the nobility. After long discussions forty-nine *capitoli*, or laws, were agreed upon.[37] They clearly show the three main streams which made up the revolution.[38] First, there were the *capitoli* designed to satisfy the mass of the common people who wanted a reduction of taxes and a general indulgence for the robberies and burnings of houses committed during the rioting. The abolition of the five gabelles

[36] Rocco Pirri, *Bibl. Stor. e Lett.*, p. 112.
[37] Printed in La Lumia's documents; also in Reina.
[38] Siciliano, *Archivio Storico*, pp. 262 ff.

was proclaimed for the whole kingdom. Secondly, there were those designed to grant the guilds greater participation in the government by reserving all offices to Palermitans, by deposing most of the legal and financial officers of the treasury and the treasury courts, by giving the guilds the appointment of local food and trade in inspectors, and by creating a special body of six *giurati*, three elected by the nobles and three by the people. Without two noble and two popular *giurati* the senate could not assemble or take decisions. Thirdly, there were the *capitoli* inserted by the middle-class intellectuals, young lawyers like Pietro Milano, for a reform of legal procedure and for a return to the ancient laws of the time of King Peter of Aragon—a typical seventeenth-century touch. For the rest, the Marquis de los Vélez was to be confirmed in his office as were also the Inquisitors, a number of judges, the treasurer and the captains of the galleys. It was a compromise in which the government had managed to retain a number of key positions thanks to the determination of Alesi to resist the more radical group of his followers and to the efforts of Trasmiera and a number of lawyers who pretended to support the captain-general. The viceroy was even permitted to choose his own bodyguard in return for procuring the acceptance of the *capitoli* in Madrid. A proposal to provide him with a citizen guard was turned down by the consuls, apparently much against the wishes of the people.

On the 20th Alesi made a speech to the people from the steps of San Giuseppe asking for the acceptance of the *capitoli*. "I will never do anything by my own simple command or caprice," he claimed, "yours must be the will, on you depends everything which is to be arranged." [39] But the populace was no longer satisfied with its leader. There had been three extra *capitoli* handing over the government to the viceroy again while Alesi resigned his title of captain-general and became *sindaco*, the official who defended the city's prerogatives and privileges, with a salary of 2,000 ducats per year for life and a bodyguard of seventy. It is possible that Alesi took this step

[39] Auria, *Bibl. Stor. e Lett.*, p. 129.

because he realized the weakness of his position as captain-general. The dismissal of so many officials had been correct from a revolutionary point of view, but had produced administrative inefficiency: it was the dilemma of all revolutions. As most of the nobles had left the town, trade had nearly come to a standstill. Moreover, Alesi had difficulties in controlling his own followers whose attempted looting and extortion from rich nobles led him into serious quarrels with the tanners, the silversmiths, and the fishing guild who were further embittered by the embargo on ships leaving the port.[40] The viceroy had secretly spent 10,000 ducats in a campaign against Alesi.[41] Rumors were spread that Alesi intended to deliver the island to the French and that he had been bribed by the viceroy to betray the people. Without a systematic plan of action, without experienced advisers, surrounded by spies and, above all, without an organized and disciplined political party, Alesi's position became impossible.

On August 21 the viceroy signed the forty-nine *capitoli* and on the next morning Trasmiera's carefully prepared counterstroke came off.

Two separate columns moved towards Alesi's house in the tanners' quarter: the fishermen's guild coming from the harbor, and the nobles with several thousand of the *basso popolo* following, armed and specially hired for the day. No one lifted a finger to save the captain-general. He and twelve of his friends, including his brother, were murdered, some with extreme cruelty and with complete disregard of the rights of ecclesiastical sanctuary.[42]

It was the first great victory of the reaction, and the viceroy decided to follow it up by the arrest of the most troublesome of the consuls. This was too much for the people. As suddenly as they had turned against Alesi they now turned against the

[40] Serio, *Bibl. Stor. e Lett.*, p. 37.
[41] From a "Volume di Provisioni dell' anno 1646–47, nell' Archivio del Commune di Palermo," quoted by La Lumia, *Storie Siciliane*, p. 131.
[42] "Breve Relazione," p. 406.

nobles, deeply regretting their faithlessness to their dead leader. Almost at once there began the growth of an Alesi legend. His weaknesses were forgotten, he became the symbol of the revolution and men claimed to have seen him at night riding in his white armor and shouting *"Serra, Serra*—To the Barricades!"

On the 23rd the viceroy, now at Castellammare, had to publish the forty-nine *capitoli,* release the arrested consuls, and agree to punish the officers who had arrested them.

From then until the death of Vélez on November 3, there was a period of armed truce and maneuvering for position with neither side strong enough to strike a decisive blow. The revolutionaries were still faced wtih the difficulty of administering the town in the absence of so many trained officials. By the end of October the deficit due to the senate's bread subsidies had risen to 140,000 ducats,[43] and there were still difficulties in paying the interest on the debt. As so often later, it was found that a national debt is one of the strongest safeguards of a government against revolution. The guild organization, built up entirely on sectional and economic interests, proved quite inadequate as a political organization, and there was no other. More than ever did it seem necessary to come to terms with the government. After Alesi the chroniclers do not mention any more individual leaders, and the artisans were divided in their attitude towards the nobility. Together with the hatred and distrust produced by centuries of aristocratic oppression there was the equally old and genuine respect for the established order of things and the superiority of the nobility; and this cleavage ran not only through the popular movement, dividing it as to what policy to pursue, but was equally present in the minds of the individuals, sapping their will to action and making impossible the development of a consistent political program.

The most serious failure in this respect was the inability of the revolutionaries to cooperate. There was not one general Sicilian revolution but a great number in the different Sicilian towns. Some of the leaders understood the social and political

[43] di Blasi, *Storia Cronologica,* p. 234.

significance of the movement in their own particular town quite well, yet they never attempted to creat a genuinely national movement by calling a meeting of representatives of all the revolutionary communes or by insisting on the calling of the Sicilian parliament and transforming the *braccio demaniale,* the aristocratic representatives of the towns, into a representative assembly of the people. Parliament had been the stronghold of the nobility and of privilege for so long and so regularly, that it never occurred to the Sicilian revolutionaries to use it as the French revolutionaries in 1789 used the States-General which, by the very fact that it had been defunct for over 150 years, could be adapted to new conditions in a way that was impossible for the well-established Sicilian parliament with its long tradition of resistance against the encroachments of the crown. The old particularism of the Sicilian towns which, but for the danger of an Angevin reconquest, would have led to the establishment of a number of independent communes after the Sicilian Vespers,[44] prevented in 1647 concerted action against the military power of the Spanish government and of the nobility. Apart from Palermo's declaration of the abolition of the five gabelles for the whole kingdom, the towns were content to shut their gates against the Spanish soldiers and remain on the defensive, while the government and the nobles were able to concentrate their forces as they pleased and retake the towns outside Palermo one by one.

On the side of the nobility, on the other hand, no compromise was possible. Upbringing and carefully cultivated traditions, religious convictions as well as economic interests prevented any possibility of accepting the people as equal partners in a government which had been an aristocratic privilege for centuries. The viceroy never meant to accept the forty-nine *capitoli* permanently as he stated quite definitely in his letter to the senate of Messina.[45] Even the middle-class chroniclers and diarists never looked on Alesi as anything but a diabolical mon-

---

[44] M. Amari, *History of the War of the Sicilian Vespers;* Earl of Ellesmeere, trans. (London, 1850), I, 188, 271 ff.

[45] Letter of Sept. 8, 1647 in Copa, *L'Idra Dicapitata,* pp. 271 ff.

ster, though they were not otherwise unsympathetic to the sufferings of the people.

The chasm between the classes appears clearly in the struggles of September, 1647. An agreement had been reached on the 5th, the so-called *Capitoli* of Peace, by which the viceroy was to move back into the royal palace. Two days later, however, he refused on the pretext that his son was ill. The scene has been described,[46] how the Marquesa de los Vélez stood with her eyes fixed on the sick child, making clear without a word her determination never to leave Castellammare and expose herself to the insults of the mob. The Spanish ladies would not even compromise to deceive the people.

By judicious threats that the viceroy and his court would move to Messina, Trasmiera had maneuvered the guilds into the position of petitioning the viceroy for the repeal of the forty-nine *capitoli* on September 17, "as being originated by the rebel Alesi and without public usefulness." It was a grave moral blow to their own position.[47] In return Vélez published a decree granting the substance of the *capitoli,* but making it dependent on acceptance by the king, a practically unobtainable condition.

Gradually the government began to regain control and take drastic action against a number of would-be leaders of new uprisings. So well, indeed, that no actual new revolts took place. But in October an attempt to disarm the people proved to be still impossible. Militarily the guilds still had the upper hand. Moreover, as long as this was so, there was the danger of French interference. Mazarin had had his agents in Sicily for a long time. He himself, although actually born in Italy, came from the Mazarino family, one of the very large number of minor noble families in Sicily, and he knew Sicilian conditions well. On 25 July he wrote to Fontenay-Mareuil, the French ambassa-

[46] Reina, *Delle rivolutioni,* pp. 245 ff.

[47] The Messinian Jesuit Samperi, writing under the pseudonym of M. A. Sestini, pointed out these implications shortly afterwards in his dialogues, *La Felicita Caduta* . . . (Perugia, 1648).

dor in Rome: "His Majesty is highly satisfied with the trouble you have taken in this matter [i.e., the revolt in Naples] and with fomenting the rising in Sicily."[48] But he was careful not to commit himself too far, being at that time more interested in forcing Spain to make peace than in establishing a precedent of revolt against a lawful sovereign, a precedent which might have unfortunate repercussions on his own position in France.[49] Despite the memories of the Sicilian Vespers, of the strength of which he was well aware,[50] he did consider in August the possibilities of a Sicilian republic under the protection of the French king,[51] though he was not prepared to act until called upon by the Sicilians themselves.[52] Vélez took the French danger seriously enough; for on October 2 he issued an order expelling all Catalans, Portuguese, Piedmontese, and Savoyards with less than ten years' residence.[53] This measure was undoubtedly aimed at French agents as well as at the influence of members of nations in revolt against the Habsburg monarchy. Characteristically the guilds did not object.

In December, 1647, the French fleet was anchored off Naples and Cardinal Teodoro Trivulzio, who had succeeded Vélez after the latter's death in November, was still faced with a critical situation—made no easier by his unpopularity as an Italian among the Spanish nobles. He had, however, the great advantage over the guilds of having a definite policy and lifelong political experience. He restored confidence by moving the court back into Palermo; he kept the people amused by sumptuous festivities and elaborate tournaments while doing his best to provide corn during a winter which was nearly as difficult as the preceding one.

In December was discovered the plot of Vaira Sirletti, a Calabrian priest, and Francesco Albamonte, a writer. They had wanted to rescue Baronio from prison and make him head of a

[48] *Lettres du Cardinal Mazarin*, ii, 465.
[49] Cf. Merriman, *Six Contem. Revs.*
[50] *Lettres du Cardinal Mazarin*, ii, 561 ff.     [51] *Ibid.*, p. 476.
[52] *Ibid.*, p. 471.     [53] Auria, *Bibl. Stor. e Lett.*, p. 179.

Sicilian republic. Their plan was to kill several of the consuls and to blame this on the government so as to rouse the people, and to follow it up by calling the Turks into the country.[54] There was, however, a strong suspicion at the time that Trivulzio purposely spread the rumor about the Turks, and it is probable that he also spread the story of the planned murder of the consuls.[55]

The next conspiracy is worth telling in some detail for its air of romantic tragi-comedy.[56] Gabriele Platanella, a companion of Alesi, had escaped to France. In Marseilles he impressed the authorities sufficiently to be sent to Paris. He told Mazarin that he was a relative of the chief consul of Palermo and that the consuls were ready to hand the city over to the French.[57] Mazarin sent him with a letter of introduction to Fontenay-Mareuil. On the passage to Rome Platanella met a Flemish nobleman who pretended to be French and to whom he confided his plans. The nobleman was very sympathetic and promised to give him a personal introduction to the French ambassador. Arriving in Rome he hurried to the Spanish ambassador, the Count d'Oñate, and arranged that the latter should dress up as the French ambassador. The Count's servants, in French livery, then escorted Platanella to the Spanish embassy where d'Oñate showed himself very interested and had a list given him of all persons supposedly involved in the conspiracy. Platanella was then sent by ship to Palermo with orders to be arrested, but still under the impression that he had talked to the French ambassador. He was executed in May, 1648, but the consuls were found to have been innocent of his plot.

They were equally innocent in April of the conspiracy of

---

[54] *Ibid.*, pp. 228 ff.

[55] Siciliano accepts Auria's version of this, but there seems to be no more reason for accepting it than the stories of the armies of demons which Sirletti was supposed to have called—stories which Auria and Collurafi accept as uncritically.

[56] Collurafi, "Tradimento del Platanella," in *Tumultuationi.*

[57] *Lettres du Cardinal Mazarin,* II, 561. Letter of Dec. 20, 1647, to the French Resident in Sweden.

Pietro Milano, the young friend of Alesi. Gradually it was becoming evident that the guilds were no longer capable of revolutionary action. They were disunited, and as the fishing guild had not been trusted since Alesi's death, the others demanded to take over the fishing guild's fortifications. Trivulzio was only too pleased to agree, thus driving a permanent wedge between the fishermen and the rest of the artisans. In March appeared the first signs that the artisans were becoming heartily tired of manning the fortifications in every kind of weather to the detriment of their trade.[58] The guild's position was further weakened by the news of the collapse of the Neapolitan revolt in April and of the impending approach of the Spanish fleet. The French fleet had long since returned to its own ports and no further help could be expected from it.

On June 14 the people forced the dismissal of the *pretore* of Palermo who had been selling rotten corn. This was their last success. On July 7 the last plot was betrayed and its leaders executed. Trivulzio decided to strike while the people were still terrified by the swiftness of the execution of the plotters. He had gradually managed to introduce troops into the city and the consuls knew it. He now demanded—and obtained—the surrender of the fortifications. Then the consuls were induced to submit a memorandum for the reintroduction of the five gabelles in the same way as they had been induced to petition for the abolition of the forty-nine *capitoli*. The next step was to banish every one without definite employment from Palermo and then ask for the handing over of all arms.[59]

On July 25 a deputation was elected for the imposition of new gabelles. The new taxes were a return to the system of indirect taxation, but without the privileged exemptions. The rate of interest on the debt was reduced from 5 to 3.5 per cent and a sinking fund was established—seventy years before Wal-

---

[58] Auria, *Bibl. Stor. e Lett.,* p. 274.

[59] Another decree for disarmament was necessary in August as it was found that people had several sets of arms from Alesi's storming of the armories.

pole. The new financial deputation, with powers of a court of first instance, and the whole financial system remained in force with only slight alterations until 1860.[60] The popular senators survived for a few more years until finally this first achievement of the revolution was also lost. Trivulzio's Machiavellian policy had proved successful—contrary to the opinion of many of the Spanish nobles who would have preferred the cruder method of a general massacre of the artisans.

When it was all over and Trivulzio had been succeeded by Don John of Austria, the illegitimate son of Philip IV, some of the nobles started a belated aristocratic revolt.[61] In 1649 there was a rumor of Philip IV's death, and two lawyers, Antonio del Giudice and Giuseppe Pesce, who had played ambiguous roles in the Alesi revolt, conceived the idea of proclaiming a Sicilian nobleman as king. The count of Mazzarino, head of the great house of Branciforte, was first suggested, but later the choice fell on the duke of Montalto, the former viceroy of Sardinia. Both Mazzarino—not a relation of Mazarin—and Montalto (Montault) belonged to old Sicilian or Norman families who had had little or no intermarriage with Catalans and Spaniards. Either because he was jealous or because he had been a spy from the beginning, Mazzarino disclosed all to Don John. The two lawyers were imprisoned and confessed. Most of the implicated nobles fled and were condemned in their absence, but neither Mazzarino nor Montalto was touched. It was the last of the mid-century revolts in Sicily.

As in Naples, the year of revolution had achieved practically no permanent results. It had, however, produced a surprising number of interesting constitutional experiments and ideas. Alesi and his friends seem to have conceived some idea—although it was never worked out as a systematic theory or program—of a mixed government in which the viceroy, the nobles, and the people were to share equally and the popular representatives were to act in accordance with the wishes of the people.

[60] La Lumia, *Storie Siciliane*, pp. 187 ff.
[61] di Blasi, *Storia Cronologica*, pp. 281ff.

The institution of the two popular senators on the model of the Roman tribunes, and the later proposal to set up a Sicilian republic, for which there was no tradition apart from the two unsuccessful attempts in 1254 and 1282, show a survival of Renaissance ideas in the small intellectual middle class of Sicily. The attempt to create a system of direct and luxury taxes, together with the abolition of tax exemptions for privileged classes, foreshadows policies which did not become common until after the French Revolution. It is doubtful whether the scheme would have worked in the absence of adequate machinery for collection and with the corruption of Sicilian officials; for it was abolished before it had time to prove itself. Unlike the Neapolitan revolt in which there were wholesale massacres and ferocious reprisals, the revolt in Palermo was marked by a comparative absence of atrocities. Very few on the nobles' side were killed and most of those in open clashes; and while the government executed a number of individual leaders of the people there was, apart from the action against Alesi, at no time a reign of terror. The credit for this moderation must go in the first place to Alesi and to Trivulzio and in the second place to the absence of large contingents of regular troops.

The role of the central government of the Spanish Empire in Madrid is more difficult to evaluate. De los Vélez's first letter about the riots in May of 1647 came as a complete shock to Madrid, and the Council of Italy felt very apologetic about having to present Philip IV with the news of yet another major disaster.[62] There was, moreover, very little that the government in Madrid could do about it; for the distance between Palermo and Madrid, and the consequent time lag in the arrival of dispatches, would render specific orders or good advice out of date before they arrive. The Council of Italy felt that it was particularly regrettable that the viceroy had ordered the squadron of Sicilian galleys to remain at Palermo when they were urgently needed elsewhere; but they did not dare to recommend

[62] *Consulta* of June 17, 1647. Archivo General de Simancas, Secreterías Provinciales, legajo 1020 (no folio numbers).

a reversal of the viceroy's decision. It seemed best, so the Council advised the king, to write to the viceroys of Naples and Sardinia and ask them to send all the grain they could to Sicily. For the rest, the king should write to Vélez expressing his appreciation of his actions. He should also enclose personal letters to prelates and other dignitaries outside Palermo which the viceroy should forward at his discretion in order to encourage the recipients in their loyalty to the king. The Council ended their *consulta* by wondering whether the riots had not been caused by the viceroy's reputation for "natural goodness and mildness" and whether he should not be immediately replaced by the duke of Alva who had been previously nominated as his successor.

At this point the king rejected the idea of an immediate recall of Vélez. But in the course of the summer the news from Palermo became more and more alarming, and the question of the recall of the viceroy came to dominate the discussion of the Sicilian problem in Madrid, almost to the exclusion of all other considerations.[63] Thus when the viceroy urgently asked for 100,000 scudi, the Council of Italy supported his request but Philip IV did not even bother to comment on it.[64]

Vélez's death conveniently solved for Madrid the still undecided question of his recall, but it did not solve the financial problems of the Sicilian government. In December, or in early January of 1648, Cardinal Trivulzio tried to arrange for a secret and, apparently, unsecured loan from the Bank of Palermo. One of the bank's three governors violently opposed the scheme. The proposal leaked out and there was an immediate run on the bank. Trivulzio had to fall back on the very inefficient and unpopular device of a forced loan from rich Sicilians. Faced with the prospect of a complete collapse of the credit of the Sicilian government and the almost certain mutinies of the troops which would follow, the Council of Italy once more urged the king to send 70,000 or 80,000 ducats from Spain to

[63] *Consultas* of July 7 and Aug. 3, 1647. *Ibid.*, leg. 1444.
[64] *Consulta* of Sept. 24, 1647. *Ibid.*

Sicily. This time Philip IV wearily agreed with his councilors, "despite the lack of means which you know of." [65] This sum (if indeed it was ever sent) seems to have been the only tangible help which the Spanish monarchy gave to its government in Sicily during its greatest crisis.

The most immediate reason for the failure of the revolution was the impossibility of establishing a revolutionary constitution with the cooperation of people and nobles in the government. Yet for a complete overthrow of the social order the revolutionary forces were not strong enough. The Sicilian revolutionaries had almost none of the advantages of the contemporary English parliamentarians. They did not represent a rising class of prosperous country gentlemen and capitalist merchants; they had no leaders of the caliber of Pym and Cromwell, educated men, schooled by long experience of political life, and not handicapped by social inferiority. They lacked the great moral strength which the English Puritans drew from their religious beliefs—in harmony with their political aspirations. Though no less religious, the Sicilians found that their religion became the strongest weapon in the hands of the established order. The Sicilian revolution was never backed by a consistent political philosophy.

Added to this fundamental weakness was the constant rivalry between Palermo and Messina which prohibited united action in 1647, as in 1672, when Messina revolted and received no help from Palermo. Such successes as were achieved were therefore due almost entirely to the weakness and momentary embarrassment of Spain. Once the crisis had been overcome the revolt was doomed.

[65] *Consulta* of April 12, 1648. *Ibid.*

# CHAPTER 11

# Decadence or Shift? Changes in the Civilization of Italy and Europe in the Sixteenth and Seventeenth Centuries

THE IDEA that certain periods and certain countries were outstanding in their contribution to civilization is as old as the writing of literary and art history. "All ages have produced heroes and politicians," wrote Voltaire in his *Siècle de Louis XIV*,[1] "all peoples have experienced revolutions: all histories are practically equal for him who does not want to remember anything but facts. But whoever thinks and, what is rarer still, whoever has good taste, will count only four centuries in the history of the world." According to Voltaire, one needed to remember only the Greece of the fifth and fourth centuries B.C., the Rome of Caesar and Augustus, Medicean Italy, and France in the century of Louis XIV. Almost two hundred years earlier, Vasari had pointed to the same phenomenon in Italy. In the introduction to his *Life of Michelangelo* he says that God in his mercy had shown pity on the vain endeavors of man by sending down to earth a spirit who could work perfection in every art and profession, in painting, sculpture, and architecture, no less than in moral philosophy and poetry. And since Florence was more deserving of this grace than all other cities, because of the great and marvellous achievements of Cimabue and Giotto, of Donatello, Brunelleschi, and Leonardo, he wanted "to crown the perfection merited by all these achievements through one of her citizens."[2]

---

[1] Voltaire, *Siècle de Louis XIV* (Paris, 1919), pp. 1–2.
[2] G. Vasari, *Le Vite*, C. Ricci, ed. (Milan, 1930), IV 391.

The appearance of a Michelangelo, as the appearance of a Shakespeare or a Mozart, must always remain a divine miracle. Yet, unlike Vasari, the modern historian of civilization cannot rest content with divine providence as an explanation for the astonishing concentration of artistic talent in Renaissance Italy. Indeed, one may well question whether Vasari's pretty parable was much more than an elegant literary device to introduce his greatest hero. Vasari knew well the tradition of craftsmanship, the hard apprenticeship through which the young artist had to pass in the workshops of the masters. In spite of his immense admiration for the work of great individuals, he was aware of the cumulative nature of the development of Italian art.

Yet craftsmanship and tradition are not in themselves a sufficient explanation of a concentration of creative activity. Moreover, while concentration of outstanding talent has often occurred in quite a wide range of activities, it has rarely embraced all of them. In some countries, at some periods of their history, there occurred shifts in the concentration of talent from some creative activities to others. It is the purpose of this chapter to investigate such shifts in the cultural history of Europe in the sixteenth and seventeenth centuries, and to show by historical analysis why shuch shifts occurred in some countries and not in others. Such an approach will allow us to drop not only Vasari's metaphor of divine providence but also the fashionable, but no less mystical, metaphor of growth and decadence.

Consider Italy. Whatever historians may think of the term Renaissance, few will deny that, for some two hundred years up to the early sixteenth century, Italy was outstanding in Europe for the great wealth and quality of her production in the visual arts, in literature and classical learning, as well as in the theory and practice of political and economic organization. The social basis and the political and economic framework for these achievements was the medieval Italian city-state. Whereas the civilization of transalpine Europe was feudal, courtly, and ecclesiastical, the civilization of Italy was urban, republican, and secular. By republican I mean a social organization in which the mass of small artisans and craftsmen, as well as the wealthy merchants, were free citizens of their state, not vassals of a suzerain, subjects of a prince, or serfs of a lord. The political control of most Italian city-states remained in the hands of a wealthy patriciate. The lower classes managed to participate only rarely in the political control of their cities. But the sense of citizenship and personal freedom remained. The citizens were not irreligious. The great cathedrals, with their frescoes representing the stories of the Bible, symbolized the common achievements and hopes of their Christian community. But despite the great number of monks and friars in the Italian cities, most of the scholars, writers and artists were not clerics; their public was the whole body of citizens, not the exclusive court society of a king of France or a duke of Burgundy.

With the economic decline of the late fourteenth and of the fifteenth century, the social and political basis of this society began to change. In city after city, local *condottieri* established a one-man rule, often with popular support, against the oligarchy of the patricians. As the tyrannies of the *condottieri* became respectable, they changed into principalities, for which popular support was deemed unnecessary. The new courts and the new aristocratic court-societies now tended to become the centers of the civilization of the city-states. But, at least until the end of the fifteenth century, the new miniature monarchies still retained many of the characteristics of the medieval city-state. The Italian artist, through the exigencies of patronage, was becoming more and more a courtier, but he was still a citizen. Nowhere is this development clearer than in Florence. The rule of Cosimo and Lorenzo de Medici was as effective as that of the Sforza of Milan or the Gonzaga of Mantua; but they remained nominally private citizens. Their court still had some of the informality and egalitarian character of a summer school for artists and scholars. Even after the turn of the century, Leonardo and Michelangelo, whom we regard primarily as court artists, still affirmed their Florentine citizenship by working as military engineers in the wars of the restored republic.

By contrast Rome, which had never been a genuine city-state, did not become an outstanding cultural center until the popes of the mid-fifteenth century began to attract artists and scholars to their courts. The greatest masters of the Roman Renaissance were not Romans, but Tuscans and Umbrians.

It was inevitable that both literary and artistic styles and art forms should be influenced by these shifts in the social center of gravity. Already in the fifteenth century the greatest of the communal enterprises, the building of the cathedrals, began to slow down. The tardy completion of the *duomo* of Florence was a typical phenomenon. Ghiberti and Brunelleschi, at least, were still employed by the guilds. Bramante and Michelangelo, the architects of St. Peter's in Rome, however, were employed by the popes; and St. Peter's, although a symbol for the religious aspirations of the whole of Christianity, was not the cathedral of a Christian commune in the sense in which the cathedrals of Pisa, Lucca, or Siena had been. Frescoes were giving way to easel paintings, commissioned by private patrons and hung in private *palazzi*. Michelangelo's Sistine ceiling is a fresco, but it was painted for the private chapel of the pope. His frescoes in the Pauline Chapel are not even now open to the public. The whole difference between republic and monarchy lies in the conception of the Or San Michele in Florence (the public hall built by the guilds, to which all the great sculptors of the time contributed their sculptures) and the conception of Michelangelo's tombs of Julius II and the Medici.

Such examples could be multiplied at will, and they are paralleled in literature in the change from Petrarch and Boccaccio to Ariosto. In the first decade of the sixteenth century the humanist Castiglione produced a literary portrait of the ideal courtier, a type of book which, even a generation earlier, would have been inconceivable in Italy; but in transalpine, courtly Europe, it would have fitted into a respectable literary tradition, as the popularity of Olivier de la Marche's writings testify. Castiglione's famous book, despite its new subject, still preserves much of the earlier Italian tradition. With its fusion of different elements and traditions, it is an example of the stylistic perfection and classical balance which Italy achieved for a brief generation when the new Italian courts could still draw on the living traditions of the late medieval city-state and blend them with their own splendor and the individualism of the new rulers.

This much will be conceded by most historians. The later sixteenth and the seventeenth centuries are much more controversial. Sixty years of war between the great powers of Europe, France and Spain, with Italy as their battleground, killed what was left of the city-states and their traditions. The tyrants obtained ducal or grand-ducal titles. They modelled their courts on those of Spain and France. Naples, Sicily and Milan were ruled by viceroys and governors general. Only Venice survived as a true republic.

Could the small principalities, with their increasingly exclusive and rigid courts, satisfy the spiritual needs of their citizens as the Christian commune of the city-state had done? It soon became apparent that they could not. The career of Savonarola had shown in which direction the new currents would flow. It was not a coincidence that his success came at the end of the first period of Medicean rule in Florence, or that his preaching could affect even members of the Medicean élite, like Pico della Mirandola and Botticelli. In Italy, as in the rest of Europe, the later sixteenth century became an age of religious mass movements. The reformers of the earlier part of the century, mostly humanists and intellectuals, could never slake the craving for new values and certainties of a populace cut off from the direction of its own destinies. This task was left to the extremist preachers of religious reform, the Ochino and Valdés, until these, in turn, had to flee before the power of the state and the Inquisition and their place was taken by the fiery Theatine, Dominican, and Jesuit preachers of the Counter Reformation. The Milanese and Neapolitans might rise against the attempted introduction of the Spanish Inquisition; but they were fanatically Catholic, and their hero was San Carlo Borromeo.

It is not really surprising that, in these circumstances, the classical style in the visual arts should have broken down. Already the later work of Raphael, for instance the *Fire of the Borgo*, 1517–1518, points the way to the new style of mannerism. Michelangelo's work after about 1520 is famous for its nonclassical qualities. The stylistic development of the late works of artists like Michelangelo tends to follow laws of its own, and I do not want to attach too much importance to them in this context. But it is only necessary to compare a portrait by Bronzino with one by Raphael to see that we have entered a different world. The stiffness and formality, both of dress and bearing, of the sitter, as for instance in the portrait of Eleonora of Toledo, faithfully reflects the stiffness and formality of the new court society.[3] Where the face of Raphael's Castiglione or Titian's Paul III is open to the beholder, Bronzino's faces are like masks, but masks behind which one may discern a hidden nervous tension. The age was no longer one of integrated personalities, whether honest humanists like Castiglione or sly diplomats like Paul III.

Together with a change in style there was also a change in the quality of Italian painting and sculpture. My own opinion is that Parmigianino, Cellini, Vasari, the Carracci, and even Bronzino, for all the fine qualities of their work, were lesser artists than the great painters of the *quattrocento* and early *cinquecento*. Only Caravaggio might be counted among the giants, and even the claims made for him have often been disputed. In the seventeenth century the decline continues. The rhetoric of Guido Reni and the romanticism of Salvatore Rosa were no substitute for the creative fire of the Renaissance.

In sculpture, the decline was even more rapid. The classical tradition of Donatello, Verrocchio, and the early Michelangelo found no successors. Giambologna, a Frenchman living in Italy, possessed superb technical skill, and some of his work, especially the animal sculptures in the Bargello in Florence, has

[3] *Cf.* W. Pinder, "Zur Physiognomik des Manierismus," *Festschrift Ludwig Klages* (Leipzig, 1932), pp. 152–53.

great charm. But he was no Donatello. After him, there came Ammanati and other unhappy epigones of Michelangelo's later style. Not until Bernini, in the seventeenth century, did Italy produce another sculptor of the first rank; and there was no one else of a comparable stature. One does not have to go all the way with Benedetto Croce and call the whole baroque period (which, for Croce, included mannerism) "variations on ugliness," [4] yet to accept the phenomenon of decline in the visual arts.

This decline was paralleled in literature and political philosophy. Marino, who considered himself, and was considered by his contemporaries, as the greatest of all poets, ancient or modern, is now read only by specialist literary historians.[5] Tassoni's reputation has not survived any better. "No great book," says Croce, "that is, one which reveals man more profoundly to man, was inspired by the Counter Reformation. Nor did any poet do this, not even Torquato Tasso . . . Neither did any artist, because the art of the seventeenth century, when it did not serve practical ends . . . appeared frankly sensual. Austere men, heroic missionaries, open and generous minds certainly abounded still in the Roman Church, but this is not the point; these most worthy men lacked moral inventiveness, the ability to create new and progressive forms of ethical life." [6]

The splendid tradition of politically *engagé* historical writing in Florence died in the 1540's when it became clear that a return to a republican form of government had ceased to be a political possibility.[7] The political theorists of the later six-

[4] Quoted in V. Titone, *La politica dell'Età Barocca* (Caltanissetta, 1950), p. 37.

[5] *Ibid.*, p. 47. G. B. Ciotti, the publisher of Marino's *Rime*, wrote in his preface, in 1602: " . . . this divine mind, esteemed in the universal opinion of all judicious Italians as one of the greatest lights of lyrical poetry, even a miracle of our times. . . ."

[6] B. Croce, *Storia dell' Età Barocca in Italia* (Bari, 1929), pp. 16–17 (my translation).

[7] L. von Albertini, *Das florentinische Staatsbewusstsein im Übergang von der Republik zum Prinzipat* (Berne, 1955).

teenth century, Botero, Scipio di Castro, Campanella, and the rest of them, are both dull writers and unoriginal thinkers when compared with Machiavelli and Guicciardini. Boccalini, the most acute and honest of them, had Machiavelli expelled from Parnassus because he taught blind and harmless sheep to use their teeth and "give sight to those moles whom Mother Nature, with great foresight, had created blind." [8] This ironical argument overruled his own powerful defence of Machiavelli.[9] Boccalini's is the most bitter indictment of the political society of the Counter-Reformation era. Botero, the best known of the political writers of the time, only purveyed the most widely accepted platitudes of the day. His ideas and his method of writing he copied from Bodin. Botero, the secretary of San Carlo Borromeo, set up Louis XI as his political hero.[10] The moral advance from Machiavelli's hero, Cesare Borgia, does not appear very striking.

Nevertheless, Croce was wrong in stigmatizing the Italian Counter Reformation and baroque periods as inferior to the Renaissance in all aspects of creative endeavor. First, I want to argue that architecture did not share in the decline of the other visual arts. There is much prejudice in this country against the baroque in architecture, and the attempts, by Vanbrugh and others, to introduce the style here, have not always been wholly successful. Yet from the Gesù in Rome, from Longhena's Santa Maria della Salute—and who would wish to see Venice without this superb contrast to its Byzantine, Gothic, and Palladian buildings?—to Borromini's and Bernini's palaces and churches, baroque buildings at their best can at least compare with the buildings of Brunelleschi, Bramante, and Michelangelo. In the colonnades of St. Peter's, Bernini created, on his own terms, a

---

[8] T. Boccalini, *Ragguagli di Parnasso* (Bari, 1910), I, 328.

[9] *Ibid.*, p. 327. For an excellent analysis of Boccalini's thought, see F. Meinecke, *Die Idee der Staatsraison* (Munich, 1929), Bk. 1, chap. 3; translated by D. Scott, *Machiavellism*, W. Stark, ed. (London, 1957).

[10] G. Botero, *The Reason of State*, P. J. and D. P. Waley, trans. (London, 1956).

structure as elegant and aesthetically satisfying as Brunelleschi's façade of the Ospedale degli Innocenti.

Perhaps even more significant was Italian achievement in philosophy, the natural sciences and, above all, in music. Yet it is curious that Croce should have all but ignored this phenomenon. This is not the place to present an outline of the history of science in Italy. It is sufficient to mention the towering figure of Galileo, his pupils Torricelli and Viviani, or names such as those of the zoologist Stelluti and the anatomist Malpighi. Modern science came of age with the work of the Academia dei Lincei, of Rome, and the Academia del Cimento, of Florence— both of them earlier foundations than the Royal Society. For the eclecticism of Leonardo, even though it was the eclecticism of genius, the academies sustituted the principles of systematic investigation and rational analysis on which all further advances in science have come to be based.

Perhaps the most revolutionary shift in Italian creative activity was towards music.[11] The Italians had, of course, always been an intensely musical nation. In the Middle Ages they had played a prominent part in the invention of musical notation, an invention comparable to that of the alphabet. But throughout the Renaissance, music had to give pride of place to poetry and the visual arts. Dante and Petrarch never set their poems to music in the manner of the French and German troubadours. A foreigner, Henricus Isaac, arranged the tunes for Lorenzo de Medici's popular songs.[12] Even at the beginning of the sixteenth century Castiglione tells us that Italian composers were at a discount and that no piece of music was fashionable unless it was thought to have been composed by Josquin des Prés.[13] Northwestern Europe, England, Flanders, and northern

[11] As far as I am aware, L. Olschki, in *The Genius of Italy* (Oxford, 1949), is the only author to have appreciated the significance of this shift in creative activity.

[12] *Ibid.*, pp. 402–405.

[13] B. Castiglione, *Il libro del Cortegiano*, V. Cian, ed., 4th ed. (Florence, 1947), pp. 190–91.

France were the true home of the finest Renaissance music. The first of the great line of organists of St Mark's in Venice was the Netherlander Adriaen Willaert, appointed in 1527. He was the founder of the great Venetian school of music. In the second half of the sixteenth century this school achieved its first great climax in the rich brocade of the compositions of Merulo and Andrea and Giovanni Gabrieli. Well might Francesco Sansovino exclaim, in 1581, that musc had her very own home in Venice.[14] It could not truthfully have been said fifty years earlier.

Independently of the school of Venetian organists and instrumentalists, there developed the school of sacred choral music with Palestrina as its greatest master. The secular counterpart of Palestrina's masses were the unaccompanied madrigals. Monteverdi, the finest of the Italian madrigalists, is still popular with modern singers. From about 1580 the circle of the musical amateur, Giovanni Bardi, Vincenzo Galilei, Caccini and Peri, experimenting with the typically sixteenth-century notion of re-creating Greek musical drama, invented a completely new musical form, opera.[15] It was little more than ten years from the first opera, Peri's *Dafne,*[16] to Monteverdi's *Orfeo,* the earliest opera still to enjoy successful productions. From then on, Italian music went from strength to strength. The modern gramophone companies have proved conclusively that Italian seventeenth-century music is still very much alive.

Much of this development centered in Venice. It is Venice which may provide a clue to the whole development of Italian civilization in the sixteenth and seventeenth centuries. Venice was the one Italian state which maintained its old character as an independent city-state and a true republic throughout the

[14] G. M. Cooper, "Instrumental Music," *The Oxford History of Music,* 2d ed., II, 422.

[15] *Grove Dictionary of Music and Musicians,* E. Blom, ed., 5th ed. (1954), VI, 195.

[16] Significantly, the first performance of this opera took place in the house of another musical amateur, Count Corsi; see M. F. Bukofzer, *Music in the Baroque Era* (London, 1948), p. 56.

sixteenth century. She suffered political and economic setbacks, but the Venetian fleet could still vindicate its old reputation and the strength of the Venetian civic spirit in the great victory of Lepanto. Only in the seventeenth century were the Venetian merchants driven off the seas by the successful competition of the Dutch and English in the spice trade of the Indies and the carrying trade of the Mediterranean. This continued political and economic vitality of the Venetian city-state was paralleled by the continued vitality of the great school of Venetian painters. From about the middle of the sixteenth century, when Michelangelo had painted his last fresco, there was in the rest of Italy no painter of the stature of Titian, Tintoretto, and Veronese. With Palladio and his school, Venice produced not only a new style in architecture which was to be almost as influential in Europe as the baroque, but in their Palladian country houses the Venetian patricians created a new form of social center for a cultured, aristocratic, and noncourtly style of living, which was still to bear fruit in eighteenth-century England.

Life in Venice had become different from life almost everywhere else in Italy. In Venice the artist remained the citizen of a free republic; in Florence, Rome, and Milan he had become the subject of a petty prince or, worse, a distant monarch. The Venetian participated, however indirectly, in the political and public life of a free community; the Florentine, the Roman, and the Milanese was excluded from the political and public life of his state except through the cramping formalities of a court. The Venetians were well aware of their advantages. When Iacopo Sansovino fled to Venice after the sack of Rome, in 1527, Titian and Aretino counseled him to remain in the republic and not be tempted by the false allurements of the court life of Rome or France.[17] Titian enjoyed the patronage of Charles V and Philip II, but he visited their courts only for short periods and always returned to Venice. His correspon-

[17] *Enciclopedia Italiana*, XXX, 758; G. Lorenzetti, *Itinerario Sansoviniano a Venezia* (Venice, 1929), p. 21.

dence with Philip II shows the relationship of patron and artist, but without a hint of that of a prince and his subject.[18]

It is now possible to draw some general conclusions. Venice throughout the sixteenth century retained much of the spirit of the late medieval city-state. Despite its efficient Inquisition, Venice never became a center of the Counter Reformation like Rome and Milan. Its great religious figures of the sixteenth century, a Contarini or a Sadoleto, remained in the old tradition of intellectual Christian humanists. Paolo Sarpi's *History of the Council of Trent* showed that, even in the seventeenth century, traditional anti-Romanism was allowed to flourish in a Catholic state. At the same time, Venice was sufficiently open to new ideas to be able to play her part in the working out of the new styles in architecture and music.

In the rest of Italy, patronage had become centralized almost exclusively in the courts—courts which had lost even the semblance of a genuine leadership of the citizen body. In such a society, the scope of the painter and writer was much more limited than before. Narrowness, formality, intolerance, the Index, and the Inquisition inhibited the free expression of artistic, literary, and political genius. Castiglione's *Courtier* was put on the Index. Ammanati publicly repented of having sculpted nudes. Michelangelo's *Last Judgment* was bowdlerized on the orders of the papal court; his plans for St. Peter's were changed for purely doctrinal reasons.[19] The theoreticians of art, who flourished as never before, were questioning the very basis of Renaissance art. Where Alberti and Leonardo had spoken of

[18] *Cf.* Boccalini, who admired Venice more than any other state: "Apollo firmly believes that in free countries, more than under any other form of government, the laws are directed towards the common good of men; that under such laws the minds of the citizens are more inspired to undertake and accomplish splendid works, and that the sciences and all forms of civic life flourish more readily. He holds in particular abomination those tyrants who commit the crime of subduing the liberty of a well-ordered republic . . ." (*Ragguagli di Parnasso*, I, 63).

[19] *Enciclopedia Italiana*, XXI, 830.

art as representing nature, Danti and Lomazzo now insisted that the artist must improve on nature.[20] Aesthetic considerations aside, these theories were undoubtedly the expression of a formalized court society. Worse still, the Italian states were becoming provincial. A free city-state derives much of its vitality from the intimacy of a small community. A monarchy centralizes cultural life in court and capital, and therefore needs a larger hinterland of talent to draw upon. It needs greater wealth and power than the city-state to compete with its rivals in status; for status is the peculiar virtue of a court society. Goldoni who knew this society intimately starts one of his most famous satirical plays, *La Locandiera,* with one character saying to another: "Between you and me there is a difference in status."

Most of the political writers of the period were as narrow-minded and provincial as the courts in which they lived. Botero's and his successors' theory of reason of state was, as Professor Titone of Palermo has acutely observed, essentially conservative. Their treatises were handbooks on how to preserve, rather than how to conquer, states. Their rejection of Machiavelli was motivated not least by their fear of a theory of state which could be used to overturn the established social and political order.[21] By the seventeenth century, Tassoni, Persio and Muratori came to see virtue in the very mediocrity of the small Italian state.[22]

But princes and popes, nobles and cardinals were still great builders. The Italian sense of visual form could still find at least a partial outlet in creating churches and palaces, country houses and integrated city squares. In the seventeenth century, capital was withdrawn from industry, trade, and banking, but it was still being invested in building. This was not enough for the vitality of the Italians: they turned to speculative philosophy and natural science, where the creative thinker could escape

[20] E. Panofsky, *Idea* (Leipzig—Berlin, 1924), pp. 41 ff.

[21] V. Titone, *La politica dell'Età Barocca* (Caltanissetta, 1950), pp. 90–91, and *passim.*

[22] *Ibid.,* p. 255.

from the social problems of his time. Significantly, wealthy and learned amateurs, such as Duke Federigo Cesi, played a leading role in the foundation of the Italian scientific academies. Even some princes, like Grand Duke Ferdinand II and Cardinal Leopold of Tuscany, took an active interest in the new science, buying the services of the finest instrument makers and importing the latest lenses, barometers, and thermometers from abroad.[23] For as long as the Inquisition would let it, Italian science led Europe. The fate of Bruno and Galileo showed how precarious, even in these fields, the free exercise of genius had become.[24]

Eventually, only music was left. Into musical expression was poured the finest part of Italian creative genius. It enjoyed advantages which all other fields of creative activity had lost. In church music, the composer could keep that vitalizing contact with the whole Christian community which the painter had lost, even while he was still painting madonnas and crucifixions. It is no accident that Caravaggio, the tragic rebel and fugitive from the established society of his day, found himself attracted to the circle of San Filippo Neri for whom music formed an outstanding part of their spiritual devotions.[25] Bernini, the one great Italian sculptor of the seventeenth century, was convinced that he was God's instrument. "All that we know," he said, "comes from God, and teaching others means taking His place." [26] It was this mystical view of the religious significance of art which enabled this most feted of court artists to transcend the narrowness of court life.

But Bernini remained alone, while the number of musicians, composers, and violin builders of genius was steadily growing. The small courts, whatever their other limitations, provided the ideal setting for the development of music. Gifted aristo-

[23] A. R. Hall, *The Scientific Revolution, 1500–1800* (London, 1954), pp. 188–190.

[24] See Milton's remarks on his meeting with Galileo in "Areopagitica," *Works* (New York, 1931), IV, pp. 330–331. I am indebted to Professor P. Zagorin for drawing my attention to this point.

[25] W. Friedlaender, *Caravaggio Studies* (Princeton, N. J., 1955), p. xiii.

[26] R. Wittkower, *Gian Lorenzo Bernini* (London, 1955), p. 41.

cratic amateurs collected groups of musicians in their houses, who developed the modern forms of instrumental and chamber music. It was court society which financed the new operas. In creating this "spectacle for princes," as it was called, the seventeenth-century artist could develop a universality which rivaled that of the great Renaissance figures. In 1644, John Evelyn noted in his diary in Rome: "Bernini . . . gave a public opera wherein he painted the scenes, cut the statues, invented the engines, composed the music, writ the comedy, and built the theatre." [27] But more important than such a tour de force was the fact that opera, for all its need of court patronage, did not in fact remain the spectacle of princes. It became that of the whole Italian people, from the claque of gondoliers in the seventeenth-century opera house of Venice,[28] to your donkey guide in Taormina, who will sing to you all the most famous arias from the operas of Rossini, Verdi, and Puccini.

The theory that what occurred in Italy in the sixteenth and seventeenth centuries was a phenomenon of shift, rather than of overall decadence, is borne out by a comparison of Italian history with that of other European countries in the same period. Only a very rapid survey is possible here, and not all the implications of my theory for the rest of Europe can be considered.

Only one other country had a history at all similar to that of Italy, and that was Germany. In Germany, as in Italy, the late fifteenth and the early sixteenth centuries saw the culmination of a long development of the visual arts. In Germany, as in Italy, they had flourished in the city-states where the skilled medieval craftsman had developed into the individual artist. If the style of Veit Stoss, of Riemenschneider, Grünewald, and even of Dürer remained Gothic, rather than Renaissance and classical, the technical quality of their work and its artistic content made it comparable with that of the great Italian and

[27] *Ibid.*, p. 1.
[28] Bukofzer, *Music in the Baroque Era,* pp. 395–396.

Flemish masters of the fifteenth century. The collapse, when it came, was much more sudden and much more catastrophic than in Italy. The change to the mannerist style in the later portraits of Cranach and Holbein took place practically without an intervening classical style like that of the High Renaissance in Italy. In Germany, the intermediate phase of the early court society based on the traditions of the city-state never occurred. The territorial princes, helped by the secularization of church property and, in the case of the Lutherans, the control of a state church, crushed the independent knights and the peasants and strangled the economy of the independent cities. Nuremberg, Augsburg, and Strasbourg did not become principalities, as did Milan and Florence. But all their energies were taken up by the fight for economic and political survival in the face of more powerful and efficient rivals. The south German city-states had been much smaller than their Italian counterparts; their economic basis much narrower. Their financiers tied them as effectively and, in the end, even more disastrously, to the fortunes of the great western monarchies. Already Holbein found more congenial scope for his work in England. After his death and that of Cranach, Germany barely produced epigones in the visual arts. Only towards the end of the seventeenth century was there a genuine revival with the south German and Austrian baroque style. What little secular literature there had been, and it had been little enough, suffered equal collapse. Not until the second half of the eighteenth century did Germany produce a literary figure of European stature.

In Germany, as in Italy, it was the triumph of the small principalities with their rigid court society, aping that of France and Spain, which had this blighting effect on the visual arts and on literature. If the collapse was worse in Germany than in Italy, this was partly due to the aridity of Lutheranism, after the first heroic generation of reformers had passed away—an aridity paralleled in the narrow Catholicism of the Jesuit-dominated courts of the Catholic princes—and to a provincialism much more pervading still than in Italy. There were more of these German courts; they were poorer and, having developed apart from the city-state, they lacked the urbanity which the Florentine tradition could still impart to the grand duchy of Tuscany.

But, as in Italy, creative energies found other outlets. There is a grain of truth in Marx's malicious remark that the censorship of the German princes whipped the German philosophers into the highest spheres of metaphysical speculation. It was not true of Kepler; but Kepler, though imperial court astronomer, was forced to spend much of his time on astrology; he was never given enough money to buy instruments and died in abject poverty. It was true of the later seventeenth-century philosophers. Divorced from the political life of their states and the social problems of their day, the German philosophers (all good *Untertanen*—subjects of their princes) developed the science and the philosophical systems which were to make German thought famous from the end of the seventeenth century on: but these great philosophers also called forth a well-deserved mockery for their Panglossian lack of a sense of reality.

Even in philosophy, it had taken the Germans until the second half of the seventeenth century to pass through the intellectual desert which followed in the wake of the Reformation and the triumph of the small territorial states. In music, however, the development was much more rapid. To an even greater degree than in Italy, music was the art in which the artist maintained his contact with the community through the church service. The greatest of German seventeenth-century composers, Heinrich Schütz, composed much of his finest religious music while Germany was devastated by the armies of Wallenstein, Gustavus Adolphus, and Richelieu. The Thirty Years' War was undoubtedly a great catastrophe for Germany, but it was not the main factor determining German cultural development. Again, as in Italy, the small courts became excellent centers and sponsors of musical life. If, in the eighteenth century, J. S. Bach, the greatest of all German composers, spent most of his working life as organist and cantor of the church of

St. Thomas in Leipzig, it was not for want of trying to obtain a position as court composer. Nor was it perhaps entirely fortuitous that Frederic the Great of Prussia was one of the first to appreciate the full greatness of Bach.

The cultural history of western Europe shows no such fundamental shifts as the history of Italy and Germany. In the sixteenth century, the aristocratic court societies of Spain and France were able to assimilate the artistic influence of Renaissance Italy in their own artistic and literary traditions. France and Spain were world powers who played roles in the political, economic and religious crises of the sixteenth and seventeenth centuries which Florence, Milan, or even Rome could no longer rival. The amazing efflorescence of the Spanish genius in the "golden century"—the paintings of Greco, Velázquez, Zurbarán, and Murillo, the plays of Lope de Vega, Tirso de Molina, and Calderón, the Don Quixote of Cervantes, the mystic poetry of St. John of the Cross, the political and moral debates of the Jesuit and Dominican jurists—these were the achievements of a society which saw itself as the moral leader of a Catholic Christianity, whose kings were arbiters of the destinies of Europe, whose soldiers defended Christendom from Turks and heretics, and whose explorers and missionaries were conquering continents for Spain and Christ. In the long run, Spain had her own weaknesses. With economic collapse and political defeat, the material and psychological basis of the "golden century" disappeared. The baneful influence of the Spanish Inquisition, already evident in the middle of the sixteenth century in its sinister victory over the Spanish illuminists and Erasmians, became an ever greater handicap to literary production. By the second half of the seventeenth century, Madrid had become as provincial as Milan. There is much that still needs investigating in the decline of Spain in the seventeenth century. But in the early eighteenth century, she could still produce the elegant baroque architecture of Churriguera, and it is perhaps not without significance that Domenico Scarlatti chose to live in Madrid, rather than in his native Italy.

The cultural history of the Netherlands is more difficult to interpret than that of Italy, Germany, and Spain, but its pattern is fairly clear. In painting, the fifteenth-century tradition of van Eyck and Memling continued unbroken in the sixteenth, except of course for stylistic changes. In the seventeenth century, with the political division between the bourgeois north and the aristocratic south, the two constituent characteristics of the Netherlands style, the courtly and the urban, split as well. But it was a sign of the growing provincialism of the south that its two greatest artists, Rubens and Van Dyck, became cosmopolitan court painters, seeking their patrons as far afield as London, Madrid and Genoa.

By contrast, the cultural development of France and England is much clearer. Nowhere else was it as unbroken as in the two great western monarchies. Politically and economically successful and, in consequence, superbly self-confident, they could allow the free development of the creative spirit of their citizens. Neither the Counter Reformation in France nor Puritanism in England developed the stifling characteristics of Spanish Catholicism and German Lutherism—perhaps because they never managed to dominate their respective societies for more than very short periods. Frenchmen and Englishmen never became mere subjects of their rulers, and it is significant that, in both countries, political philosophy continued to flourish. Unlike the Germans, English and French philosophers continued to debate the social problems of their day and especially the fundamental problem of the moral justification of political power, that most fruitful debate which the Christian Middle Ages have bequeathed to modern European civilization. Literature, science, philosophy, and architecture in England, literature, science, philosophy, and all the visual arts in France, these varied forms of creative activity showed that these two countries had successfully adapted at least some of the virtues of the city-state to the dimensions of growing nation-states. At the same time, neither in England nor in France was there the shift of creative activity towards music which was so characteristic of Italy and

Germany. Despite great names, such as Byrd and Purcell, Lully and Couperin, music remained only one, and not perhaps the most typical, expression of the English and French genius.

In this chapter I have not attempted to explain the phenomenon of genius. All European countries have had their share of it. Their histories show periods of greater or lesser creative activity. I do not believe that, at least for the last five or six hundred years, it is possible to speak of the decadence of any European nation in the sense of a biological change. I believe rather that different social developments provide a greater or lesser stimulus, a more or less favorable environment for creative activity in different fields of human endeavor. Neither do I want to propound a theory of social determinism. Styles in art, literature, or music depend on developments inherent in their nature, as well as on outside influences. Art and music historians have long since recognized that the work of even the most revolutionary genius must be seen within the tradition of his own art and does not exclude the writing of a meaningful, systematic history of style. What I have attempted to do here is to widen this approach and to relate the whole complex of cultural histories to the history of European society. It is in this way, I believe, that a more profound understanding of western civilization may be found.

# Index